RELIABILITY IN
COMPUTER SYSTEM DESIGN

THE ABLEX SERIES IN SOFTWARE ENGINEERING

SERIES EDITOR

MARVIN V. ZELKOWITZ

Reliability in Computer System Design
B.S. Dhillon

in preparation

Requirements for a Software Engineering Environment
Edited by Marvin V. Zelkowitz

RELIABILITY IN
COMPUTER SYSTEM DESIGN

by

B.S. Dhillon
Professor
Faculty of Engineering
University of Ottawa

 Ablex Publishing Corporation, Norwood, N.J. 07648

Library of Congress Cataloging-in-Publication Data

Dhillon, B. S.
   Reliability in computer system design.

   (Ablex series in software engineering)
   Bibliography: p. ix
   Includes index.
   1.   System design. 2.   Electronic digital computers—
Reliability. 3.   Computer software—Reliability.
I. Title. II. Series.
QA76.9.S88D49   1987   004.2′1   87-1164
ISBN 0-89391-412-6

Ablex Publishing Corporation
355 Chestnut Street
Norwood, New Jersey 07648

TABLE OF CONTENTS

BIOGRAPHY OF THE AUTHOR

Dr. Dhillon is a full professor in the Faculty of Science and Engineering, University of Ottawa.

He attended the University of Wales where he received a B.Sc. in Electrical and Electronic Engineering and a M.Sc. in Industrial and Systems Engineering. His Ph.D. in Reliability Engineering was received from the University of Windsor. He wrote his doctoral thesis on reliability evaluation of networks composed of three state devices. He is Advisory Editor of "Microelectronics and Reliability: An International Journal", Associate Editor of "International Journal of Energy Systems", and Editor-at-Large for Engineering Books (Marcel Dekker, Inc.). Dr. Dhillon served as an associate editor of the 10th–13th Annual Modeling and Simulation Proceedings, Pittsburgh, Pennsylvania, USA. He has published over 170 articles on Reliability Engineering as well as nine books on various aspects of Engineering Reliability and related areas. Three of his books are translated into Russian and Chinese.

Serving as a referee to many national and international journals, book publishers and other bodies, he has presented keynote and invited lectures at various national and international conferences. Dr. Dhillon has several years of experience in electronics and nuclear power industries.

He is recipient of the American Society for Quality Control's Austin J. Bonis Reliability Award and the Society of Reliability Engineers' Merit Award, as well as several appreciation certificates from various American professional societies. A registered Professional Engineer in Ontario, Professor Dhillon is listed in the American Men and Women of Science, Dictionary of International Biography, Men of Achievement, Who's Who in Technology, Personalities of America, etc.

PREFACE

Computers are increasingly being used at an alarming rate for various purposes. Some people have predicted that those days are not very far off when the computer business will be the largest single component of the US economy. As computer failures or mistakes can effect our daily lives, their reliability is important to all of us. In addition, the reliability of computers used in critical areas such as defense, aerospace and nuclear power generation is of utmost importance because their failures could be very costly and catastrophic.

In computers, the reliability problem is associated with both hardware and software. Therefore, both these items have to be reliable for their successful operations. At the moment, to the author's knowledge, there is no published book that effectively covers the reliability of computer hardware and software within the framework of a single volume. In order to design and produce reliable computers, the knowledge in reliability of computer hardware and software is important to concerned engineers. An engineer needing information in both these two areas generally faces inconvenience because the information on these two topics is available in some texts and in various technical articles but not in a single volume. This book is an attempt to fulfil this vital need. The computer hardware and software reliability (and related) topics are treated in such a manner that the reader require no previous knowledge to understand the contents. The emphasis is on the structure of the concepts rather than the minute details. Sources for most of the material presented are given in the References. The book contains over 850 references on computer system reliability and several examples along with their solutions. The references will be useful to the reader who wishes to delve more deeply into a specific area of computer system reliability.

This book should be useful to anyone concerned with design and production of computers. In particular computer design engineers, software specialists, system engineers; reliability, quality control and safety engineers; electronics engineers, project engineers and managers, engineering administrators, and senior undergraduate and graduate students of computer science, computer engineering, reliability and quality control should benefit the most.

The book is composed of twelve chapters plus appendix. The appendix contains 717 references on computer system reliability. The references are separated into two major categories; i.e. computer hardware reliability and software reliability.

I wish to thank many leading professionals and friends whose invisible inputs have shaped my thinking on many areas of this text. The author is deeply greatful to Dr. S.N. Rayapati for the preparation of diagrams for this book. I am indebted to my relatives and friends in and outside Ottawa for their interest and encouragement throughout. Finally, I thank my wife, Rosy, for typing the entire manuscript and for her help in proofreading. During the preparation of the manuscript the disturbances of my little daughter, Jasmine, have also helped because they led to many rest and coffee breaks!

B.S. Dhillon
Ottawa, Ontario

1
INTRODUCTION

1.1 NEED FOR RELIABILITY

Nowadays computers have become very complex and sophisticated, and their applications have increased at an alarming rate. For example, according to the *Wall Street Journal* of January 23, 1979, computer costs accounted for 1% (i.e. $25.65 billion) of the gross national product (GNP) of the United States. Furthermore, according to some predictions, the computer business in the United States will overtake the automobile business in the 1980s. This means that the computer business will be the largest single component of the U.S. economy.

Computers are used in critical areas such as aerospace, nuclear power generation, and defense. For such applications their reliability is of utmost importance because a computer failure in these areas could be very costly and catastrophic. Other factors such as increasing repair costs, harsher operating environments, use by novices, and the existence of bigger systems are also responsible for the increasing emphasis on reliability of computer systems. To improve reliability and assist field service personnel in fault isolation, computer hardware manufacturers such as International Business Machines (IBM), Amdahl, and Univac make use of redundancy. However, in computers the reliability problem is not only confined to the hardware aspect, but also extends to software. Both hardware and software have to be reliable for successful operation of a computer. Therefore there is a definite need to place emphasis on the reliability of both the computer hardware and the software.

1.2 HISTORY OF COMPUTER SYSTEM RELIABILITY

Relays and electronic tubes were extensively used in the earlier-day digital computers. In those computers, because of the poor reliability of such devices, a considerable amount of effort was directed to the areas of computer checking and self-repair [1]. In computers composed of relays, intermittent faults dominated the scene relative to permanent faults. To overcome this problem extensive use of dynamic checking was made.

The invention of the transistor may be regarded as an important milestone in the history of computer system reliability because transistors possessed a higher inherent reliability than did electronic tubes or relays. In the 1950s transistors found their way into the computer market.

Works of C.E. Shannon [2], W.R. Hamming [3], J. Von Neumann [4], and E.F. Moore and C.E. Shannon [5] have played an important role in computer system reliability. For example, it was J. Von Neumann who first proposed the replication scheme called triple modular redundancy (TMR) to improve the reliability of a system in 1956. Three years later, R. Eldred [6] considered efficient methods of test generation for combinational circuits. Efficient diagnostic tests for digital circuits were developed by S. Seshu and D.N. Freeman [7], S. Seshu [8], and J.M. Galey, R.E. Norby and J.P. Roth [9]. In 1962 a symposium on Redundancy Techniques for Computing Systems was held in Washington, D.C. The proceedings of that symposium were published by Spartan Books [10] under the editorship of R.H. Wilcox and W.C. Mann. In 1965 W.H. Pierce published a book [11] entitled "Failure Tolerant Design." This was probably the first book concerned with computer system reliability.

Over the past number of years many persons have contributed to the field of computer system reliability. Articles published by W.C. Carter and W.G. Bouricius [1], A. Avizienis [12,13], C.V. Ramamoorthy [14], M.Y. Hsiao, W.C. Carter, J.W. Thomas and W.R. Stringfellow [15], R.A. Short [16] and J. Goldberg [17] provide a very good overview of the subject. A comprehensive list of selected references is given in reference [18].

1.2.1 Software Reliability

Although the reliability of computer software is as important as that of computer hardware, effort in this direction did not surface until the 1960s. It was at Bell Laboratories [19] where the serious effort on software reliability probably started first in 1964. A histogram of problems per month reported for the first switching system software is an evidence of this effort [20]. In this case the software was composed of 100,000 words. Three years later in 1967, R.W. Floyd [21] considered methods for formal validation of software programs. In the same year G.R. Hudson [22] developed Markov birth–death models. Two conferences on software engineering, sponsored by the North Atlantic Treaty Organization (NATO), were held in West Germany and Italy in 1968 and 1969, respectively. Issues on reliable software were addressed in both these meetings [23]. In 1966, R. Barlow and E.M. Scheuer [24] published a mathematical model concerned with reliability growth (hardware system) during a development testing program. This model could also be applied for software debugging. Works of R.L. London [25] and J.L. Sauter [26] concerned with software reliability were published in 1969. Contributions of Z. Jelinski and P.B. Moranda [27], M.L. Shooman [28], G.J. Schick and R.W. Wolverton [29], N.F. Schneidewind [30], and J.D. Musa [31] are briefly discussed in Chapter 11. Many other researchers and authors have contributed to software reliability. A list of selective references is given in reference [32].

References on computer hardware reliability and software reliability listed in the appendix of this book attest the effort of other research workers and authors.

1.3   TERMS AND DEFINITIONS

This section presents selected terms and definitions used in computer system reliability [33-36].

Reliability: the probability that an item will carry out its required mission satisfactorily for a specified period of time when used according to designed conditions.

Availability: the probability that an item is functioning satisfactorily at any instant of time when used according to designed conditions. (In this situation the elements of the total time considered are the operating time, the logistic time, the active repair time, and the administrative time.)

Redundancy: the existence of two or more means for carrying out a specified function.

Failure: the termination of the ability of a unit to carry out its assigned mission.

Mean time to repair: the total corrective maintenance time over the total number of corrective maintenance actions performed during a defined time period.

Fault: an attribute which adversely affects an item's reliability.

Effectiveness: the capability of the item to carry out its assigned mission.

Debugging: the process of rectifying and isolating errors.

Software testing: the process of executing software to find out whether the results it generates are valid [35].

Fault-tolerant computing: the ability to execute given algorithms successfully regardless of computer software errors and hardware failures [12].

Software: computer program items in the form of magnetic tapes, disks or card decks as well as all kinds of descriptive documentation, including flow charts, listings, etc.

Software error: a clerical, conceptual or syntactic discrepancy which causes one or more faults in the software.

Software failure: failure which occurs in a situation when a computer program fault is elicited by some kind of input data, leading to the computer program incorrectly computing the specified function [36].

Software Fault: a discrepancy in the computer software which makes worse its capability to perform as intended.

Software reliability: the probability of a specified software functioning for a given period, without an error, when used within the framework of designed conditions on the specified machine.

1.4 SCOPE OF THE TEXT

Today applications of computers are increasing at an alarming rate. They are used in areas such as national defense, aerospace, nuclear power generation, and so on. A large number of engineers, programmers, etc. are employed in the computer industry. What is generally expected from these persons is the production of a reliable product at the minimum cost. In order to fulfil this expectation effectively, understanding by these persons of both computer hardware related reliability and software reliability concepts is necessary.

At present, to the best of author's knowledge, there is no published work that covers the topics of computer software reliability and computer hardware reliability within the framework of a single book. Furthermore, according to a literature search study conducted by the author, there are over 350 articles published on computer hardware related reliability but only a few books. Similarly, in software reliability, there are only a limited number of published books. None of these books cover the hardware aspect. At present, persons needing information in both these areas generally face a great deal of difficulty, because they have to study various books or articles. This process is time consuming and rather cumbersome to follow. This book is an attempt to combine computer hardware related reliability and software reliability concepts into a single volume. Previous knowledge is not essential to digest the contents, since two chapters on mathematics and basic reliability principles are provided for background.

The topics treated in the book are of current interest and have a large applicability (imagine the size of the computer industry throughout the world!). This book should be useful to persons such as reliability and quality control engineers, system engineers, electrical and electronics engineers, software specialists, engineering administrators, computer design engineers, project engineers, and senior undergraduate and graduate students of reliability, quality control, computer science and computer engineering.

1.5 SUMMARY

This chapter covered general topics associated with computer system reliability along with scope of the book. The need for reliability with respect to computers was discussed. The history of the computer system reliability was reviewed. A separate section was specifically devoted to the history of software reliability. A number of relevant selective terms and definitions were presented. The scope of the text was outlined.

1.6 EXERCISES

1. Define the following terms:

   i) Reliable software
   ii) Hazard rate
   iii) Maintainability
   iv) Mean time between failures
   v) Active redundancy
   vi) Inherent reliability.

2. Write an essay on fault-tolerant computing.
3. Discuss the history of fault-tolerant computing.
4. Write an essay on "need for software reliability".
5. Discuss the history of electronic computers.

1.7 REFERENCES

1. W.C. Carter and W.G. Bouricius, "A Survey of Fault Tolerant Computer Architecture and Its Evaluation", Computer, January/February, 1971, pp. 9–16.

2. C.E. Shannon, "A Mathematical Theory of Communications", Bell System Tech. Journal, Vol. 27, 1948, pp. 379–423 and 623–656.

3. W.R. Hamming, "Error Detecting and Error Correcting Codes", Bell System Tech. Journal, Vol. 29, 1950, pp. 147–160.

4. J. Von Neumann, "Probabilistic Logics and the Synthesis of Reliable Organisms from Reliable Components", in *Automata Studies* Edited by C.E. Shannon and J. McCarthy, Princeton University Press, Princeton, 1956, pp. 43–98.

5. E.F. Moore and C.E. Shannon, "Reliable Circuits Using Less Reliable Relays", Journal of Franklin Institute, Vol. 262, 1956, pp. 191–208.

6. R. Eldred, "Test Routines Based on Symbolic Logic Statements", Journal of the Association for Computing Machinery, January 1959.

7. S. Seshu and D.N. Freeman, "The Diagnosis of Asynchronous Sequential Switching Systems", IRE Transactions on Electronic Computers, Vol. 11, 1962, pp. 459–465.

8. S. Seshu, "On an Improved Diagnosis Program", IEEE Transactions on Electronic Computers, Vol. 14, 1965, pp. 76–79.

9. J.M. Galey, R.E. Norby and J.P. Roth, "Techniques for Diagnosis of Switching Circuit Failures", IEEE Transactions on Communications Electronics, Vol. 83, 1964, pp. 509–514.

10. R.H. Wilcox and W.C. Mann, Eds., *Redundancy Techniques for Computing Systems,* Spartan Books, Washington, D.C., 1962.

11. W.H. Pierce, *Failure Tolerant Design,* Academic Press, New York, 1965.

12. A. Avizienis, "Fault-Tolerant Computing: An Overview", Computer, January/February, 1971, pp. 5–8.

13. A. Avizienis, "Fault-Tolerant Systems", IEEE Transactions on Computers, Vol. 25, 1976, pp. 1304–1312.

14. C.V. Ramamoorthy, "Fault-Tolerant Computing: An Introduction and An Overview", IEEE Transactions on Computers, Vol. 20, 1971, pp. 1241–1244.

15. M.Y. Hsiao, W.C. Carter, J.W. Thomas and W.R. Stringfellow, "Reliability, Availability and Serviceability of IBM Computer Systems: A Quarter Century of Progress", IBM Journal of Research and Development, Vol. 25, 1981, pp. 453–465.

16. R.A. Short, "The Attainment of Reliable Digital Systems Through the Use of Redundancy: A Survey", IEEE Computer Group News, Vol. 2, March 1968, pp. 2–17.

17. J. Goldberg, "A Survey of the Design and Analysis of Fault-Tolerant Computers", in *Reliability and Fault Tree Analysis* edited by R.E. Barlow, J.B. Fussell and N.D. Singpurwalla, Society for Industrial and Applied Mathematics, Philadelphia, 1975, pp. 687–704.

18. B.S. Dhillon and K.I. Ugwu, "Bibliography of Literature on Computer Hardware Reliability", Microelectronics and Reliability, Vol. 26, 1986, pp. 99–122.

19. G.J. Schick and R.W. Wolverton, "An Analysis of Competing Software Reliability Models", IEEE Transactions on Software Engineering, Vol. 4, 1978, pp. 104–120.

20. G. Haugk, S.H. Tsiang and L. Zimmerman, "System Testing of The No. 1 Electronic Switching System", Bell System Tech. Journal, Vol. 43, 1964, pp. 2575–2592.

21. R.W. Floyd, "Assigning Meanings to Programs", Mathematical Aspects of Computer Science, Vol. XIX, 1967, pp. 19–32. (American Mathematical Society, Providence, Rhode Island).

22. G.R. Hudson, "Programming Errors as a Birth-and-Death Process", Report No. SP-3011, System Development Corporation, December, 1967.

23. P. Naur, Editor, *Software Engineering Concepts and Techniques*, Petrocelli/Charter Books, Inc., New York, 1976.

24. R. Barlow and E.M. Scheuer, "Reliability Growth During a Development Testing Program", Technometrics, Vol. 8, 1966, pp. 53–60.

25. R.L. London, "Proving Programs Correct: Some Techniques and Examples", BIT, Vol. 10, 1969, pp. 168–182.

26. J.L. Sauter, "Reliability in Computer Programs", Mechanical Engineering, Vol. 91, 1969, pp. 24–27.

27. Z. Jelinski and P.B. Moranda, "Software Reliability Research", in *Statistical Computer Performance Evaluation* edited by W. Freiberger, Academic Press, New York, 1972, pp. 465–484.

28. M.L. Shooman, "Probabilistic Models for Software Reliability Prediction", in *Statistical Computer Performance Evaluation* edited by W. Freiberger, Academic Press, New York, 1972, pp. 485–502.

29. G.J. Schick and R.W. Wolverton, "Assessment of Software Reliability", presented at 11th Annual Meeting of German Operations Research Society, Hamburg, West Germany, Sept. 6–8, 1972; in Proceedings of the Operations Research, Physica-Verlag, Wurzburg-Wien, 1973, pp. 395–422.

30. N.F. Schneidewind, "An Approach to Software in Reliability Prediction and Quality Control", Proceedings of the American Federation of Information Processing Societies (AFIPS) Fall Conference, Published by AFIPS Press, Montvale, New Jersey, 1972, pp. 837–847.

31. J.D. Musa, "A Theory of Software Reliability and Its Applications", IEEE Transactions on Software Engineering, Vol. 1, 1975, pp. 312–327.

32. B.S. Dhillon, "Software Reliability—Bibliography", Microelectronics and Reliability, Vol. 22, 1982, pp. 625–640.

33. W.H. Von Alven, Editor, *Reliability Engineering,* Prentice-Hall, Inc., Englewood Cliffs, New Jersey, 1964.

34. R.T. Anderson, *Reliability Design Handbook,* Published by Rome Air Development Center, Griffiss Air Force Base, New York, 1976.

35. R.L. Glass, *Software Reliability Guidebook,* Prentice-Hall, Inc., Englewood Cliffs, New Jersey, 1979.

36. M. Lipow, "Prediction of Software Failures", The Journal of Systems and Software, Vol. 1, 1979, pp. 71–75.

2
BASIC RELIABILITY MATHEMATICS FOR COMPUTER SYSTEMS

2.1 INTRODUCTION

Just as in any other engineering discipline, mathematics plays an important role in reliability. Probability theory is an indispensible tool of the reliability discipline. In comparison to general mathematics, the history of probability is not old; it had its beginnings in the seventeenth century in France. Blaise Pascal and Pierre Fermat are regarded as the fathers of the origin of modern probability theory. However, it was the ardent gambler, Chevalier de Méré, who put forward the problem of dividing winnings in a game of chance to Blaise Pascal. In turn Blaise Pascal consulted Pierre Fermat. Ever since many researchers have contributed to the probability theory. It has been applied in reliability problems since World War II.

This chapter presents several mathematical concepts concerned with probability and the reliability discipline. These concepts are essential in understanding the subsequent chapters of this book.

2.2 PROBABILITY

The probability $P(Y)$ of the outcome of event Y is defined as given below:

$$P(Y) = \lim_{m \to \infty} \left[\frac{M}{m} \right] \tag{2.1}$$

In the above definition, it is assumed that the event Y occurs M times out of m repeated trials. Generally, the value of $P(Y)$ is approximated from the following relationship since it is impossible to carry out infinite trials:

$$P(Y) = \frac{M}{m} \tag{2.2}$$

9

2.2.1 Properties of Proability

Some of these are as follows:

i. The probability of the sample space S is

$$P(S) = 1 \tag{2.3}$$

ii. For each event Y, the event probability is always

$$0 \leqslant P(Y) \leqslant 1 \tag{2.4}$$

iii. The probability of the intersection of events Y_1 and Y_2 is

$$P(Y_1 \cap Y_2) = P(Y_1/Y_2)P(Y_2) \tag{2.5}$$

In Eq. (2.5) $P(Y_1/Y_2)$ is the probability of Y_1 given that Y_2 has happened. The intersection of events Y_1 and Y_2 is denoted by the symbol $\cap$. $P(Y_2)$ is the probability of event Y_2.

In the case of independent events, the above equation becomes

$$P(Y_1 \cap Y_2) = P(Y_1) \cdot P(Y_2) \tag{2.6}$$

For k number of independent events, the above equation is generalized as follows:

$$P(Y_1 \cap Y_2 \cap \cdots \cap Y_j \cap \cdots \cap Y_k) = \prod_{j=1}^{k} P(Y_j) \tag{2.7}$$

Alternatively

$$P(Y_1 Y_2 Y_3 \cdots Y_k) = P(Y_1)P(Y_2)P(Y_3) \cdots P(Y_k) \tag{2.8}$$

Where

$P(Y_j)$ is the probability of event Y_j; $j = 1, 2, 3, \ldots, k$.

iv. The probability of the union of k independent events is given by

$$P(Y_1 + Y_2 + Y_3 + \cdots + y_k) = 1 - \prod_{j=1}^{k} \{1 - P(Y_j)\} \tag{2.9}$$

In the above equation the union of events is denoted by the symbol $+$.

Example 2.1

A system is controlled by two independent computers A and B. At least one computer must work normally for the successful operation of the system.

The reliabilities of computers A and B are 0.75 and 0.85, respectively. Calculate the probability that the system will be controlled successfully by the computers.

With the aid of the above given data and Eq. (2.9) we get

$$P(A + B) = 1 - [1 - P(A)][1 - P(B)]$$

$$= 1 - (1 - 0.75)(1 - 0.85)$$

$$= 0.9625$$

Where

$P(A)$ is the reliability of computer A.
$P(B)$ is the reliability of computer B.

Thus the probability that the system will be controlled successfully by the computers is 0.9625.

Example 2.2

In Example 2.1 if both the computers are required for the successful operation of the system, determine the probability that the system will be controlled successfully by the computers.

Applying Eq. (2.6) and the specified data results in

$$P(AB) = P(A) \cdot P(B)$$

$$= (0.75)(0.85)$$

$$= 0.6375$$

Thus the probability that the system will be controlled successfully by the computers is only 0.6375.

2.3   PROBABILITY DISTRIBUTIONS

2.3.1   Continuous Distributions

These probability distributions are quite useful for describing failures as a function of continuous random variable time t. Examples of such distributions are Weibull, gamma, exponential, lognormal, and Rayleigh. The cumulative distribution function $F(t)$ of a continuous distribution is defined as

$$F(t) = \int_{-\infty}^{t} f(y)dy \tag{2.10}$$

Where

    t is time.

    $f(t)$ is the probability density function of a continuous distribution.

Therefore, from relationship (2.10) we get

$$F(\infty) = \int_{-\infty}^{\infty} f(y) \cdot dy = 1 \tag{2.11}$$

and

$$f(t) = \frac{dF(t)}{dt} \tag{2.12}$$

The mean value, μ, and the variance, σ^2, respectively, are defined by

$$\mu = \int_0^\infty t f(t) dt \tag{2.13}$$

and

$$\sigma^2 = \int_0^\infty (t - \mu)^2 f(t) dt \tag{2.14}$$

Where

    μ is the mean value.

The hazard rate, $\lambda(t)$, is defined by

$$\lambda(t) = \frac{f(t)}{1 - F(t)} \tag{2.15}$$

Exponential Distribution. This is probably the most widely used probability distribution in reliability studies. Usually, this is the distribution used to describe the failure times of electronic parts. Its simplicity is probably one of the factors for its wide applications in reliability engineering. The probability density function of the distribution is defined as

$$f(t) = \theta e^{-\theta t} \qquad \theta > 0, \, t \geqslant 0 \tag{2.16}$$

Where

    t is time.

    θ is the scale parameter. In reliability work it is known as the constant failure rate of an item.

By substituting the above relationship into Eq. (2.10) we get

$$F(t) = \int_0^t \theta e^{-\theta y} dy$$

$$= \left[\frac{\theta e^{-\theta y}}{-\theta} \right]_0^t = 1 - e^{-\theta t} \qquad (2.17)$$

Similarly, by substituting relationship (2.16) into Eq. (2.13) and (2.14) respectively, we get

$$\mu = \int_0^\infty t \theta e^{-\theta t} dt$$

$$= \frac{1}{\theta} \qquad (2.18)$$

and

$$\sigma^2 = \int_0^\infty \left[t - \frac{1}{\theta} \right]^2 \cdot \theta e^{-\theta t} dt$$

$$= \frac{1}{\theta^2} \qquad (2.19)$$

With the aid of equations (2.15) through (2.17) we get

$$\lambda(t) = \frac{\theta e^{-\theta t}}{1 - (1 - e^{\theta t})} = \theta \qquad (2.20)$$

The above result demonstrates that the constant failure rate is associated with the exponential distribution.

Example 2.3

The failure times of a lineprinter are described by the density function

$$f(t) = \theta e^{-\theta t} \qquad (2.21)$$

Where

t	is time.
$\theta = 0.002$	failure/hour, the constant failure rate of the line printer.

Calculate the failure probability of the lineprinter for a 15 hour mission.

By substituting the given data into Eq. (2.17) we get

$$F(15) = 1 - e^{-(0.002)(15)}$$

$$= 0.0296$$

Thus the failure probability of the lineprinter is 2.96%.

Example 2.4

Assume that the constant failure rate of a computer is 0.0005 failure/hour. Determine the computer's mean time to failure.

Substituting the above data into Eq. (2.18) results in

$$\mu = \frac{1}{\theta} = \frac{1}{0.0005} = 2,000 \text{ hours}$$

Thus the mean time to failure of the computer is 2,000 hours.

Weibull Distribution. This probability distribution was developed by W. Weibull in 1951 [1]. It is a very flexible and a widely used distribution that can represent various types of physical phenomena. Exponential and Rayleigh probability distributions are the special cases of the Weibull distribution. The distribution probability density function, the cumulative distribution function, the hazard rate, the mean value, and the variance are

$$f(t) = \frac{b}{\gamma} \left[\frac{t - \alpha}{\gamma} \right]^{b-1} \exp\left[-\left(\frac{t - \alpha}{\gamma} \right)^{b} \right] \qquad (2.22)$$

$$\text{for } \gamma > 0, b > 0, 0 \leqslant \alpha \leqslant t \leqslant \infty$$

Where

b   is the shape parameter.
t   is time.
α   is the location parameter.
γ   is the scale parameter.

$$F(t) = 1 - \exp\left[-\left(\frac{t - \alpha}{\gamma} \right)^{b} \right] \qquad (2.23)$$

$$\lambda(t) = \frac{b}{\gamma} \left[\frac{t - \alpha}{\gamma} \right]^{b-1} \qquad (2.24)$$

$$\mu = \alpha + \gamma\Gamma\left[1 + \frac{1}{b}\right]$$ (2.25)

and

$$\sigma^2 = \gamma^2\left\{\Gamma\left[1 + \frac{2}{b}\right] - \left[\Gamma\left[1 + \frac{1}{b}\right]\right]^2\right\}$$ (2.26)

Where

$$\Gamma(\beta) = \int_0^\infty t^{\beta-1} e^{-t} dt$$ (2.27)

Example 2.5

In Eq. (2.22) set $b = 2$ and $\alpha = 0$. Comment on the resulting probability density function.

By setting $b = 2$ and $\alpha = 0$ in Eq. (2.22), we get

$$f(t) = \frac{2}{\gamma}\left[\frac{t}{\gamma}\right]\exp\left[-\left[\frac{t}{\gamma}\right]^2\right]$$ (2.28)

The above function is the probability density function of the Rayleigh distribution.

Example 2.6

In Eq. (2.22) set $b = 1$ and $\alpha = 0$. Comment on the resulting probability density function.

Setting $b = 1$ and $\alpha = 0$ in Eq. (2.22) results in

$$f(t) = \frac{1}{\gamma} e^{-\frac{1}{\gamma}t}$$ (2.29)

The above function is the probability density function of the exponential distribution.

2.3.2 Discrete Distributions

Binomial and Poisson distributions described below belong to the family of discrete distribution.

Binomial Distribution. Often it is used to perform reliability analysis. The following general expression in many cases is used to represent the distribution:

$$(R + F)^k \tag{2.30}$$

Where R is the probability of success; F is the probability of failure; k is the fixed number of known trials.

The following assumptions are associated with the above expression

  i.   Trials are independent.
 ii.   Each trial has only two possible outcomes, i.e. a success or a failure.
iii.   All the k trials have the same probabilities of success and the same probabilities of failure.
 iv.   For each trial $(R + F) = 1$.

The expression (2.30) may be rewritten to the following form:

$$(R + F)^k = \sum_{n=0}^{k} \left[\frac{k!}{n!(k-n)!} \right] R^n F^{k-n} = 1 \tag{2.31}$$

The probability of exactly n successes in k trials is given by

$$P_{sn} = \left[\frac{k!}{n!(k-n)!} \right] R^n F^{k-n} \tag{2.32}$$

Example 2.7

A subsystem of a computer has three identical and independent modules. The probability of success of each module operating normally is 0.8. Calculate the probability of success of exactly two modules operating normally.

Thus the probability of failure F of a module is $1 - R = 1 - 0.8 = 0.2$.

By substituting the specified data into Eq. (2.32) we get

$$P_{s2} = \frac{3!}{2!(3-2)!} R^2 F^{3-2}$$

$$= 3R^2 F$$

$$= 3(0.8)^2(0.2)$$

$$= 0.384$$

Thus the probability of success of exactly two modules operating normally is 38.4%.

Poisson Distribution. This distribution can be approximated from the binomial distribution when the probability of success of each trial is small and the total number of trials is large. The distribution becomes quite useful in reliability studies when one is interested in the occurrence of a number of the same kind of events. Each event represents a failure in reliability studies. The probability that exactly n occurrences will take place is given by

$$P(n) = \frac{(\mu t)^n e^{-\mu t}}{n!}, \quad n = 0, 1, 2, \cdots \tag{2.33}$$

Where

μ is the average failure or arrival rate.
t is time.

Example 2.8

A subsystem used in a computer has an average failure rate of 0.0005 failures/hour. Calculate the probability of having one failure in a 200 hour period.

By substituting the specified data into Eq. (2.33) we get

$$P(1) = \frac{[(0.0005)(200)] e^{-(0.0005)(200)}}{1!}$$

$$= 0.0905$$

Thus the probability of having one failure in a 200 hour period is 9.0484%.

2.4 LAPLACE TRANSFORMS

The Laplace transform method was developed by P.S. de Laplace over 170 years ago [2]. It is a quite useful technique to obtain the solution of constant-coefficient linear differential equations. By definition, the Laplace transform of function $f(t)$ is

$$F(s) = \int_0^\infty f(t) e^{-st} dt \tag{2.34}$$

Where

$f(t)$ is a function of time t.
s is the Laplace transform variable.

Example 2.9

Find the Laplace transform of the following two functions:

$$f(t) = 1 \tag{2.35}$$

$$f(t) = e^{-\lambda t} \tag{2.36}$$

Where

t is time and λ is a constant.

By substituting Eq. (2.35) into relationship (2.34) we get

$$F(s) = \int_0^\infty 1 \cdot e^{-st} dt$$

$$= \left[\frac{e^{-st}}{-s} \right]_0^\infty$$

$$= \frac{1}{s} \tag{2.37}$$

Similarly, substituting Eq. (2.36) into relationship (2.34) results in

$$F(s) = \int_0^\infty e^{-\lambda t} \cdot e^{-st} dt$$

$$= \left[\frac{e^{-(\lambda + s)t}}{-(\lambda + s)} \right]_0^\infty = \frac{1}{(\lambda + s)} \tag{2.38}$$

Example 2.10

Find the Laplace transform of the function given below

$$f(t) = e^{-\sum_{i=1}^{n} \lambda_i t} \tag{2.39}$$

Where

λ_i is the ith constant; $i = 1, 2, 3, \ldots, n$.
n is the number of constants.
t is time.

With the aid of relationships (2.34) and (2.39) we get

$$F(s) = \int_0^\infty e^{-(s + \sum_{i=1}^{n} \lambda_i)t} dt$$

$$= \frac{1}{(s + \sum_{i=1}^{n} \lambda_i)} \tag{2.40}$$

Laplace transforms of five selected functions are presented in Table 2.1.

2.5 FINAL VALUE THEOREM

The final value of a function $f(t)$ can be obtained with the aid of the following relationship:

$$\lim_{t \to \infty} f(t) = \lim_{s \to 0} sF(s) \tag{2.41}$$

Where

t is the time variable.
s is the Laplace transform variable.

Table 2.1   Laplace Transforms of Selected Functions

$f(t)$	$F(s)$
$\mu e^{-\mu t}$ Where μ is a constant.	$\dfrac{\mu}{s + \mu}$
μ	$\dfrac{\mu}{s}$
$\dfrac{t^{k-1}}{(k-1)!}$, $k = 1, 2, 3, 4, \cdots$	$\dfrac{1}{s^k}$
$\dfrac{t^{k-1}e^{-\mu t}}{(k-1)!}$, $k = 1, 2, 3, 4, \cdots$	$\dfrac{1}{(s + \mu)^k}$
$\dfrac{df(t)}{dt}$	$sF(s) - f(0)$

Example 2.11

The Laplace transform of availability of a large computer is

$$A_c(s) = \frac{(s + \mu)}{s(s + \lambda + \mu)} \tag{2.42}$$

Where

λ is the constant failure rate of the computer.
μ is the constant repair rate of the computer.
s is the Laplace transform variable.

Obtain, with the aid of the right hand side of Eq. (2.41), the steady state availability of the computer.
The steady state availability A_{cs} of the computer is

$$A_{cs} = \lim_{s \to 0} s A_c(s)$$

$$= \lim_{s \to 0} \frac{s(s + \mu)}{s(s + \lambda + \mu)}$$

$$= \frac{\mu}{\lambda + \mu} \tag{2.43}$$

Example 2.12

The inverse Laplace transform of Eq. (2.42) is

$$A_c(t) = \frac{\mu}{(\lambda + \mu)} + \frac{\lambda}{(\lambda + \mu)} \cdot e^{-(\lambda + \mu)t} \tag{2.44}$$

Where

t is time.

Obtain with the aid of the left hand side of Eq. (2.41) the steady state availability of the computer. Comment on the end result.
Thus the steady state availability A_{cs} of the computer is

$$A_{cs} = \lim_{t \to \infty} A_c(t)$$

$$= \lim_{t \to \infty} \left[\frac{\mu}{(\lambda + \mu)} + \frac{\lambda}{(\lambda + \mu)} e^{-(\lambda + \mu)t} \right]$$

$$= \frac{\mu}{\lambda + \mu}$$

The above result is the same as given in Eq. (2.43). It proves the fact that both methods yield the same end result.

2.6 MARKOV MODELING

Often used in reliability studies, this method can handle both repairable and nonrepairable systems. The following assumptions are associated with Markov modeling:

    i.   Occurrences are independent.

    ii.   The transition rate, say λ, from one state to another is constant.

    iii.   The probability of occurrence of a transition from one state to another in the small time interval Δt is $\lambda \Delta t$, where λ is the transition rate.

    iv.   The probability of more than one occurrence in the small time interval Δt is very small and therefore it is ignored.

This method is demonstrated in Example 2.13.

Example 2.13

Assume that a computer system can fail in m number of mutually exclusive failure modes as shown in the state–space diagram of Figure 2.1. In the diagram, λ_j denotes jth computer system failure mode's constant failure rate, for $j = 1, 2, 3, 4, \ldots, m$. Develop expressions for state probabilities with the aid of the Markov modeling method and Figure 2.1.

The following symbols were used to develop equations for the computer system model shown in Figure 2.1.

j is the jth state of the computer system: $j = 0$ (computer system functioning successfully), $j = 1$ (computer system failed: failure mode type 1), $j = 2$ (computer system failed: failure mode type 2), $j = 3$ (computer system failed: failure mode type 3), $j = m$ (computer system failed: failure mode type m).

$P_j(t)$ is the probability that computer system is in state j at time t, $j = 0\ 1, 2, 3, \ldots, m$.

Δt is the time interval.

λ_i is the constant failure rate of the computer system failing in failure mode type i, for $i = 1, 2, 3, \ldots, m$.

m is the total failure modes of the computer system.

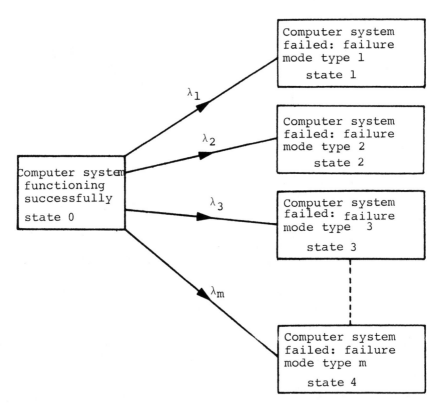

Figure 2.1 State Transition Diagram of a Computer System with *m* Failure Modes.

The following equations are associated with Figure 2.1:

$$P_0(t + \Delta t) = P_0(t)(1 - \lambda_1\Delta t)(1 - \lambda_2\Delta t) \cdots (1 - \lambda_m\Delta t)$$

$$= P_0(t)\left[1 - \sum_{i=1}^{m} \lambda_i\Delta t\right] \tag{2.46}$$

$$P_i(t + \Delta t) = P_i(t)(1 - 0\Delta t) + \lambda_i\Delta t P_0(t) \tag{2.47}$$

$$\text{for } i = 1, 2, 3, \ldots, m.$$

Where

$P_0(t)$ is the probability that the computer system is in operating state 0 at time t.

$P_i(t)$ is the probability that the computer system is in failed state i, for $i = 1, 2, 3, \ldots, m$.

$P_0(t + \Delta t)$ is the probability of the computer system being in operating state 0 at time $t + \Delta t$.

$P_i(t + \Delta t)$ is the probability of the computer system being in failed state i at time $(t + \Delta t)$, for $i = 1, 2, 3, \ldots, m$.

$(1 - \sum\limits_{i=1}^{m} \lambda_i \Delta t)$ is the probability of no failure in small time interval Δt when the computer system is in state 0.

The results of rearranging Eq. (2.46) and (2.47) and taking limit as $\Delta t \rightarrow 0$ are

$$\lim_{\Delta t \rightarrow 0} \frac{P_0(t + \Delta t) - P_0(t)}{\Delta t} = \frac{dP_0(t)}{dt} = - \sum_{j=1}^{m} \lambda_j P_0(t) \qquad (2.48)$$

and

$$\lim_{\Delta t \rightarrow 0} \frac{P_i(t + \Delta t) - P_i(t)}{\Delta t} = \frac{dP_i(t)}{dt} = \lambda_i P_0(t) \qquad (2.49)$$

for $i = 1, 2, 3, \ldots, m$.

At time $t = 0$, $P_0(0) = 1$, $P_i(0) = 0$ for $i = 1, 2, 3, \ldots, m$. The results of solving differential Eqs. (2.48) and (2.49) are

$$P_0(t) = e^{-\lambda_{cs} t} \qquad (2.50)$$

where

$$\lambda_{cs} = \sum_{i=1}^{m} \lambda_i \qquad (2.51)$$

$$P_i(t) = \frac{\lambda_i}{\lambda_{cs}} (1 - e^{-\lambda_{cs} t}), \text{ for } i = 1, 2, 3, \ldots, m. \qquad (2.52)$$

2.7   THE METHOD OF MAXIMUM LIKELIHOOD

This is a well-known method used to estimate parameters of a distribution. It tends to produce better estimates than any other techniques [3], and is usually straightforward to apply. For a single unknown parameter, the likelihood function of the sample is defined as

$$F(t_1, t_2, \ldots, t_m; \lambda) = f(t_1; \lambda)f(t_2; \lambda) \cdots f(t_m; \lambda) \qquad (2.53)$$

Where

$(t_1, t_2, \ldots, t_m)$ is a random sample drawn from the population distribution with probability density function $f(t; \lambda)$.

λ is the parameter of the distribution.

$f(t_j; \lambda)$ is the probability density function of the random variable t_j; for $j = 1, 2, 3, \ldots, m$.

The method of maximum likelihood is concerned with determining the value of λ in Eq. (2.53) which maximizes the likelihood function of the sample. Thus by taking the natural logarithm of Eq. (2.53), differentiating it with respect to λ, and then setting it equal to zero, we get

$$\frac{\partial \ln F(\cdot)}{\partial \lambda} = 0 \qquad (2.54)$$

The value of λ can easily be obtained from Eq. (2.54)

Example 2.14

The failure times of a computer are described by the following probability density function:

$$f(t; \mu) = \frac{1}{\mu} e^{-\frac{1}{\mu}t} \qquad (2.55)$$

Where

t is time.

μ is the distribution parameter, or more specifically, the mean time to failure of the computer.

Derive the maximum likelihood estimation for the distribution parameter μ. With the aid of Eqs. (2.53) and (2.55) we get

$$F(t_1, t_2, \ldots, t_m; \lambda) = \frac{1}{\mu^m} \exp\left[-\frac{1}{\mu} \sum_{j=1}^{m} t_j \right] \qquad (2.56)$$

Taking the natural logarithm of the above equation results in

$$\ln F(\cdot) = -m \ln \mu - \frac{1}{\mu} \cdot \sum_{j=1}^{m} t_j \qquad (2.57)$$

Taking the derivatives of Eq. (2.57) with respect to μ and setting the resulting expression equal to zero yields

$$\frac{\partial \ln F(\cdot)}{\partial \mu} = -\frac{m}{\mu} + \frac{1}{\mu^2} \sum_{j=1}^{m} t_j = 0 \qquad (2.58)$$

Rearranging Eq. (2.58) leads to

$$\hat{\mu} = \frac{1}{m} \sum_{j=1}^{m} t_j \qquad (2.59)$$

Where

m is the sample size.
$\hat{\mu}$ is the maximum likelihood estimation of μ.

2.8 SUMMARY

This chapter reviewed essential mathematical concepts. Four important properties of probability were presented. Essential continuous and discrete probability distributions were covered. These distributions are exponential, Weibull, binomial, and Poisson. The Laplace transform method was presented and Laplace transforms of five selected functions were given in table form. The final value theorem was presented. The Markov modeling technique was demonstrated with the aid of a solved example. The method of maximum likelihood was covered. A number of examples along with their solutions were presented.

2.9 EXERCISES

1. Write an essay on the history of mathematics.
2. Discuss the history of probability theory.
3. Find the inverse Laplace transform of the following function:

$$F(s) = \frac{1}{(s + \lambda_1)(s + \lambda_2)} \qquad (2.60)$$

Where

λ_1 and λ_2 are the constants.

s is the Laplace transform variable.

4. Prove that the Laplace transform of $df(t)/dt$ is $sF(s) - f(0)$.
5. Prove that the mean value m of a continuous probability distribution is given by

$$m = \int_0^\infty [1 - F(t)]\, dt \tag{2.61}$$

Where

$F(t)$ is the cumulative distribution function.

t is time.

6. The mean time to failure of a computer is 1500 hours. If its failure times are described by an exponential distribution, calculate the probability of success (of the computer) for a 40 hour mission.
7. With the aid of Eq. (2.23), prove that the reliability function associated with the Rayleigh distribution is

$$R(t) = \exp\left[-\left(\frac{t}{\gamma}\right)^2 \right] \tag{2.62}$$

8. Obtain an expression for the time-dependent total failure probability of the computer system described in example 2.12. You may make use of Eq. (2.52).

2.10 REFERENCES

1. W. Weibull, "A Statistical Distribution Function of Wide Applicability", Journal of Applied Mechanics, Vol. 18, 1951, pp. 293–297.

2. F.E. Nixon, *Handbook of Laplace Transformation*, Prentice-Hall Inc., Englewood Cliffs, N.J., 1965.

3. D.K. Lloyd and M. Lipow, *Reliability: Management, Methods and Mathematics*, Prentice-Hall, Englewood Cliffs, NJ, 1962.

3
INTRODUCTION TO QUALITY CONTROL AND RELIABILITY

3.1 INTRODUCTION

Quality control and reliability fields have much in common. In many engineering companies, both are practiced within the framework of a single department. However, the origin of quality control is much older than that of reliability. The history of statistical quality control goes back as far as 1916, when C.N. Frazee of Telephone Laboratories applied statistical methods to inspection problems. The concept of the operating characteristics curve is credited to him. Eight years later in 1924, Walter A. Shewhart of Western Electric developed well-known quality control charts. These charts are regarded as a major milestone in the development of the modern quality control discipline. Another important event in the history of quality control took place in 1946 when the American Society for Quality Control (ASQC) was formed. Ever since its formation, ASQC has played an instrumental role in the development of the quality control field. Today quality control principles are being practiced in many industries to produce various kinds of products. The computer is one of them.

The history of reliability goes as far back as World War II when its basic principles were applied during the development of V1 rockets in Germany. It was also in the 1940's when the need for reliability was recognized in the Armed Forces of the United States. In 1950, the Department of Defense formed an ad hoc committee on reliability. From this committee emerged the permanent group called Advisory Group on the Reliability of Electronic Equipment (AGREE), who produced a report known as the AGREE report in 1957. Ever since, various researchers and authors have contributed to the field of reliability. Today it has advanced to a level where it is beginning to be separated into various specialized areas. Computer reliability is one of them.

Although this chapter covers some general aspects of quality control, the emphasis is on reliability.

3.2 QUALITY CONTROL

Quality control concepts play an instrumental role in producing reliable computers. As computers become larger, more complex and costly to produce, the importance of quality control concepts is increasing. Some of the advantages of a quality control program are as follows:

i.   Reduction in rework and production cost;
ii. Customer satisfaction;
iii. Lesser number of defectives;
iv. Better confidence in produced goods;
v.   Reduction in overall cost.

3.2.1 Acceptance Sampling

Acceptance sampling may be described as a process for making statistical decisions regarding the quality of products in a lot. For judging quality, the concept of acceptance sampling is probably the oldest method. Its basis is that a sample of reasonable size drawn from a large population will exhibit the characteristics of the entire population. Some of the advantages of this method are as follows:

i.   Reduces the cost of inspection
ii. Requires less manpower to carry out inspection
iii. Helps to save time needed for inspection
iv. Incurs less product handling damage
v.   Is applicable in cases where it is physically impossible to perform 100% inspection (e.g. testing ammunition).

Similarly, some of the drawbacks of acceptance sampling are the risk of accepting bad lots or rejecting good ones, that knowledge of probability theory is required to a certain level, that less information is provided, and so on.

3.2.2 Inspection Related Formulas

This section presents three formulas concerned with determining the percentage of defects correctly identified by the inspector, actual inspector efficiency, and reliability of redundant inspectors [1], respectively.

Formula I. This is concerned with determining the percentage of defects correctly identified by the inspector. In this model it is assumed that the work performed by the inspector is assessed by the check inspector. Thus the percentage of defects, D, correctly identified by the inspector is expressed as follows:

$$D = \left[\frac{n_i - n_g}{n_i - n_g + n_m} \right] \times (100) \qquad (3.1)$$

Where

n_g is the number of defect-free units rejected by the inspector.
n_m is the number of defects overlooked by the inspector.
n_i is the number of defects discovered by the inspector.

Example 3.1

A lot of certain units was inspected by an inspector who found 80 defects. A check inspector was assigned to re-examine the entire number of units inspected by the inspector. The check inspector found that the inspector missed 8 defects and rejected 4 units without defects. Compute the value of the percentage of defects correctly identified by the inspector.

In this example values of n_i, n_g, and n_m are defined as:

$$n_i = 80$$

$$n_g = 4$$

$$n_m = 8$$

By substituting the above values into Eq. (3.1) we get

$$D = \left[\frac{80 - 4}{80 - 4 + 8} \right] \times (100)$$

$$= 90.48\%$$

In this case 90.48% of defects were correctly identified by the inspector.

Formula II. This formula is the refined version of Formula I. In Formula I we assumed that the check inspector is perfect or not prone to error and the regular (i.e. original) inspector is prone to error. However in real life situations this assumption may not be valid because there is the possibility that the check inspector may also make errors during the reinspection process. Therefore in order to improve the accuracy of Formula I we introduce a new factor R into Eq. (3.1) as follows:

$$D_m = \left[\frac{(n_i - n_g \cdot R)}{n_i - R \cdot n_g + n_m \cdot R} \right] \times (100) \qquad (3.2)$$

Where

D_m is the actual inspector efficiency.
R is the reliability of the check inspector.

Formula III. This formula is concerned with evaluating the reliability of two independent inspectors working in parallel. More specifically, the same components are checked by both inspectors. The reliability R_{ns} of inspectors working in parallel is given by

$$R_{ns} = 1 - \prod_{i=1}^{2} (1 - D_i) \qquad (3.3)$$

Where

D_i is the percentage of defects correctly identified by inspector i; for $i = 1, 2$.

3.2.3 Control Charts

These charts were originally developed by Walter A. Shewhart and are widely used in quality control work. A control chart may simply be described as a graphical method used to determine whether or not a process in question is under a "state of statistical control". Control charts keep track of process variations such as variations in absenteeism, dimensions, manpower turnover, and so on. All the control charts have the following common features:

   i.   The average value of the process;
  ii.   lower control limit;
 iii.   upper control limit.

If a process parameter under the state of control is within the upper and lower control limits, then the process in question is functioning satisfactorily. If it is not, then the process is not functioning satisfactorily and there is a definite need for action to correct the process. The most commonly used control charts are the p chart and the $\bar{s}$–r chart. In the case of the p chart the population consists of both defective and good items. Therefore the binomial distribution is used to develop the upper and lower control limits. The fraction of defectives in samples taken periodically from a process is recorded periodically on the chart. On the other hand, the $\bar{s}$–r chart jointly records the samples' mean ($\bar{s}$) and range (r). As in the case of the p chart, the samples are taken periodically from the process.

3.2.4 Activities of a Quality Control Department

There are various activities performed in a quality control department. They may vary from one department to another. Some of these are quality planning, training, inspection, statistical analysis, auditing, inspection planning, process and measurement control, developing programs to prevent defects, conducting research and development studies, analyzing quality costs, and performing analysis of quality field complaints.

3.3 BASIC RELIABILITY CONCEPTS

3.3.1 General Reliability Function

This section presents derivations for the general reliability function [5]. This function can be applied to all kinds of probability distributions used in reliability theory. Examples of such distributions are Weibull, exponential, Rayleigh, and normal.

Suppose K number of identical items are being tested; after some time t, $K_s(t)$ survive and $K_f(t)$ fail. In this case, at any time t, the reliability function $R(t)$ is

$$R(t) = \frac{K_s(t)}{K} \qquad (3.4)$$

The total number of identical items put under test is given by

$$K = K_s(t) + K_f(t) \qquad (3.5)$$

Therefore,

$$K_s(t) = K - K_f(t) \qquad (3.6)$$

After substituting Eq. (3.6) into Eq. (3.4) we get

$$R(t) = \frac{K - K_f(t)}{K}$$

$$= 1 - \frac{K_f(t)}{K} \qquad (3.7)$$

The derivative of Eq. (3.7) with respect to time t is

$$\frac{dR(t)}{dt} = -\frac{1}{K}\frac{dK_f(t)}{dt} \qquad (3.8)$$

As dt approaches zero we obtain from Eq. (3.8) the following probability density function

$$\frac{dR(t)}{dt} = \frac{dF(t)}{dt} = -f(t) \qquad (3.9)$$

Where

$F(t)$ is the cumulative failure distribution function.

$f(t)$ is the failure density function.

The above relationship can be used to obtain the failure density function of a probability distribution or an item whose reliability or cumulative distribution function is known.

Dividing both sides of Eq. (3.8) by $K_s(t)$ we get

$$-\frac{K}{K_s(t)} \cdot \frac{dR(t)}{dt} = \frac{1}{K_s(t)} \cdot \frac{dK_f(t)}{dt}$$

$$= z(t) \tag{3.10}$$

Where

$z(t)$ is the instantaneous failure rate (hazard rate).

Substituting Eq. (3.4) into Eq. (3.10) results in

$$-\frac{1}{R(t)} \frac{dR(t)}{dt} = z(t) \tag{3.11}$$

The above relationship can be used to obtain the hazard rate function of a probability distribution or an item whose reliability function is given.

Therefore, with the aid of Eq. (3.9) and (3.11) we get

$$z(t) = -\frac{1}{R(t)} \cdot [-f(t)]$$

$$= \frac{f(t)}{R(t)} \tag{3.12}$$

The above relationship can also be used to obtain the hazard rate function of a probability distribution when its failure density and reliability functions are known.

In order to obtain the general reliability function, we rewrite Eq. (3.11) to the following form:

$$\frac{dR(t)}{R(t)} = z(t) \cdot dt \tag{3.13}$$

Integrating both sides of Eq. (3.13) from time zero to time t gives

$$\int_0^t \frac{1}{R(t)} \cdot dR(t) = -\int_0^t z(t) \cdot dt \tag{3.14}$$

At time $t = 0$, $R(0) = 1$, the above equation is rewritten to the following form:

$$\int_1^{R(t)} \frac{1}{R(t)} \cdot dR(t) = -\int_0^t z(t) \cdot dt$$

$$[\ln R(t)]_1^{R(t)} = -\int_0^t z(t) \cdot dt$$

$$\ln R(t) = -\int_0^t z(t) \cdot dt \qquad (3.15)$$

Therefore, from Eq. (3.15) we get

$$R(t) = \exp\left[-\int_0^t z(t) \cdot dt \right] \qquad (3.16)$$

The above relationship can be used to obtain the reliability function for a probability distribution or for an item whose hazard rate function is known.

In Table 3.1 a number of useful relationships used in reliability analysis are presented.

Example 3.2

Failure times of a computer are described by the following probability density function:

$$f(t) = \lambda e^{-\lambda t} \qquad (3.17)$$

Where

t is time.
λ is the scale parameter.

Obtain expressions for reliability and hazard rate. From Table 3.1 we get

$$R(t) = 1 - \int_0^t f(t)\, dt \qquad (3.18)$$

Substituting relationship (3.17) into Eq. (3.18) results in

$$R(t) = 1 - \int_0^t \lambda e^{-\lambda t} dt$$

$$= 1 - [1 - e^{-\lambda t}]$$

$$R(t) = e^{-\lambda t} \qquad (3.19)$$

1">B.S. Dhillon

Table 3.1 Some of the Relationships Used in Reliability Analysis

$$R(t) = \exp[-\int_0^t z(t)\cdot dt]$$

$$R(t) = \int_t^\infty f(t)\cdot dt$$

$$R(t) = 1 - \int_0^t f(t)\cdot dt$$

$$\int_0^t f(t)\cdot dt + \int_t^\infty f(t)\cdot dt = \int_0^\infty f(t)\cdot dt = 1$$

$$R(t) + F(t) = 1$$

$$F(t) = \int_0^t f(t)\cdot dt$$

$$F(t) = 1 - R(t) = 1 - \int_t^\infty f(t)\cdot dt$$

$$F(t) = 1 - \exp[-\int_0^t z(t)\cdot dt]$$

$$z(t) = \frac{f(t)}{R(t)}$$

$$z(t) = -\frac{1}{R(t)}\cdot\frac{dR(t)}{dt}$$

$$z(t) = \frac{f(t)}{\int_t^\infty f(t)\cdot dt}$$

$$\frac{dF(t)}{dt} = f(t)$$

$$\frac{dR(t)}{dt} = \frac{-dF(t)}{dt} = -f(t)$$

With the aid of Eq. (3.11) and (3.19) we get

$$z(t) = -\frac{1}{R(t)}\cdot\frac{dR(t)}{dt}$$

$$= -\frac{1}{e^{-\lambda t}}\cdot\frac{d(e^{-\lambda t})}{dt}$$

$$= \lambda \tag{3.20}$$

Computer's reliability and hazard rate expressions are given by Eqs. (3.19) and (3.20), respectively.

Example 3.3

The failure rate λ of a specific computer system is 0.004 failure/hour. Calculate the system reliability for a 15 hour mission with the aid of Eq. (3.16).

In this example it is obvious that the failure rate of the computer system is constant. Therefore

$$z(t) = \lambda \tag{3.21}$$

Substituting the above relationship into Eq. (3.16) leads to

$$R(t) = \exp\left[-\int_0^t \lambda \cdot dt \right]$$

$$= e^{-\lambda t}$$

By substituting the specified data for λ and time t into Eq. (3.22) we get

$$R(15) = e^{-(0.004)(15)}$$

$$= 0.9418$$

Thus the reliability of the computer system is 0.9418.

3.3.2   Failure Rate Models for Parts and Equipment

This section presents two models to compute failure rates of electronic parts and equipment. For many electronic parts or components, an equation of the following general form is used to predict their failure rates:

$$\lambda_p = \lambda_{bs} \cdot \alpha_1 \cdot \alpha_2 \cdots \tag{3.23}$$

Where

λ_p is the total failure rate of the part.

α_1 is the factor which accounts for the influence of environmental factors, excluding temperature.

α_2 is the factor which accounts for the effects of different quality levels on the part in question.

λ_{bs} is the base failure rate. This is related to electrical and temperature stresses on the component or the part.

To predict the failure rate of an item of equipment during bid proposal and early design phases, the parts count method is frequently used. In order to make use of this method the information required is equipment environment, generic part types and quantities, and part quality levels. For a defined equipment environment, the failure rate of the equipment is expressed as follows [2]:

$$\lambda_e = \sum_{K=1}^{m} P_{qK} (\lambda \alpha)_K \qquad (3.24)$$

Where

m is the number of distinct generic component categories.

λ is the generic failure rate of the generic component K; expressed in failures/10^6 hr.

P_{qK} is the quantity of the generic component K.

α is the quality factor of the generic component k.

λ_e is the failure rate of the equipment expressed in failures/10^6 hr.

Equation (3.24) is applicable only if all the equipment or the total system will be operated in a single environment.

3.3.3 Reliability Configurations

This section presents reliability configurations being used from time to time in computers. These configurations are as follows:

Series Configuration. This is the simplest configuration. An m unit series configuration is shown in Figure 3.1. In this case, if any one of the units fail, the entire system fails. Each block in Figure 3.1 represents a unit.

For independent nonidentical units, the reliability of the series configuration is given by

$$R_{sc} = R_1 \cdot R_2 \cdot R_3 \cdot \cdots R_m \qquad (3.25)$$

Where

R_{sc} is the reliability of the series configuration (system).

R_i is the reliability of the ith unit; for $i = 1, 2, 3, 4, \ldots, m$.

m is the number of units.

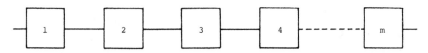

Figure 3.1 An m Unit Series Configuration

For the constant failure rate of a unit, using Eq. (3.19), the ith unit reliability is

$$R_i(t) = e^{-\lambda_i t} \tag{3.26}$$

$$\text{for } i = 1, 2, 3, \ldots, m.$$

Where

$R_i(t)$ is the reliability of unit i at time t; for $i = 1, 2, 3, \ldots, m$.
λ_i is the constant failure rate of unit i; for $i = 1, 2, 3, \ldots, m$.
t is time.

Substitute the above equation into Eq. (3.25) yields

$$R_{sc}(t) = e^{-\lambda_1 t} \cdot e^{-\lambda_2 t} \cdot e^{-\lambda_3 t} \cdots e^{-\lambda_m t}$$

$$= e^{-\left(\sum\limits_{i=1}^{m} \lambda_i\right)t} \tag{3.27}$$

The mean time to failure $MTTF$ of an item is given by

$$MTTF = \int_0^\infty R(t) \cdot dt \tag{3.28}$$

Where

$R(t)$ is the item's reliability at time t.

Alternatively,

$$MTTF = \lim_{s \to 0} R(s) \tag{3.29}$$

Where

s is the Laplace transform variable.
$R(s)$ is the Laplace transform of the item's reliability.

Taking the Laplace transform of Eq. (3.27) we get

$$R(s) = \frac{1}{s + \sum\limits_{i=1}^{m} \lambda_i} \tag{3.30}$$

Applying Eqs. (3.29) and (3.30) results in

$$MTTF = \lim_{s \to 0} \frac{1}{\left[s + \sum\limits_{i=1}^{m} \lambda_i \right]}$$

$$= \frac{1}{\sum\limits_{i=1}^{m} \lambda_i} \qquad (3.31)$$

The variance of the time to failure distribution of an item is defined by

$$\sigma^2 = \int_0^\infty (t - MTTF)^2 f(t) \cdot dt \qquad (3.32)$$

Where

$f(t)$ is the failure density function of the item.

Alternatively,

$$\sigma^2 = -2 \lim_{s \to 0} R'(s) - (MTTF)^2 \qquad (3.33)$$

Where

$$R'(s) = \frac{dR(s)}{ds}$$

Taking the derivative of Eq. (3.30) with respect to s leads to

$$\frac{dR(s)}{ds} = -\frac{1}{\left[s + \sum\limits_{i=1}^{m} \lambda_i \right]^2} \qquad (3.34)$$

$$\sigma^2 = -2 \lim_{s \to 0} \frac{1}{\left[s + \sum\limits_{i=1}^{m} \lambda_i \right]^2} - \frac{1}{\left[\sum\limits_{i=1}^{m} \lambda_i \right]^2}$$

$$= \frac{1}{\left[\sum\limits_{i=1}^{m} \lambda_i \right]^2} \qquad (3.35)$$

Example 3.4

A subsystem of a computer has three critical and independent units. If any one of the units fails, the subsystem will fail completely. Units 1, 2 and 3 reliabilities are 0.9, 0.85, and 0.95, respectively. Calculate the subsystem's reliability.

In this example the critical units of the subsystem are connected in series. Thus by substituting the given data into Eq. (3.25) we get

$$R_{sc} = R_1 \cdot R_2 \cdot R_3$$

$$= (0.9)(0.85)(0.95)$$

$$= 0.7268$$

The reliability of the subsystem is 72.68%.

Parallel Configuration. In this case a system is composed of m active units. More specifically all the m units operate simultaneously. At least one unit must work for the system to be successful. For independent and nonidentical units, the parallel configuration reliability is expressed as follows:

$$R_{pc} = 1 - \prod_{i=1}^{m} (1 - R_i) \qquad (3.36)$$

Where

R_{pc} is the reliability of the parallel configuration.
R_i is the reliability of unit i, for $i = 1, 2, 3, \ldots, m$.
m is the number of units.

For identical units, the above equation reduces to

$$R_{pc} = 1 - (1 - R)^m \qquad (3.37)$$

Where

R is the reliability of a unit.

Rearranging Eq. (3.37) and taking a natural logarithm results in

$$m = \frac{\ln(1 - R_{pc})}{\ln(1 - R)} \qquad (3.38)$$

From the above equation one can estimate the value of m for the given values of R_{pc} and R.

For the constant failure rate of unit i, substituting Eq. (3.26) into Eq. (3.36) results in

$$R_{pc}(t) = 1 - \prod_{i=1}^{m} (1 - e^{-\lambda_i t}) \tag{3.39}$$

Where

t is time.

λ_i is the constant value rate of unit i, for $i = 1, 2, 3, \ldots, m$.

For identical units, the above equation simplifies to

$$R_{pc}(t) = 1 - (1 - e^{-\lambda t})^m \tag{3.40}$$

Where

λ is the constant failure rate of a unit.

With the aid of Eqs. (3.29), (3.33), and (3.40), we get the following formulas for mean time to failure $MTTF_p$ and variance σ_p^2:

$$MTTF_p = \sum_{j=1}^{m} \frac{1}{j\lambda} \tag{3.41}$$

and

$$\sigma_p^2 = \sum_{j=1}^{m} \frac{1}{(j\lambda)^2} \tag{3.42}$$

Example 3.5

A computer has two identical and independent central processing units functioning in parallel. At least one of the central processing units must operate normally for the system's success. Calculate the reliability of the two central processing unit parallel subsystem if the reliability of a single central processing unit is 0.90.

By substituting the above given data into Eq. (3.37) we get

$$R_{cps} = 1 - (1 - 0.90)^2$$

$$= 0.99$$

Thus the reliability of the two central processing unit parallel subsystem is 0.99.

Example 3.6

The specified reliability of a subsystem used in a computer is 0.98. However, its estimated reliability is only 0.85. Calculate the number of independent and identical subsystems to be used in parallel to achieve the specified reliability of 0.98.

Substituting the above data into Eq. (3.38) yields

$$m = \frac{\ln(1 - 0.98)}{\ln(1 - 0.85)}$$

$$= \frac{-3.9120}{-1.8971}$$

$$= 2.0621$$

$$\cong 2$$

In order to achieve the specified reliability of 0.98, two subsystems have to be placed in parallel.

N-out-of-*m* Unit Configuration. This is another configuration used to improve system reliability. In this case a system contains *m* simultaneously operating units. At least *N* number of them must work normally for the system's success. For independent and identical *m* units, the N-out-of-*m* unit configuration reliability is given by

$$R_{N/m} = \sum_{j=N}^{m} \left[\frac{m!}{j!(m - j)!} \right] R^j (1 - R)^{m-j} \tag{3.43}$$

Where

R is the reliability of a unit.

For $N = m$ and $N = 1$, the above equation reduces to the one for an identical unit series system and for an identical unit parallel system, respectively. For the constant failure rate λ of a unit, substituting Eq. (3.22) into Eq. (3.43) results in

$$R_{N/m} = \sum_{j=N}^{m} \left[\frac{m!}{j!(m - j)!} \right] (e^{-\lambda t})^j (1 - e^{-\lambda t})^{m-j} \tag{3.44}$$

By substituting the above equation into Eq. (3.28), we get

$$MTTF_{N/m} = \int_0^\infty \left[\sum_{j=N}^m \left[\frac{m!}{j!(m-j)!} \right] (e^{-\lambda t})^j (1 - e^{-\lambda t})^{m-j} \right] dt$$

$$= \sum_{j=N}^m \frac{1}{j\lambda} \tag{3.45}$$

In Table 3.2 reliability expressions for selective special cases of the N-out-of-m unit configuration are presented [2].

Example 3.7

A subsystem of a computer is composed of four independent, identical and active modules. At least three of the four modules must function normally for the subsystem's success. The reliability of a module is 0.8. Calculate the subsystem's reliability.

Table 3.2   Reliability Equations for Selective Special Cases of the N-out-of-m Unit Configuration

Number	Situation	Reliability Equation
1	At least 2 units of 3 operating normally for success.	$R_s = 3R^2 - 2R^3$ Where R_s is the system reliability R is the reliability of a unit.
2	At least 1 unit of m operating normally for success.	$R_s = \sum_{i=1}^m (-1)^{i+1} \binom{m}{i} R^i$
3	At least $(m-1)$ units of m operating normally for success.	$R_s = mR^{m-1} - (m-1)R^m$
4	At least $(m-2)$ units of m operating normally for success.	$R_s = \binom{m}{2} R^{m-2} + (2m - m^2)R^{m-1} + \binom{m-1}{2} R^m$

For the specified data, from Eq. (3.43) we get

$$R_{3/4} = \sum_{j=3}^{4} \left[\frac{4!}{j!(4-j)!} \right] R^j (1-R)^{4-j}$$

$$= 4R^3 - 3R^4$$

$$= 4(0.8)^3 - 3(0.8)^4$$

$$= 0.8192$$

Thus the subsystem's reliability is 81.92%.

Example 3.8

In Example 3.7 the constant failure rate of each module of the computer subsystem is 0.0002 failures/hour. Calculate the mean time to failure of the subsystem.

By substituting the specified data into Eq. (3.45) we get

$$MTTF_{3/4} = \sum_{j=3}^{4} \frac{1}{j\lambda}$$

$$= \sum_{j=3}^{4} \frac{1}{j(0.0002)}$$

$$= 2916.67 \text{ hours}$$

Thus the mean time to failure of the computer subsystem is 2916.67 hours.

Series–Parallel Configuration. The block diagram of this configuration is shown in Figure 3.2. Each block in this figure represents a unit. In this case two independent and active parallel subsystems are connected in series. Each of these two subsystems is composed of two independent units in parallel. If any one of the subsystems fails, the system fails.

This kind of configuration is quite useful in a situation when the primary unit failure mode is open. The reliability of the configuration shown in Figure 3.2 is

$$R_{spc} = [1 - (1 - R_1)(1 - R_2)][1 - (1 - R_3)(1 - R_4)] \qquad (3.46)$$

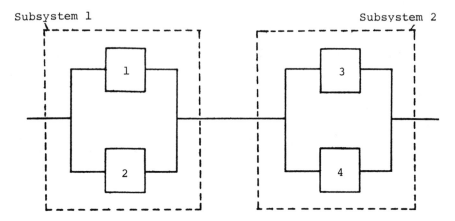

Figure 3.2 A Series–Parallel Network

Where

R_{spc} is the series–parallel configuration's reliability.
R_i is the reliability of unit i; for $i = 1, 2, 3, 4$

For identical units the above equation becomes

$$R_{spc} = [1 - (1 - R)^2]^2 \tag{3.47}$$

Where

R is reliability of a unit.

As for the series configuration, one can develop equations for mean time to failure and variance [3].

Example 3.9

Four independent and identical units of a computer are forming a series–parallel configuration. The reliability of each unit is 0.85. Calculate the reliability of the series–parallel network.

For the specified data, use of Eq. (3.47) results in

$$R_{spc} = [1 - (1 - 0.85)^2]^2$$

$$= 0.9555$$

Thus the reliability of the series–parallel configuration is 95.55%.

Parallel–Series Configuration. The block diagram of this configuration is shown in Figure 3.3. Each block in this figure represents a unit. The figure shows two subsystems forming a parallel system. Each subsystem contains two units in series. The parallel–series system fails only when both its subsystems fail.

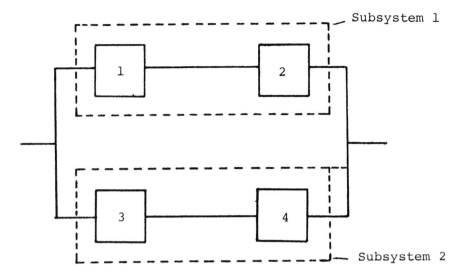

Figure 3.3 A Parallel–Series Configuration.

This type of network is quite useful in situations where primary unit failure mode is short. For independent units, the configuration reliability is given by

$$R_{psc} = 1 - (1 - R_1 \cdot R_2)(1 - R_3 \cdot R_4) \qquad (3.48)$$

Where

R_{psc} is the reliability of the parallel–series configuration.
R_i is the reliability of unit i; for $i = 1, 2, 3, 4$.

In the case when all four units are identical, the above equation becomes

$$R_{psc} = 1 - (1 - R^2)^2 \qquad (3.49)$$

Where

R is the unit's reliability.

As for the series configuration, one can develop expressions for mean time to failure and variance [3].

Example 3.10

Four identical and independent elements of a subsystem used in a computer are arranged in a parallel–series configuration. Each element's reliability is 0.8. Determine the reliability of the subsystem in question.

45

With the aid of the specified data and Eq. (3.49) we get

$$R_{psc} = 1 - \{1 - (0.8)^2\}^2$$

$$= 0.8704$$

Thus the reliability of the parallel–series subsystem is 87.04%.

Standby Redundant Configuration. In this case only one unit is operating and $(m - 1)$ units are on standby. As soon as the operating unit fails, it is immediately replaced with one of the $(m - 1)$ standbys. The system fails only when all the m units fail. In order to develop a reliability expression for the configuration, the following were assumed:

    i.   All the units are identical and independent.
    ii. Failure times of each unit are exponentially distributed.
   iii. The switching mechanism is perfect.
   iv. A failed unit is never repaired.
    v. Standby units remain as good as new.

Thus the reliability of the standby system is

$$R_{sc}(t) = e^{-\lambda t} \sum_{K=0}^{m-1} (\lambda t)^K / K! \tag{3.50}$$

Where

$R_{sc}(t)$	is the reliability of the standby configuration.
λ	is the constant failure rate of a unit.
t	is time.
m	is the total number of units in the system.

With the aid of Eqs. (3.50), (3.29), and (3.33) we obtained the following formulas for mean time to failure $MTTF_{sc}$ and variance σ_{sc}^2:

$$MTTF_{sc} = \frac{m}{\lambda} \tag{3.51}$$

and

$$\sigma_{sc}^2 = \frac{m}{\lambda^2} \tag{3.52}$$

Example 3.11

A system is composed of two identical and independent computers. One computer is operating and the other one is on standby. As soon as the operating computer fails, it is immediately replaced with the standby computer. The constant failure rate of a computer is 0.0004 failures/hour. Calculate the system mean time to failure by assuming that

i.   The switching mechanism is perfect.
ii. A failed computer is never repaired.
iii. The standby computer cannot fail in its standby mode and remains as good as new.

By substituting the above given data into Eq. (3.51) we get

$$MTTF_{sc} = \frac{2}{0.0004}$$

$$= 5,000 \text{ hours}$$

Thus the mean time to failure of the computer system is 5,000 hours.

Bridge Configuration. This configuration is shown in Figure 3.4. Each block in the diagram represents a unit. The configuration is composed of five units. For independent and identical units, the reliability of the bridge configuration shown in Figure 3.4 is given by

$$R_{bd} = 2R^5 - 5R^4 + 2R^3 + 2R^2 \tag{3.53}$$

Where

R_{bd} is the reliability of the bridge network.
R is the reliability of a unit.

As for the series configuration, one can develop expressions for mean time to failure and variance.

3.3.4 Fault Trees

This method is widely used to analyze complex systems. The history of the method goes back to the early 1960s when H.A. Watson of Bell Telephone Laboratories developed it to perform the analysis of the Minuteman Launch Control System. Since then many others have contributed to the method [4] which is described in detail in reference [5].

The fault tree analysis begins by identifying an undesirable event of the system under study. This event is commonly referred to as the top event of the system. Events which could cause this top event to occur are generated and connected by logic operators such as OR and AND.

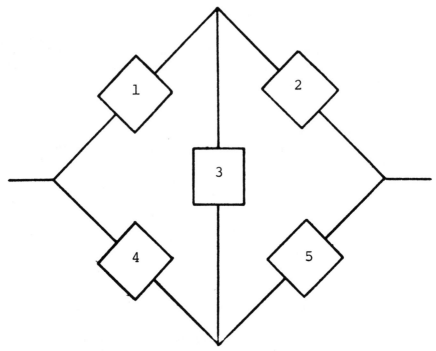

Figure 3.4 A Five-Unit Bridge Network

In developing fault trees, one successively reiterates the question "How could this event occur?" This way the construction of a fault tree proceeds by generation of events in a successive manner until the primary events are reached; more specifically, until there is no need to develop events any further. A fault tree may simply be described as a logic structure relating the top fault event of a system to its primary fault events.

To construct a fault tree various kinds of symbols are used. Many of these are described in reference [5]. Here, in order to construct a simple fault tree, we will make use of the symbols shown in Figures 3.5 and 3.6. Figure 3.5 presents two symbols to represent events. The rectangle represents a resultant event, that is, an event resulting from the combination of fault events through the input of a logical gate such as shown in Figure 3.6. The circle represents a basic (primary) fault event or the failure of an elementary unit.

Figure 3.6 presents symbols for AND and OR gates. The symbol for the AND gate signifies that an output fault event occurs only if all the input fault events occur. Similarly, the symbol for the OR gate signifies that an output fault event occurs if at least one of the input fault events occur.

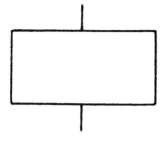
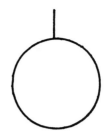

Resultant Event   Basic Fault Event

Figure 3.5 Symbols Used to Represent Events

For independent input fault events, the probability of occurrence of the OR gate's output fault event is given by

$$F_{OR} = 1 - \prod_{i=1}^{m} (1 - F_i) \qquad (3.54)$$

Where

m is the number of input fault events.

F_{OR} is the probability of occurrence of the OR gate's output fault event.

F_i is the probability of the occurrence of the input fault event i; for $i = 1, 2, 3, \ldots, m$.

Similarly for independent input fault events, the probability of occurrence of the AND gate's output fault event is

$$F_{AND} = \prod_{i=1}^{m} F_i \qquad (3.55)$$

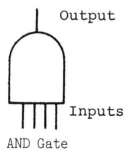
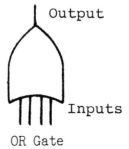

AND Gate   OR Gate

Figure 3.6 Symbols For AND and OR Gates

Where

F_{AND} is the probability of occurrence of the AND gate's output
            fault event.
m is the number of input fault events.
F_i is the probability of the occurrence of the input fault event i;
            for $i = 1, 2, 3, \ldots, m$.

Example 3.12

Develop a fault tree for the independent unit parallel–series configuration
shown in Figure 3.3. Assume that this figure represents a computer system.
Obtain an expression for the failure probability of that parallel–series
configuration (computer system).

With the aid of symbols shown in Figures 3.5 and 3.6, the fault tree shown
in Figure 3.7 was developed.

With the aid of Eqs. (3.54) and (3.55) we obtained the probability of the
occurrence of the top event shown in Figure 3.7 as follows:

$$F_T = F_{s1} \cdot F_{s2} \tag{3.56}$$

Where

F_T is the failure probability of the series–parallel configuration.
F_{s1} is the failure probability of the subsystem 1.
F_{s2} is the failure probability of the subsystem 2.

With the aid of Eq. (3.54), the failure probabilities of subsystems 1 and 2,
respectively, are

$$F_{s1} = 1 - (1 - F_1)(1 - F_2) \tag{3.57}$$

and

$$F_{s2} = 1 - (1 - F_3)(1 - F_4) \tag{3.58}$$

Where

F_i is the failure probability of unit i; for $i = 1, 2, 3, 4$.

By substituting Eqs. (3.57) and (3.58) into Eq. (3.56) we get:

$$F_T = [1 - (1 - F_1)(1 - F_2)][1 - (1 - F_3)(1 - F_4)] \tag{3.59}$$

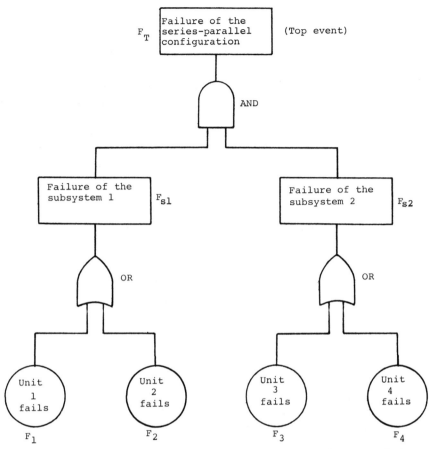

Figure 3.7 A Fault Tree Representing the Parallel–Series Configuration of Figure 3.3

3.4 COMPARATIVE RELIABILITY ANALYSIS OF SIMPLEX AND REDUNDANT SYSTEMS

Redundancy is one of the methods used to increase system reliability. In theory, it enables one to increase a system reliability to close to unity. There are various types of redundant networks which are used to increase system reliability. The type of redundancy used in real life situations depends on factors such as cost, the reliability problem in question, preference, and so on. In this section, for comparison purposes with a simplex system (a single-unit system), we selected four redundant types of configurations: k-out-of-n:G (the configuration is good if at least k of its n units are good. G stands for good), bridge network, series–parallel, and parallel–series [6].

The reliability of the redundant configuration may not always be better than that of the simplex system. In some situations, the reliability of a simplex system is better than that of a redundant system after a certain time interval. System mean time to failure may be a misleading indicator of performance for mission-oriented systems [7]. If the mission period of these systems is less than the crossover point or time (i.e., when the reliability of a simplex system is equal to the reliability of a redundant system), then it is wise to introduce redundancy. Otherwise, it is better to have a single-unit system. Therefore, this section is concerned with investigating the crossover points of the simplex and the already specified redundant configurations.

The crossover point was determined by equating the reliability of simplex and redundant systems under consideration. The crossover points or times are found when the simplex and redundant systems' (under consideration) unit failure rates are constant and time dependent. In other words, when the unit failure times are described by exponential, Rayleigh, and bathtub distributions. In the case of bathtub distribution, its hazard rate can also represent the shape of a bathtub. That is why it is called bathtub distribution. It is described in detail in references [8-9].

In the subsequent analysis the following symbols are used:

R	reliability of a single unit (i.e., reliability of a simplex system).
k	number of units needed for the system's success.
n	total number of units in a system.
$R_{k/n}$	reliability of k-out-of-n:G configuration.
R_b	reliability of bridge configuration.
R_s	reliability of series configuration.
R_p	reliability of parallel configuration.
R_{sp}	reliability of series–parallel configuration.
R_{ps}	reliability of parallel–series configuration.
$R_{sp(3)}$	reliability of three-unit series–parallel configuration.
t	time.
λ	unit constant failure rate.
λt	normalized time.
α	scale parameter
β	scale parameter.

3.4.1 Analysis

k-out-of-n:G Configuration. The system reliability expression [8] for k-out-of-n number of independent and identical units is given by

$$R_{k/n} = \sum_{i=k}^{n} \binom{n}{i} R^i (1 - R)^{n-i} \tag{3.60}$$

Where

R denotes single-unit reliability and $\begin{pmatrix} n \\ i \end{pmatrix} = n!/i!(n - i)!$

To determine the crossover point, we equate Eq. (3.60) with the reliability of a simplex system as follows:

$$R_{k/n} = R$$

i.e.,

$$\sum_{i=k}^{n} \begin{pmatrix} n \\ i \end{pmatrix} R^i(1 - R)^{n-i} = R \tag{3.61}$$

Equation (3.61) was solved analytically (in some cases) and numerically for different combinations of k and n as given in Table 3.3.

Example 3.13

In Eq. (3.61), by setting $n = 3$ and $k = 2$, solve the resulting equation.

$$\sum_{i=2}^{3} \begin{pmatrix} 3 \\ 2 \end{pmatrix} R^i(1 - R)^{3-i} = R$$

$$3R^2 - 2R^3 = R \tag{3.62}$$

Rearranging Eq. (3.62) we get

$$3R^2 - 2R^3 - R = 0 \tag{3.63}$$

or

$$2R^2 - 3R + 1 = 0 \tag{3.64}$$

The above equation is a quadratic equation and its roots are

$$R = \frac{3 + \sqrt{9 - (4)(2)(1)}}{(2)(2)} = 1$$

and

$$R = \frac{3 - \sqrt{9 - (4)(2)(1)}}{2(2)} = \frac{1}{2}$$

Crossover points for different configurations are given in column 4 of Table 3.3. Figures 3.8 and 3.9 show the single-unit reliability versus system reliabil-

Table 3.3 System Reliability Expressions and Crossover Point Results for Different Combinations of k and n

Case No.	Configuration	System Reliability Expression	Crossover Point (i.e., the value of R)
1	2-out-of-3:G	$R_{2/3} = 3R^2 - 2R^3$	0.500000
2	2-out-of-4:G	$R_{2/4} = 6R^2 - 8R^3 + 3R^4$	0.232408
3	2-out-of-5:G	$R_{2/5} = 10R^2 - 20R^3 + 15R^4 - 4R^5$	0.131123
4	3-out-of-4:G	$R_{3/4} = 4R^3 - 3R^4$	0.767592
5	3-out-of-5:G	$R_{3/5} = 10R^3 - 15R^4 + 6R^5$	0.500000
6	4-out-of-5:G	$R_{4/5} = 5R^4 - 4R^5$	0.868879
7	2-out-of-6:G	$R_{2/6} = 15R^2 - 40R^3 + 45R^4 - 24R^5 + 5R^6$	0.083645
8	3-out-of-6:G	$R_{3/6} = 20R^3 - 45R^4 + 36R^5 - 10R^6$	0.347129
9	4-out-of-6:G	$R_{4/6} = 15R^4 - 24R^5 + 10R^6$	0.652871
10	5-out-of-6:G	$R_{5/6} = 6R^5 - 5R^6$	0.916354

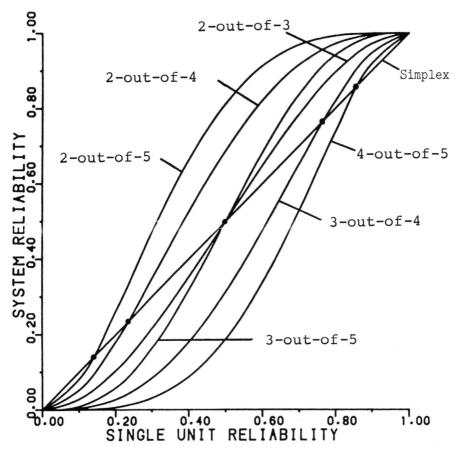

Figure 3.8 Unit Reliability Versus System Reliability—Plot I

ity plots for different values of k and n. The crossover points of Table 3.3 can also be obtained from Figures 3.8 and 3.9 where the non-simplex system reliabilities intercept the simplex system reliability.

From Figure 3.8 it is observed that for 2-out-of-3:G and 3-out-of-5:G configurations the crossover point is the same. Before the crossover $R_{3/5}$ $< R_{2/3}$ and after the crossover $R_{2/3} < R_{3/5}$. Furthermore, the plots indicate that the crossover point exists for 2-out-of-3:G, 2-out-of-4:G, 2-out-of-5:G, 3 out-of-4:G, 3-out-of-5:G, and 4-out-of-5:G configurations with respect to the simplex system. In addition, it is noticed that $R_{2/5} > R_{2/4} > R_{3/4} > R_{4/5}$.

Similarly, Figure 3.9 demonstrates the existence of crossover points for 2-out-of-6:G, 3-out-of-6:G, and 5-out-of-6:G configurations with respect to the simplex system. As expected, $R_{2/6} > R_{3/6} > R_{4/6} > R_{5/6}$.

The series and parallel configurations are special cases of the k-out-of-n:G configuration when $k = n$ and $k = 1$, respectively.

55

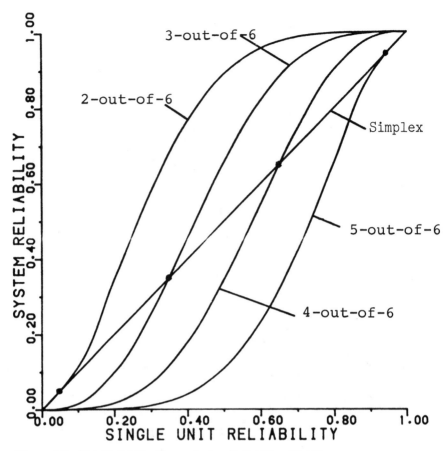

Figure 3.9 Unit Reliability Versus System Reliability—Plot II

Series–Parallel Configuration. In this case the system is composed of m independent and active k-out-of-n unit subsystems in series. More clearly, each subsystem forms the k-out-of-n unit system. If any one of these subsystems fails, the entire system fails. The system reliability is given by

$$R_{sp} = \prod_{j=1}^{m} R_j \qquad (3.65)$$

Where

$R_j = R_{k/n}$, already defined in Eq. (3.60).

This configuration could be compared with the simplex system for the fixed values of m, k and n.

Thus the series–parallel system reliability for $m = 2$, $k = 2$ and $n = 3$ is given by

$$R_{sp} = 9R^4 - 12R^5 + 4R^6 \qquad (3.66)$$

Equating R_{sp} with the reliability of the simplex system (i.e., R) and solving for R, we get the crossover point $R = 0.796138$. The plots of Eq. (3.66) and the simplex system reliability are shown in Figure 3.10. Both system reliabilities are the same at $R = 0.796138$.

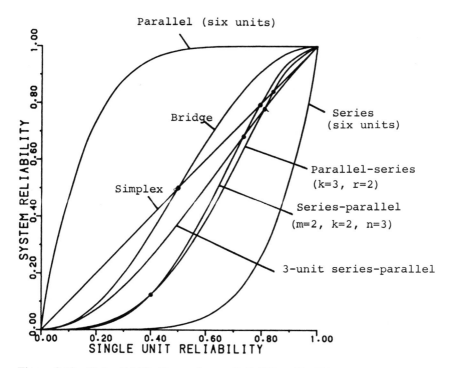

Figure 3.10 Unit reliability Versus System Reliability—Plot III

Parallel–Series Configuration. The parallel–series network is composed of r independent and active subsystems in parallel. Each series subsystem contains K independent units. At least one subsystem must function successfully for the system's success. If all the subsystems are identical, then reliability of the parallel–series system is given by

$$R_{ps} = 1 - (1 - R^k)^r \tag{3.67}$$

Where

R is the reliability of a single unit.

For $k = 3$ and $r = 2$, reliability of the parallel–series system is given by

$$R_{ps} = 2R^3 - R^6 \tag{3.68}$$

Equating Eq. (3.68) with the reliability of the simplex system and solving for $R(0 < R < 1)$ leads to the crossover point $R = 0.848375$. This result can also be obtained from the plots of Figure 3.10.

General Configurations. This section is concerned with six-unit series, parallel, and three-unit series–parallel networks. The reliability of a six independent and identical unit series system is given by:

$$R_s = R^6 \tag{3.69}$$

Where

R is single-unit reliability.

Similarly, the reliability of a six-unit (independent and identical) active parallel system is given by

$$R_p = 6R - 15R^2 + 20R^3 - 15R^4 + 6R^5 - R^6 \tag{3.70}$$

Where

R is the single unit reliability.

The reliability of a three-unit (independent and identical) series–parallel system (comprised of two subsystems in series; Subsystem I is 1-out-of-2:G and subsystem II is 1-out-of-1:G) is given by

$$R_{sp(3)} = 2R^2 - R^3 \tag{3.71}$$

Where

R is the single unit reliability.

Equating Eqs. (3.69) through (3.71) with the reliability of the simplex system separately, and solving each of the resultant equations leads to the conclusion that there is no crossover point for parallel, series and three-unit series–parallel configurations. The plots of Eqs. (3.69) through (3.71) are shown in Figure 3.10. These plots show that crossover points exist between three-unit series–parallel, six-unit parallel–series, and series–parallel networks.

Bridge Configuration. For identical and independent units, the five-unit bridge network reliability from reference [8] is:

$$R_b = 2R^5 - 5R^4 + 2R^3 + 2R^2 \tag{3.72}$$

Where

R is the reliability of a single unit.

Equating R_b with the reliability of a simplex system and solving for $R(0 < R < 1)$ leads to the crossover point $R = 0.500000$. The plot of Eq. (3.72) is shown in Figure 3.10.

From Figure 3.10 it is to be noted that the reliabilities of series–parallel and parallel–series configurations are equal (i.e., $R_{sp} = R_{ps}$) when single-unit reliability $R = 0.4$. Furthermore, $R_{sp} < R_{ps}$ (for $0 < R < 0.4$), $R_{sp} = R_{ps}$ (for $R = 0.4$), and $R_{sp} > R_{ps}$ (for $0.4 < R < 1.0$). As expected, for the special case configurations under consideration, $R_p > R_b > R_s$. The crossover points between the simplex system and series–parallel, parallel–series, and bridge networks are given in Table 3.4.

3.4.2 Time-Dependent Analysis

The simplex system reliability equations for exponential, Rayleigh, and bathtub distributions, respectively from references [3,9], are:

$$R(t) = e^{-\lambda t} \tag{3.73}$$

$$R(t) = e^{-\alpha t^2} \tag{3.74}$$

$$R(t) = \exp[1 - e^{(\beta t)^{1/2}}] \tag{3.75}$$

Table 3.4 Crossover Points for Three Configurations

Case No.	Configuration	Crossover Point (i.e. the value of R)
1	Series–parallel	0.796138
2	Parallel–series	0.848375
3	Bridge	0.500000

Where

t   is time and λ, α, and β are the parameters of the respective distribution.

For exponential distribution, the crossover normalized time is

$$\lambda t = \ln(1/R^*) \tag{3.76}$$

Where

$R^*(0 < R^* < 1)$ is the single-unit reliability at the crossover point for a given system configuration.

For Rayleigh distribution, the crossover normalized time is

$$\sqrt{\alpha} \cdot t = \sqrt{\ln(1/R^*)} \tag{3.77}$$

For bathtub distribution, the crossover normalized time is

$$\beta t = [\ln(1 - \ln R^*)]^2 \tag{3.78}$$

With the aid of R^* values from Tables 3.3 and 3.4 and Eqs. (3.76) through (3.78), we obtained the crossover normalized times for different system configurations and failure time distributions as given in Table 3.5.

For exponential, Rayleigh, and bathtub distributions, the comparative reliability plots for various configurations are shown in Figures 3.11 through 3.16.

The plots of Figure 3.11 show that the reliabilities of 2-out-of-3:G, 3-out-of-5:G, bridge, and simplex configurations have the same crossover point, i.e., $\lambda t = 0.6931472$. Furthermore, it is observed that before the crossover $R_{3/5} > R_b > R_{2/3} > R$, and after the crossover $R_{3/5} < R_b < R_{2/3} < R$.

Similarly, Figure 3.12 shows the plots of $\sqrt{\alpha} \cdot t$ versus system reliability. It is evident from these plots that the reliabilities of 2-out-of-3:G, 3-out-of-5:G, bridge, and simplex configurations have the same crossover point; i.e., $\sqrt{\alpha} \cdot t = 0.8325546$. The plots indicate that before the crossover $R_{3/5} > R_b > R_{2/3} > R$ and after the crossover $R_{3/5} < R_b < R_{2/3} < R$.

The plots of Figure 3.13 exhibit that the reliabilities of 2-out-of-3:G, 3-out-of-5:G, bridge, and simplex configurations have the same crossover point, i.e., $\beta t = 0.2772956$. In addition, it is observed that before the crossover $R_{3/5} > R_b > R_{2/3} > R$ and after the crossover $R_{3/5} < R_b < R_{2/3} < R$.

Additional time-dependent reliability plots for several distinct configurations are shown in Figures 3.14, 3.15, and 3.16.

Figure 3.14 shows the plots of λt versus system reliability. It is observed that before the crossover with respect to simplex system reliability, $R_{2/4} > R_{3/5} > R_b > R_{sp} > R_{ps} > R$ and after the crossover $R_{sp} < R_{ps} < R_{3/5} <$

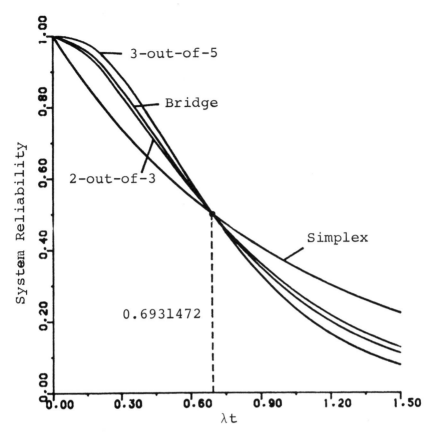

Figure 3.11 Reliability Plots for Various Configurations when the Unit Failure Time Distribution is Exponential

$R_b < R_{2/4} < R$. Furthermore, there is a crossover between reliabilities of series–parallel and parallel–series configurations. Therefore, between parallel–series and series–parallel configurations, it is observed that before the crossover $R_{sp} > R_{ps}$ and after the crossover $R_{sp} < R_{ps}$.

Figure 3.15 shows the plots of $\sqrt{\alpha} \cdot t$ versus system reliability for various configurations. From the plots it is observed that before the crossover with respect to simplex system reliability, $R_{2/4} > R_{3/5} > R_b > R_{sp} > R_{ps} > R$ and after the crossover $R_{sp} < R_{ps} < R_{3/5} < R_b < R_{2/4} < R$. Furthermore, it is observed that there exists a crossover within parallel–series and series–parallel configurations. Prior to this crossover $R_{sp} > R_{ps}$ and after the crossover $R_{sp} < R_{ps}$.

Figure 3.16 shows plots of βt versus system reliability for several distinct configurations.

Table 3.5   Crossover Normalized Times for Various Configurations

Case No.	Configuration	Exponential (i.e. value of λt)	Rayleigh (i.e. value of $\sqrt{\alpha} \cdot t$)	Bathtub (i.e. value of βt)
			Crossover Normalized Times for Given Failure Time Distributions	
1	2-out-of-3:G	0.693147	0.832555	0.277296
2	2-out-of-4:G	1.459261	1.207998	0.809750
3	2-out-of-5:G	2.031620	1.425349	1.230095
4	2-out-of-6:G	2.481174	1.575174	1.555928
5	3-out-of-4:G	0.264497	0.514293	0.055072
6	3-out-of-5:G	0.693147	0.832555	0.277296
7	3-out-of-6:G	1.058059	1.028620	0.520942
8	4-out-of-5:G	0.140551	0.374902	0.017295
9	4-out-of-6:G	0.426376	0.652975	0.126122
10	5-out-of-6:G	0.087353	0.295555	0.007013
11	Series–parallel	0.227983	0.477475	0.042178
12	Parallel–series	0.164433	0.405503	0.023175
13	Bridge	0.693147	0.832555	0.277296
14	Simplex	0.693147	0.832555	0.277296

3.5   RELIABILITY ANALYSIS OF A TRIPLE-MODULAR REDUNDANT SYSTEM WITH REPAIR

This section is concerned with reliability analysis of a three independent and identical unit system with repair. The redundant system operates successfully as long as a minimum of two of three units are functioning normally. A failed unit is repaired only when the remaining two units are operating successfully. The state–space diagram of the triple-modular redundant system with repair is shown in Figure 3.17. The Markov modeling method [5] is used to develop equations for this model. The following assumptions are associated with the model:

    i.   The system contains three independent and identical units.

    ii.   All the system units are active.

    iii. The failure rate of a unit is constant.

    iv. The repair rate of a failed unit is constant.

    v.   A repaired unit is as good as new.

    vi. The system fails when more than one unit fails.

    vii. Numerals in the boxes of Figure 3.17 denote specific states of the system.

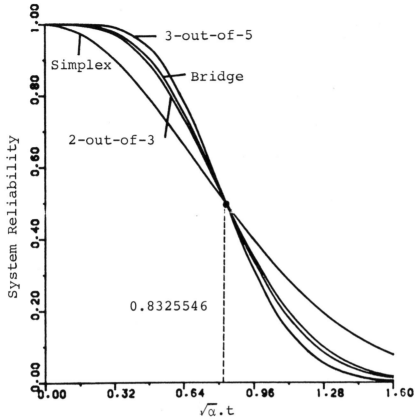

Figure 3.12 Reliability Plots for Various Configurations When the Unit Failure Time Distribution is Rayleigh

The following symbols are associated with this model:

i is the ith state of the triple-modular redundant system shown in Figure 3.17; $i = 0$ (three units operating normally), $i = 1$ (two units operating normally, one unit failed), $i = 2$ (one unit operating normally, two units failed).

$P_i(t)$ is the probability that the triple-modular redundant system is in state i at time t; for $i = 0$, 1 and 2.

λ is the constant failure rate of a unit.

α is the constant repair rate of a unit.

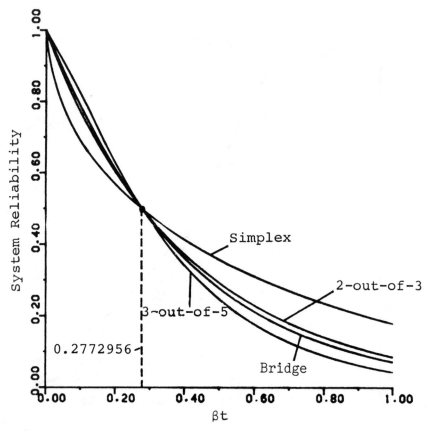

Figure 3.13 Reliability Plots for Various Configurations When the Unit Failure Time Distribution is Bathtub

With the aid of the Markov modeling technique, we write down the following differential equations associated with Figure 3.17:

$$\frac{dP_0(t)}{dt} + 3\lambda\, P_0(t) = \alpha \cdot P_1(t) \tag{3.79}$$

$$\frac{dP_1(t)}{dt} + (2\lambda + \alpha)\, P_1(t) = 3\lambda \cdot P_0(t) \tag{3.80}$$

$$\frac{dP_2(t)}{dt} = 2\lambda \cdot P_1(t) \tag{3.81}$$

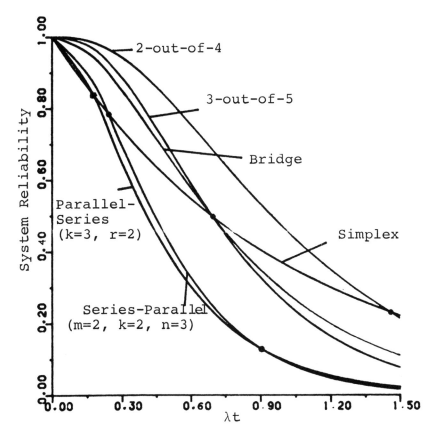

Figure 3.14 Reliability Plots for Various Configurations When the Unit Failure Time Distribution is Exponential

At time $t = 0$, $P_0(0) = 1$ and $P_1(0) = P_2(0) = 0$.
By solving the above differential equations we get

$$P_0(t) = \frac{1}{(c_1 - c_2)} [(2\lambda + \alpha)(e^{c_1 t} - e^{c_2 t}) + c_1 e^{c_1 t} - c_2 e^{c_2 t}] \quad (3.82)$$

$$P_1(t) = \frac{3\lambda}{(c_1 - c_2)} [e^{c_1 t} - e^{c_2 t}] \quad (3.83)$$

Where

$$c_1, c_2 = \frac{-(5\lambda + \alpha) \pm \sqrt{\lambda^2 + \alpha^2 + 10\lambda\alpha}}{2} \quad (3.84)$$

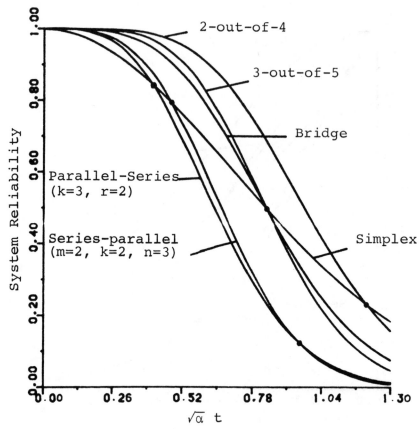

Figure 3.15 Reliability Plots for Various Configurations When the Unit Failure Time Distribution is Rayleigh

The reliability of the triple-modular redundant system with repair is

$$R_{TMRr}(t) = P_0(t) + P_1(t)$$

$$= \frac{1}{c_1 - c_2}[(5\lambda + \alpha)(e^{c_1 t} - e^{c_2 t}) + c_1 e^{c_1 t} - c_2 e^{c_2 t}] \qquad (3.85)$$

Substituting the above equation into relationship (3.28) results in

$$MTTF_{TMRr} = \int_0^\infty R_{TMRr}(t) \cdot dt$$

$$= \frac{5}{6\lambda} + \frac{\alpha}{6\lambda^2} \qquad (3.86)$$

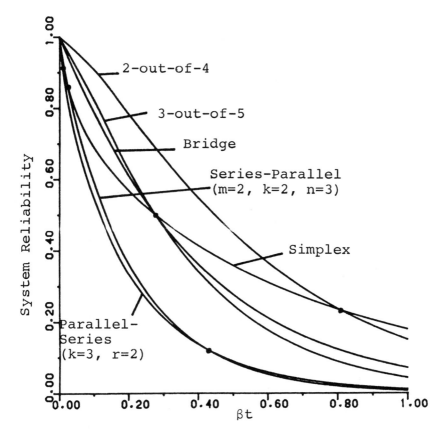

Figure 3.16 Reliability Plots for Various Configurations When the Unit Failure Time Distribution is Bathtub

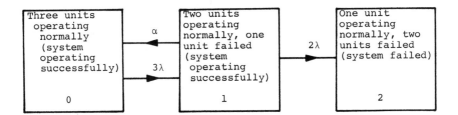

Figure 3.17 State Transition Diagram for a Triple-Modular Redundant System with Repair

Where

$MTTF_{TMRr}$ is the mean time to failure of the repairable triple-modular redundant system.

3.6 Summary

This chapter presented various aspects of quality control and reliability. Histories of statistical quality control and reliability were briefly described. Acceptance sampling and control charts were discussed, and activities of a quality control department were presented along with advantages of the quality control program. Three formulas concerned with inspection were presented.

An expression for general reliability function was developed and a mathematical model to estimate failure rate of equipment was presented. Reliability configurations such as series, parallel, N-out-of-m, series–parallel, parallel–series, and bridge were presented. Mean time to failure and variance formulas were developed for some of these configurations. With the aid of a solved example, the fault tree technique was described. Comparative reliability analysis of simplex and redundant systems was presented. Finally, the reliability equation of a repairable triple-modular redundant system was developed with the aid of the Markov modeling technique. Thirteen solved examples were presented in the chapter.

3.7 EXERCISES

1. Discuss the history of quality control.
2. Write an essay on quality assurance in the computer industry.
3. Discuss the similarities and differences between the quality control and reliability disciplines.
4. What are the functions of a Reliability Engineering department?
5. Prove that the failure density function of an item is given by

$$f(t) = \lambda(t) \cdot \exp\left[-\int_0^t \lambda(t) \cdot dt \right] \tag{3.87}$$

Where

$\lambda(t)$ is the hazard rate of an item.
t is time.

6. With the aid of Eqs. (3.44) and (3.33), obtain an expression for variance.

7. Assume that in Eq. (3.47) the failure times of a unit are exponentially distributed. Develop expressions for mean time to failure and variance.
8. Assume that in Eq. (3.53) a unit has a constant failure rate. Develop expressions for mean time to failure and variance.
9. Describe the following terms:

    i. OR gate
    ii. AND gate
    iii. Basic fault event
    iv. Simplex system

10. Prove the following equation with the aid of differential Eqs. (3.79) through (3.81):

$$P_0(t) + P_1(t) + P_2(t) = 1 \qquad (3.88)$$

3.8 REFERENCES

1. K. Stout, *Quality Control in Automation*, Kogan Page Ltd., London, 1985.

2. US MIL-HBK-217C, "Reliability Prediction of Electronic Equipment", USAF Rome Air Development Center, 1978. Available from the National Technical Information Service (NTIS), Springfield, Virginia.

3. B.S. Dhillon, *Systems Reliability, Maintainability and Management*, Petrocelli Books, Inc., New York, 1983.

4. B.S. Dhillon and C. Singh, "Bibliography of Literature on Fault Trees", Microelectronics and Reliability, Vol. 17, 1978, pp. 501–503.

5. B.S. Dhillon and C. Singh, *Engineering Reliability: New Techniques and Applications*, John Wiley & Sons, New York, 1981.

6. B.S. Dhillon and S.N. Rayapati, "Comparative Analysis of Simplex and Redundant Systems", Microelectronics and Reliability, Vol. 25, 1985, pp. 343–356.

7. W.G. Bouricius, W.C. Carter, and P.R. Schneider, "Reliability Modeling Techniques for Self-Repairing Computer Systems", Proceedings of the Twelfth Association of Computing Machinery (ACM) Conference, 1969, New York, pp. 295–309.

8. B.S. Dhillon, *Reliability Engineering in Systems Design and Operation*, Van Nostrand Reinhold Company, New York, 1982.

9. B.S. Dhillon, "Life Distributions", IEEE Transactions on Reliability, Vol. 30, 1981, pp. 369–375.

4

COMPUTER FAILURES

4.1 INTRODUCTION

Computers may fail due to software faults or hardware failures. Software faults are due to errors in programming whereas hardware failures are associated with the computer electronic, electrical and mechanical elements. Both hardware and software failures are important factors in determining the reliability of computer systems.

This chapter discusses various aspects of computer failures and separately lists the main points of software and hardware reliability.

4.2 CAUSES OF COMPUTER FAILURES

Computer failures occur due to various causes. In order to correct them, identification of these causes is absolutely necessary. Therefore this section discusses various sources of computer failure [2,3]. The major sources of system failures are listed below.

    i.   Human errors.
    ii.   Environmental and power failures.
   iii.   Gradual erosion of the data base.
   iv.   Saturation.
    v.   Processor and memory failures.
   vi.   Communication network failures.
  vii.   Peripheral device failures.
 viii.   Mysterious failures.

Although the above sources of system failures are considered self-explanatory, some of them are described below.

Human errors occur due to operator mistakes and errors in computer software. There are several occasions in which a computer system may fail due to the operator. Some of them take place in starting up, running, and shutting down the system. Software errors are discussed in detail in a subsequent section.

Other important sources of system failures are environmental and power failures. Environmental failures can occur due to failure of air conditioning equipment, electromagnetic interference, fires, earthquakes, and so on. Causes such as transient fluctuations in voltage or frequency or total power loss from the local utility company are associated with power failures.

Processor and memory failures are associated with processor and memory parity errors. Though they occur quite rarely, processor errors are generally catastrophic. There are occasions when the central processor fails to execute instructions correctly due to a "dropped bit". The memory parity errors now occur quite rarely because of improvement in hardware reliability. In addition, they are not necessarily fatal. Generally in modern computers a parity bit is used with each word or byte in memory to detect errors. Each time a word or byte is stored, the parity bit is automatically computed. In addition the bit is checked by the computer hardware when it is read. The hardware initiates an interrupt in the event when it detects a "dropped" bit and subsequently an appropriate action is taken by the operating system. However memory problems may also be caused by power failures and surges.

Communication network failures are another important source of system failures. These are associated with intermodule communication and most are of a transient nature. Such problems must be detected, if not automatically rectified, for it is very likely that an entire computer system could fail due to failures in a multiplexer, in a high-speed communication line, or in the "front-end" computer. However, on the other hand, an entire computer system normally would not malfunction due to failure in the low-speed communication lines or in the terminals. About 70% of errors in communication lines can be detected with the use of "vertical parity" logic.

Failures in the peripheral devices are quite important to consider because they too can cause serious problems. However, these failures seldom cause a system shutdown. The commonly occurring errors in peripheral devices are intermittent or transient, and the electromechanical nature of the devices is the usual reason for their occurrence. The failures of various kind of peripheral devices are discussed in detail in a subsequent section.

Finally, another major source of system failure is the mysterious or unexplained failure. In real-time systems these failures are never properly classified. When a system stops functioning suddenly without any error messages and without any indication of whether the problems was due to software, hardware, or any of the other listed reasons, the problem becomes an unexplained failure.

4.3 COMPUTER SYSTEM ERROR RECOVERY PHILOSOPHIES

Basically there are five approaches to error recovery [4]. One or more of these philosophies can be used for each of the sources of computer system failure discussed in section 4.2. The specific use of one or more philosophies will be dictated by the user's need. All the five approaches to error recovery are shown in Figure 4.1 and discussed below.

Approach I is concerned with bringing the system to a stop. In this case, when an error is detected the system is brought to a standstill to avoid further damage. For effective implementation of this approach, the system shutdown must be graceful, planned, and orderly, for the unplanned system shutdown has various drawbacks. Some of them are as follows:

    i.   It confuses the terminal users.
   ii.   The peripheral devices may be physically damaged.
  iii.   The computer operator may be confused.

The second philosophy (Approach II) is concerned with switching in a complete standby system. This philosophy calls for the backup of items such as the following:

    i.   peripheral units and power supply
   ii.   communication equipment and data bases
  iii.   processors

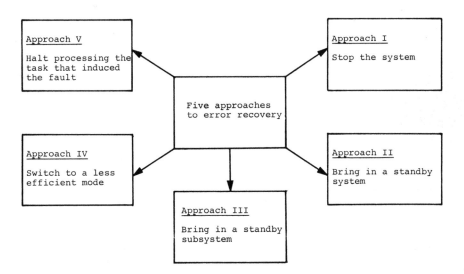

Figure 4.1 Philosophies of Error Recovery

Approach II is practiced in a situation where the requirement for high mean time between failures (MTBF) is extremely important. The obvious disadvantage of this philosophy is the high cost of the extra hardware.

Approach III is similar to the second approach, except that it calls for switching to a standby subsystem instead of a whole system as in the second philosophy. This approach is used when there is a requirement for high system mean time between failures, and obviously increases the cost due to extra hardware. However, it may be viable to introduce redundancy only in specialized units of a system. Some examples of such units are as follows:

    i.   communication lines
   ii.   multiplexers
  iii.   front-end communication computers
  iv.   terminals

The fourth philosophy is concerned with switching to a less efficient mode of operation. Approach IV calls for switching off the afflicated portion of the system only. This way the remaining system is left for the degraded mode of operation. The following are examples of the less efficient modes of operation:

    i.   When the main processor fails, it may be possible to accept transactions with the aid of the front-end computer.
   ii.   When the high-speed printers, card punches or tape drives fail, it may be feasible to send the output elsewhere.
  iii.   When a portion of the data base receives damage, it may still be possible to get some work done.
  iv.   When the front-end computer fails, it may be feasible for users to prepare their input on paper tape or cards.

Finally, Approach V is concerned with stopping processing of the task that induced the fault. When a serious error occurs, the processing of the task being performed is aborted. There are many cases where this approach becomes quite useful and the major advantages of this philosophy are its simplicity and economy. However, the common criticism of this philosophy is that it solves the system problem by passing it on to the user. Approach V is not useful for the following kinds of system failures:

    i.   power failures
   ii   memory parity errors
  iii.   processor errors.

4.4   PERIPHERAL DEVICE ERRORS

This section discusses errors associated with peripheral equipment such as paper tape and card readers, card and paper tape punches, magnetic tape units, disks, and printers. Each of these types of equipment is discussed below [5].

  i. *Paper tape and card readers:* Both of these pieces of equipment are used to read input information from paper media. In spite of parity checks, roughly 50–60% of paper tape reader's faults give incorrect results. The typical fault incident rate of card readers is two incidents per 1000 hours. There are many problems associated with card readers; some are beginning reading in the incorrect place, column double reading, and skew. Approximately between 50–60% of faults results in undiscovered misreads due to these problems.
 ii. *Card and paper tape punches:* These are used to prepare cards and paper tapes for the use in their respective readers. With regard to card punches, 30–40% of faults induce incorrect information. Many of these faults are due to punching holes outside the acceptable boundaries. Paper tape punches have the worst record with respect to faults and usually extremely low utilization. A very high percentage of paper tape faults induce the punch of incorrect characters or unacceptable spacing tolerances.
iii. *Magnetic tape units:* These are one of the important types of peripheral equipment, with roughly 10–25% of faults inducing the incorrect information on reading.
 iv. *Disks:* There are various kinds of faults associated with disks. Some examples are writing information incorrectly with errorless checking codes, spurious misreads, and reading the incorrect file.
  v. *Printers:* These are used to print outputs. The results of printer faults are missing columns of printing, semi-printed characters, and so on.

4.5   COMPUTER SOFTWARE FAILURE

In matters of reliability, software failures are as important as hardware failures. There are several well-publicized examples where software errors have led to serious problems [6]. Some of them are as follows:

  i. The first U.S. probe to Venus was lost because of an error in a FORTRAN statement.
 ii. In the onboard computer of the U.S. Apollo 8 spaceship, a software error erased a portion of the system memory.

   iii. A software error was the cause for incapacitation of a NORAD (North American Air Defense Command) exercise in 1963.

   iv. Deaths have been caused by errors in medical software [7].

    v. Delays of over two hours for at least 100 incoming flights into New York and Philadelphia airports were caused by a partial computer failure. It was speculated that the partial failure may have been caused by software error [8].

   vi. The launching of the first U.S. space shuttle was postponed about twenty minutes before the scheduled launching time on April 10, 1981 due to a software fault [9].

Some studies [10] have indicated that over 60% of software errors are committed during the requirement and design phase, while the coding phase accounts for less than 40% of the errors. This section discusses the various aspects of software errors.

4.5.1. Selected Definitions

This section presents definitions of selected terms related to software errors [10].

    i. *Software:* computer program items in the form of magnetic tapes, disks or card decks as well as all kinds of descriptive documentation, including flow charts, listings, etc.

   ii. *Software error:* a clerical, conceptual or syntactic discrepancy which causes one or more faults in the software.

   iii. *Software failure:* occurs in a situation when a computer program fault is elicited by some kind of input data, leading to the computer program incorrectly computing the specified function.

   iv. *Software fault:* a discrepancy in the computer software which worsens its capability to perform as intended.

    v. *Software reliability:* the probability of a specified software functioning for a given period, without an error, when used within the framework of designed conditions on the specified machine.

4.5.2 Failure Modes of the Software System

This section is concerned with identification of generic ways in which software will fail to carry out its system function. Some of the generic software failure modes[11] which may lead to unacceptable system hazards are shown in Figure 4.2.

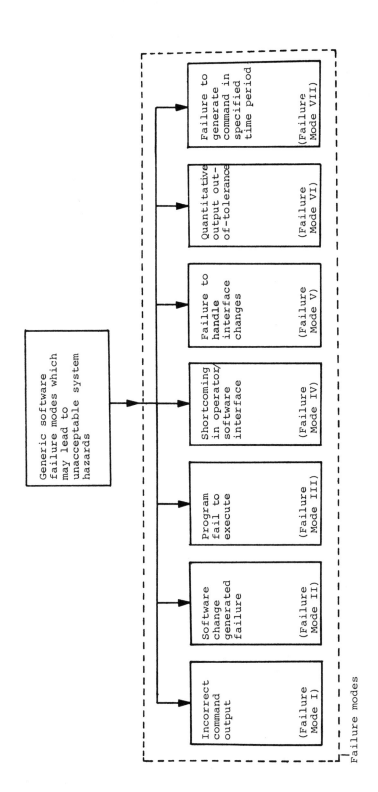

Failure modes

Figure 4.2 Software System Failure Modes

Causes for each of the failure modes shown in Figure 4.2 are presented below:

i. *Failure Mode I:* This failure mode results from causes such as inadequate parity checks, existence of power transient-generated ones or zeros, insufficient hardware status monitor information, and wrong hardware configuration for the chosen software module.

ii. *Failure Mode II:* This failure mode is due to causes such as lack of change retest requirements, insufficient independent modularity in computer software, and lack of quality assurance change control.

iii. *Failure Mode III:* This failure mode is the result of causes such as wrong input data, lack of subroutines to correct errors, inadequate memory storage space, heavy usage of "do loops" and unfinished instructions.

iv. *Failure Mode IV:* This failure mode comes from causes such as insufficiency of the automatic failsafe, lack of prioritization of warnings and alarms, insufficiency of human operator's ability to absorb data, and inadequacy of human operator/hardware/software monitors.

v. *Failure Mode V:* This failure mode is caused by inadequate flexibility in the software program to accommodate changes associated with interface, and software intolerance of credible failure modes or characteristics of computer or interfacing hardware.

vi. *Failure Mode VI:* This failure mode is the result of bit errors, rounding off, and use of the approximation algorithm, inaccurate at extremes.

vii. *Failure Mode VII:* This failure mode is caused by lack of hardware status monitor information, excessiveness of data processing time, and program time reference error.

4.5.3 Classification of Errors in Programming

This section discusses classifications of commonly found software errors in programming. Errors in programming may be classified into the following eight categories[12,13].

i. logic errors
ii. interface errors
iii. data definition errors
iv. data base errors
v. input/output errors
vi. computational errors
vii. data handling errors
viii. miscellaneous errors

Examples of the *logic errors* are excessive or inadequate number of statements in a loop, improper sequence of logic activities, logical expressions containing wrong operands, and checking on an incorrect variable. Similarly, software/software interface errors and calling in a subroutine at an incorrect place or not making the call at all are known as *interface errors*. Examples of *data definition errors* are data referred out of bounds and ill-defined data. Another important software error category is *data base errors*. Errors such as incorrectly expressed data units, initialization of data to a wrong value, and data not properly initialized in the data base fall under this category. *Input/ output errors* may include data not written at all, input read from wrong data file, and incorrectly written-out data. Missing computations, wrongly used parentheses, errors in data conversion, and equations containing a wrong operand are examples of *computational errors*. Errors associated with *data handling* may include subscripting errors, incorrect data initialization, and variables referred to by incorrect names. Finally, the *miscellaneous errors* category contains those errors which do not fall into any of the above seven categories.

4.5.4 Human Errors in Software Development

Just as in hardware development or maintenance, the occurrence of human error is important during software development or maintenance. As a result of a human error during software development or maintenance software may fail, and the consequences of that failure could be quite severe. The various factors which cause human errors during software development and maintenance may be classified into two main groups [14,15] as shown in Figure 4.3.

Factors associated with software are within the control of software designers. Furthermore, they are connected to characteristics of software components. On the other hand, the factors associated with a particular project are within the control of project managers and are connected to characteristics of software engineering project components.

The factors of groups 1 and 2 shown in Figure 4.3 are discussed below.

Group I Factors. Two major factors belong to this group. These are software perceivability and rigor of software definition. Software perceivability can be described as a measure of software components' psychometric complexity. More clearly, perceivability is a complexity measure as experienced by an individual attempting to comprehend a system with an intention to accomplish a task concerned with that system. Examples of such a task are modifying the system and examining it for faultlessness. An individual's capability to understand an abstract system depends upon system complexity aspects such as syntactic complexity, semantic complexity, and pragmatic complexity.

Firstly, the syntactic complexity aspect is related to system topology (more clearly, to the number of constituent components and the nature and variety of component interconnections).

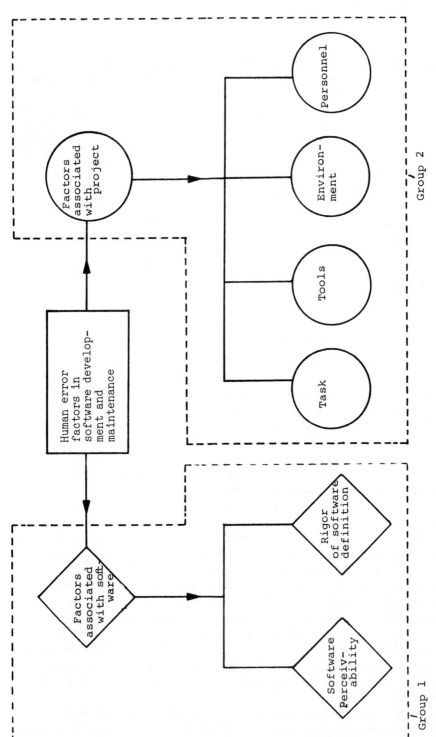

Figure 4.3 Factors Which Cause the Occurrence of Human Errors

Secondly, the semantic and pragmatic complexity aspects are related to the nature of functions accomplished by the components of the system and the system presentation format, respectively.

The second major factor, i.e. rigor of software definition, is a measure of unambiguity and completeness of the software component's definition. Software reliability is significantly effected by unambiguity and completeness of definition of the following items:

   i.   control structures
  ii.   functional specifications
 iii.   hierarchical structures
 iv.   data structures
  v.   data flow structures

Group II Factors. These factors are known as the project factors and are associated with characteristics of software engineering project components. These factors are within the project manager's control. During software development and maintenance there are several factors which bring about the occurrence of human error. These factors may be divided into the four categories given below.

   i.   *Category I:* Environmental factors.
  ii.   *Category II:* Tools (for programmer) factors.
 iii.   *Category III:* Task-related factors.
 iv.   *Category IV:* Personnel factors.

There are many factors belonging to category I, i.e. environmental factors. Some of them are as follows:

   i.   Noise level
  ii.   Morale of the team
 iii.   Management attitudes towards reliability
 iv.   Intensity of light
  v.   Team values
 vi.   Heating and ventilation levels
vii.   Level of pressure to accomplish job within a specified time limit.

Category II is concerned with tools factors. The occurrence of human error and the detection and removal of faults caused by these human errors may be affected by the availability of effective tools. For example during software development or maintenance, programmers use tools such as follow:

   i.   Methodologies
  ii.   Code generators

iii.   Rules and guidelines
iv.   Standards
v.   Computer aids for design and testing
vi.   Languages

Category III factors are task-related. More clearly, they are associated with software engineering task characteristics. Task perceivability and rigor of task definition are the parts of task factors.

Finally, Category IV factors are associated with personnel; their skills, knowledge and attitudes. To a certain extent, software feasibility is affected by these factors.

4.5.5   Software Error Cost Analysis

This section discusses software cost analysis. A large payoff is obtained by discovering software errors in initial production stages [10,16]. The following equation is developed [10] to calculate, in absence of a new tool or technique, the cost of detecting and rectifying design errors during design and test phases:

$$K_{an} = K_{cd} \cdot \alpha_{de} + K_{ct} \cdot \beta_{det} \tag{4.1}$$

Where

K_{an} is the cost of detecting and correcting design errors during design and test phases in absence of a new tool or technique.

α_{de} is the total amount of design-related errors detected and rectified in design review conducted during the design phase.

β_{det} is the total amount of design-related errors detected and rectified in the test phase.

K_{cd} is the per error cost of rectifying a design error in the design phase.

K_{ct} is the per error cost of rectifying a design error detected in the test phase.

The following two assumptions are associated with Eq. (4.1):

i.   Each detected error is permanently rectified.
ii.   Design errors are composed of both design phase errors and errors made in specifying requirements.

The number of design errors detected and rectified in the design phase with the aid of new tool or technique is given by

$$\theta_1 = \alpha_{de} + \alpha_{de} \cdot f \tag{4.2}$$

Where

θ_1 is the number of design errors detected and rectified in the
design phase with the aid of new tool or technique.

f is the additional fraction of design errors in the design phase
discovered because of using the new tool or technique.

The number of design errors detected and corrected in the test phase
because of using the new tool or technique is approximately reduced to

$$\theta_2 = \beta_{\det} - \beta_{\det} \cdot f \qquad (4.3)$$

Where

θ_2 is the number of design errors detected and corrected in the test
phase because of using the new tool or technique.

Thus the cost of detecting and rectifying design errors in design and test
phases using the new tools or technique is

$$K_{wt} = K_{nt} + K_{cd} \cdot \theta_1 + K_{ct} \cdot \theta_2 \qquad (4.4)$$

Where

K_{nt} is the development and application cost of the new technique

By substituting Eqs. (4.2) and (4.3) into Eq. (4.4), we get

$$K_{wt} = K_{nt} + K_{cd}(\alpha_{de} + \alpha_{de} \cdot f) + k_{ct}(\beta_{\det} - \beta_{\det} \cdot f) \qquad (4.5)$$

If the new tool or technique is to pay for itself, the following condition
must be satisfied:

$$K_{an} - K_{wt} > 0 \qquad (4.6)$$

4.6 SOFTWARE AND HARDWARE RELIABILITY

This section briefly discusses software and hardware reliability [17,18]. A
comparison of some of the main features of both these items is given below.

Software Reliability

1. Software does not wear out.
2. The field of software reliability is relatively new.
3. Software does not have a bathtub hazard rate curve.
4. For software, mean time to repair has no significance.
5. Software has an error rate function.

6. Well-established mathematical theory still does not exist for software reliability.
7. In software, corrective maintenance is really redesign.
8. It is impossible to repair software failures with the aid of spare modules.
9. Use of parallel redundancy in software does not improve reliability.
10. Several reliability prediction and growth models exist in software.
11. Program error is the cause for software failure.
12. Preventive maintenance (servicing and inspection) has no meaning in software.
13. For monetary savings, software reliability has a potential.
14. Obtaining failure or error data is still a problem with software.
15. Software reliability is concerned with the quality of the software design.

Hardware Reliability

1. Hardware wears out.
2. The field of hardware reliability is well established, especially in the area of electronic parts.
3. The bathtub hazard rate curve exists in hardware reliability.
4. Mean time to repair has significance in hardware reliability.
5. Hardware reliability has a hazard rate function.
6. Hardware reliability has well-established mathematical theory.
7. In hardware, to restore a failed system, corrective maintenance is performed.
8. Hardware can be repaired by making use of spare modules.
9. Hardware reliability can be improved with the application of parallel redundancy.
10. A large number of reliability prediction and growth models exist for hardware.
11. A hardware failure is (mainly) due to physical effects.
12. In hardware, preventive maintenance is used to inhibit failures.
13. For monetary savings, hardware reliability has a potential.
14. Obtaining failure data is still a problem with hardware.

4.7 SUMMARY

This chapter discussed various aspects of computer failures. A number of causes of computer failures were explained in detail. The major sources of system failures are human errors, environmental and power failures, gradual erosion of the data base, saturation, processor and memory failures, communication network failures, peripheral device failures, and mysterious failures. Five computer system error recovery philosophies were presented. These philosophies were: switch to a less efficient mode, stop the system, bring in a standby system, halt processing the task that induced the fault, and bring in a standby subsystem.

Peripheral device errors were discussed. These errors are associated with equipment such as paper tape and card readers, card and paper tape punches, printers, disks, and magnetic tape units.

The topic of computer software failures was discussed in considerable depth. Six well-publicized examples where software errors led to serious problems were given. Selective terms related to software errors were defined. Seven generic ways in which software will fail to carry out its system function were described. Classification of commonly found software errors in programming was discussed. The occurrence of human error during software development or maintenance was described in depth. A simple mathematical model to perform software error cost analysis was presented. Finally, the main points of both software and hardware reliability were listed.

4.8 EXERCISES

1. Discuss at least six well-publicized examples where software errors led to serious problems.
2. Describe the following terms:
   i.   Human error
   ii. Communication network failure
   iii. Saturation
   iv. Processor failures
   v.   Gradual erosion of the data base
3. Explain three of the five computer system error recovery philosophies.
4. Define the following two terms:
   i. Software error
   ii. Software failure
   Discuss their differences, if any.
5. Describe the meanings of the following terms:
   i.   Computational errors
   ii. Data base errors
   iii. Logic errors
   iv. Input/output errors
6. Make a comparison between software and hardware maintainability.
7. What is the difference between software reliability and maintainability?

4.9 REFERENCES

1. M. Phister, *Data Processing Technology and Economics,* Published jointly by the Santa Monica Publishing Company and Digital Press, Santa Monica, 1979.

2. E. Yourdon, "The Causes of System Failures—Part 2", Modern Data, Vol. 5, Feb. 1972, pp. 50–56.

3. E. Yourdon, "The Causes of System Failures—Part 3", Modern Data, Vol. 5, March 1972, pp. 36–40.

4. E. Yourdon, "Approaches to Error Recovery—Part 5", Modern Data, Vol. 5, May 1972, pp. 38–52.

5. R. Longbottom, *Computer System Reliability,* John Wiley & Sons, Chichester, 1980.

6. G.J. Myers, *Software Reliability Principles and Practices,* John Wiley & Sons, New York, 1976.

7. B.W. Boehm, "Software and Its Impact: A Quantitative Assessment", Datamation, Vol. 19, 1973, pp. 48–59.

8. *Newsday,* Garden City, Long Island, New York, September 7, 1978.

9. J.R. Graman, "The "Bug" Heard Around the World", ACM Sigsoft, Software Engineering Notes, Vol. 6, Oct. 1981, pp. 3–10.

10. M. Lipow, "Prediction of Software Failures", The Journal of Systems and Software, Vol. 1, 1979, pp. 71–75.

11. E.S. Dean, "Software System Safety", Proceedings of the 5th International System Safety Conference, Denver, 1981, pp. 111-A-1–111-D-18.

12. T.A. Thayer, M. Lipow, and E.C. Nelson, *Software Reliability: A Study of Large Project Reality,* North-Holland Publishing Company, Amsterdam, 1978.

13. R.D. Joshi, "Software Development for Reliable Software Systems", The Journal of Systems and Software, Vol. 3, 1983, pp. 107–121.

14. G. Rzevski, "Identification of Factors which Cause Software Failure", Proceedings of the Annual Reliability and Maintainability Symposium, 1982, pp. 157–161.

15. R.J. Lauber, "Impact of a Computer Aided Development Support System on Software Quality and Reliability", Proceedings of the Annual IEEE Computer Society International Conference (COMPSAC), 1982, pp. 248–255.

16. B.W. Boehm, "Software Engineering", IEEE Transactions on Computers, Vol. C-25, 1976, pp. 1226–1241.

17. M.B. Kline, "Software and Hardware Reliability and Maintainability: What are the Differences?" Proceedings of the Annual Reliability and Maintainability Symposium, 1980, pp. 179–185. Published by IEEE.

18. B.S. Dhillon, *Reliability Engineering in Systems Design and Operation,* Van Nostrand Reinhold Company, New York, 1983.

5
INTRODUCTION TO COMPUTER SYSTEM RELIABILITY MODELING

5.1 INTRODUCTION

Modern day computers are remarkably reliable considering their size, complexity and application areas. However, even greater reliability is increasingly needed due to factors such as stringent mission requirements, critical application areas, and so on. Through the application of standard computer engineering practice such as designing conservatively and using quality parts, with minimal redundancy it is not possible to achieve the computer reliability required for critical applications [1]. This is the reason for designing some form of built-in reliability enhancement mechanism in more and more computers over the past number of years. The general purpose of this kind of mechanism is to enable the computer system to tolerate faulty parts. Under fault conditions, it is quite possible for a computer with a high degree of built-in reliability enhancement to exhibit extremely complex behavior. Therefore, the compute reliability problem is not as simple as it may appear to be.

5.2 ISSUES IN COMPUTER SYSTEM RELIABILITY

There are various issues concerned with computer system reliability. Some factors to consider are as follows [1].

  i. Major components of computers are the logic elements, which have troublesome reliability features. In many cases it is not possible to determine effectively the reliability of such elements, and their defects cannot necessarily be healed.
 ii. The most powerful kind of self-repair in computer systems is dynamic fault tolerance, but it is extremely cumbersome to analyse. However, for certain applications it is quite vital and cannot be ignored.
iii. Failures are highly varied in character in computer systems. For example, a component used in computers may fail permanently or it may experience a transient fault caused by environment.
 iv. Current computers consist of redundancy schemes for fault tolerant and recent advances have brought improvement but there are still many practical and theoretical difficulties that remain to be overcome.

v.   Prior to the production and installation phases, it may be very cumbersome to detect mistakes associated with hardware design at lowest system levels. It is quite possible that errors in hardware design may lead to situations where operational errors due to such mistakes cannot be distinguished from those caused by transient physical faults.

5.3   REDUNDANT COMPUTER SYSTEMS

Computers with several processors are usually configured in four distinct ways to meet required reliability [2]. These are standby redundancy [3], hybrid redundancy [4], massive redundancy [4–6], and gracefully degrading redundancy [7]. Each of these is described below.

i.   *Standby Redundancy:* In this case, a system executes tasks on its operational modules. When an operational module fails, the system attempts to replace the failed module with a spare one. One of the simplest forms of a standby redundant system is a duplex system. In this case there is one active module and one spare module.
ii.   *Hybrid Redundancy:* This type of redundant system consists of a massive redundant core with a certain number of spare modules to replace faulty units.
iii.   *Massive Redundancy:* Redundant systems make use of redundancy techniques known as self-purging redundancy, triple-modular redundancy, or *N*-modular redundancy. These systems execute the same tasks on each equivalent module, and for improving the output information, "vote" on the resulting output.
iv.   *Gracefully Degrading Redundancy:* In this case, all available active units are used to execute tasks. Upon failure of an active unit, these systems attempt to reconfigure to a system having one fewer unit.

5.4   RELIABILITY MEASURES FOR COMPUTERS

This section presents several measures of computer system reliability separated into two distinct groups as given below.
   Group I. Group I measures are suitable for such configurations as standby, hybrid and massive redundant systems.

i.   System reliability
ii.   System availability
iii.   Mean time to failure
iv.   Mission time

To evaluate gracefully degrading systems, the above four measures may not be sufficient.

Group II. To handle gracefully degrading systems, five new measures are needed [2].

    i.   Computation reliability
    ii. Computation availability
    iii. Mean computation before failure
    iv. Capacity threshold
    v. Computation threshold

Firstly, *computation reliability* is defined as the failure-free probability that the system will without an error execute a task of length x initiated at time t. Secondly, *computation availability* is expressed as the expected computation capacity of the system at given time t. Thirdly, *mean computation before failure* may be described as the expected amount of computation available on the system before failure. Fourthly, *capacity threshold* is defined as that time at which a certain value of computation availability is reached. Finally, *computation threshold* may be expressed as the time at which a certain value of computation reliability is reached for a task whose length is x.

5.5   FORMULAS FOR SYSTEM AVAILABILITY AND COMPUTING EFFICIENCY

Formula I. This formula is used to determine system availability [8]. The total time that engineering, operational, or maintenance work is being carried out on the system (i.e. total power-on time) is used as a base. The system availability A_{st} is expressed as follows:

$$A_{st} = \left[t_{p0} - \left\{ \sum_{j=1}^{k} t_j + t_r + t_{ct} \right\} \right] (100/t_{p0}) \qquad (5.1)$$

Where

A_{st} is the system availability (with total power-on time used as a base).

t_{p0} is the total power-on time of the system in question.

k is the total number of interrupting failures that happened during the period the system was need for operation.

t_r is the time needed for routine maintenance.

t_{ct} is the time associated with equipment tests and engineering changes.

t_j is the time needed to put the system in question back into its operational state after an interupting failure.

Formula II. This formula is also concerned with determining system availability [8]. It makes use of only the operational and maintenance time periods as a base. The system availability A_{0m} is given by

$$A_{0m} = \left[(t_{p0} - t_{ct}) - \left(\sum_{j=1}^{k} t_j + t_r \right) \right] (100)/(t_{p0} - t_{ct}) \qquad (5.2)$$

Symbols used in formula I are also applicable for this formula.

Formula III. This formula is used in determining computing efficiency [8]. This efficiency is expressed as follows:

$$\beta = \left[S_t - \left\{ \sum_{j=1}^{k} t_j + t_{re} \right\} \right] \cdot (100)/S_t \qquad (5.3)$$

Where

t_{re} is the rerun time needed due to system errors.
S_t is the total amount of scheduled time.
t_j is defined in formula I.

5.6 MARKOV MODELING OF COMPUTER ASSOCIATED SYSTEMS

This section presents the three Markov models concerned with computing systems [2].

5.6.1 Model 1

This Markov model represents a gracefully degrading system with m number of processing modules [2]. All the processing modules are independent and identical. Additional assumptions associated with this model are as follows:

  i.   The system has m number of active modules.
 ii.   Failure times of each module are exponentially distributed.
iii.   No attempt is made to repair a failed module.
 iv.   In the boxes of Figure 5.1, m, $(m - 1)$, $(m - 2)$, 1, and 0 denote both the system state and the number of active units in that state of the system.
  v.   When the system has more than one normally operating module, a certain proportion of failures are covered.

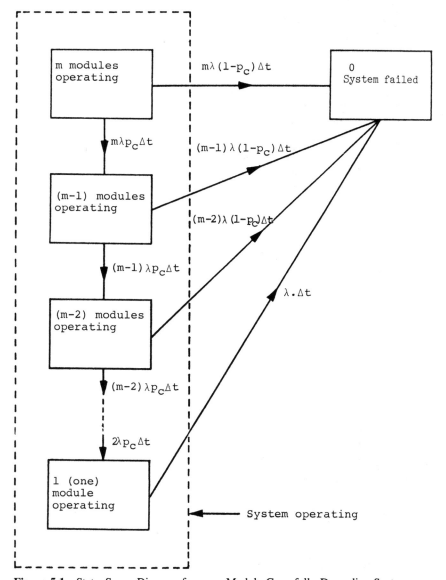

Figure 5.1 State–Space Diagram for an *m* Module Gracefully Degrading System

vi. The coverage probability is same for each state of the system with more than one active module.

The system state–space diagram is shown in Figure 5.1. The following symbols are associated with this model:

j   is the *j*th state of the system, $j = m$ [all (m) modules operating normally], $j = (m - 1)$ [($m - 1$) modules operating normally, one module failed], $j = (m - 2)$ [$(m - 2)$ modules operating normally, two modules failed], $j = 1$ [one module operating normally, $(m - 1)$ modules failed], $j = 0$ (all m modules failed).

$P_j(t)$ is the probability that the gracefully degrading system is in state j at time t; for $j = 0, 1, \ldots, (m - 2), (m - 1), m$.

λ is the constant failure rate of a module.

P_c is the (coverage) probability that the gracefully degrading system reconfigures given that a fault has been discovered while in state j, for $j = 2, 3, 4, \ldots, m$.

m is the total number of identical modules in the system.

Δt is the time interval.

The differential equations for the model shown in Figure 5.1 are:

$$\frac{dP_m(t)}{dt} + m\lambda P_m(t) = 0 \tag{5.4}$$

$$\frac{dP_j(t)}{dt} + j\lambda P_j(t) - (j + 1)\lambda p_c P_{j+1}(t) = 0 \tag{5.5}$$

for $j = 1, 2, 3, \ldots, (m - 1)$.

$$\frac{dP_0(t)}{dt} - \lambda \cdot P_1(t) - \lambda(1 - p_c)\sum_{j=2}^{m} jP_j(t) = 0 \tag{5.6}$$

At time $t = 0$, $P_m(0) = 1$, and other initial condition probabilities are equal to zero.

By solving Eqs. (5.4) through (5.6) with the aid of Laplace transforms, we get the resulting equations:

$$P_j(t) = p_c^{(m-j)} \cdot e^{-j\lambda t} \binom{m}{j} (1 - e^{-\lambda t})^{m-j} \tag{5.7}$$

for $j = 1, 2, 3, \ldots, m$.

$$\binom{m}{j} = \frac{m!}{j!(m - j)!} \tag{5.8}$$

$$P_0(t) = 1 - \sum_{j=1}^{m} P_j(t) \tag{5.9}$$

The reliability of the gracefully degrading system is given by

$$R_{gs}(t) = \sum_{j=1}^{m} p_c^{(m-j)} \cdot e^{-j\lambda t} \binom{m}{j} (1 - e^{-\lambda t})^{m-j} \tag{5.10}$$

Where

$R_{gs}(t)$ is the gracefully degrading system's reliability.

The system's mean time to failure $MTTF_{gs}$ can be obtained from the following relationship:

$$MTTF_{gs} = \int_0^\infty R_{gs}(t) \cdot dt \tag{5.11}$$

Substituting Eq. (5.10) into Eq. (5.11) yields

$$MTTF_{gs} = \int_0^\infty \left[\sum_{j=1}^m p_c^{(m-j)} \cdot e^{-j\lambda t} \binom{m}{j} (1 - e^{-\lambda t})^{m-j} \right] dt$$

$$= \frac{1}{\lambda} \sum_{j=1}^m (p_c^{m-j})/j \tag{5.12}$$

For $m = 2$ and $m = 3$ from the above equation the gracefully degrading system's mean time to failure, respectively, are

$$MTTF = \frac{1}{\lambda} \sum_{j=1}^2 (p_c^{2-j})/j$$

$$= \frac{1}{\lambda} [p_c + \tfrac{1}{2}] \tag{5.13}$$

and

$$MTTF = \frac{1}{\lambda} \sum_{j=1}^3 (p_c^{2-j})/j$$

$$= \frac{1}{\lambda} \left[p_c^2 + \frac{p_c}{2} + \frac{1}{3} \right] \tag{5.14}$$

5.6.2   Model II

In model I, if each module of the system has the same computation capacity (or ability to execute computing tasks) k, then the system state j has computation capacity jk. The computation capacity may be simply described [2] as the amount of useful computation per unit time (e.g. instructions/second). To perform reliability analysis in terms of the computation variable x instead of the time variable t, we make use of the following relationship:

$$x = kt \tag{5.15}$$

Thus we may write

$$\Delta t = \Delta x / k_j = \frac{\Delta x}{jk} \tag{5.16}$$

for $j = 1, 2, 3, \ldots, m$.

Figure 5.2 shows the computation domain representation of the Markov model for an 'm' identical module gracefully degrading system.

With the aid of Figure 5.1, the transition probability of an occurrence from state m to state $(m - 1)$ is given by

$$P_{m,m-1} = m\lambda \, p_c \, \Delta t \tag{5.17}$$

After substituting for Δt from Eq. (5.16) into Eq. (5.17) we get

$$P_{m,m-1} = m\lambda p_c \cdot \Delta x / k_m$$

$$= m\lambda p_c \cdot \Delta x / mk$$

$$= \lambda \, p_c \cdot \Delta x / k \tag{5.18}$$

Similarly, with the aid of Figure 5.1 the transition probability of an occurrence from state $(m - 1)$ to state $(m - 2)$ is given by

$$P_{(m-1),(m-2)} = (m - 1)\lambda \, p_c \Delta t \tag{5.19}$$

After substituting for Δt from Eq. (5.16) into Eq. (5.19) we get

$$p_{(m-1),(m-2)} = (m - 1)\lambda \, p_c \, \Delta x / k_{m-1}$$

$$= (m - 1)\lambda \, p_c \, \Delta x / (m-1)k$$

$$= \lambda \, p_c \, \Delta x / k \tag{5.20}$$

It is to be noted that the right hand sides of Eqs. (5.18) and (5.20) are the same. With the same reasoning as used in Eqs. (5.18) and (5.20), we obtained the remaining transition probabilities shown in Figure 5.2.

The following differential equations are associated with Figure 5.2

$$\frac{dP_m(x)}{dx} + \frac{\lambda}{k} P_m(x) = 0 \tag{5.21}$$

$$\frac{dp_j(x)}{dx} + \frac{\lambda}{k} \cdot P_j(x) - \frac{\lambda \, p_c}{k} P_{j+1}(x) = 0 \tag{5.22}$$

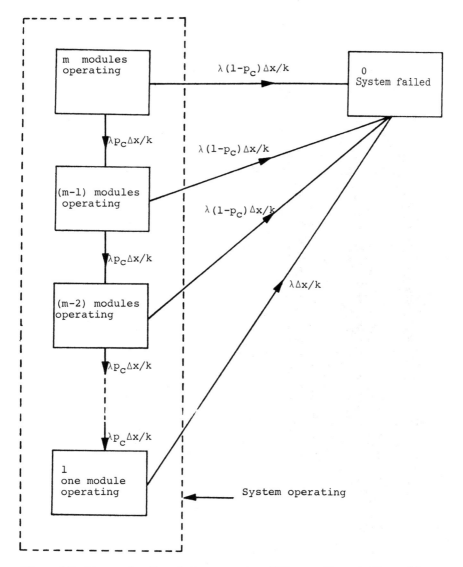

Figure 5.2 Computation Domain Representation of Diagram Shown in Figure 5.1

for $j = 1, 2, \ldots, m - 1$.

$$\frac{dP_0(x)}{dx} - \frac{\lambda}{k}P_1(x) - \frac{\lambda(1 - p_c)}{k} \sum_{j=2}^{m} P_j(x) = 0 \qquad (5.23)$$

Where

$P_j(x)$ is the probability that the gracefully degrading system is in state j after an amount x of computation; for $j = 0, 1, 2, \ldots , m$.

At $x = 0$, $P_m(0) = 1$ and other initial condition probabilities are equal to zero.

After solving the above set of differential equations we get the capacity function of each system state:

$$D_j(x) = e^{-\lambda x/k} \sum_{i=1}^{j-1} \left[\frac{\lambda p_c x}{k} \right]^i /i! \qquad (5.24)$$

for $j = 1, 2, 3, \ldots , m$.

The gracefully degrading system's mean computation before failure is

$$MCBF = \int_0^\infty D_I(x) \cdot dx$$

$$= \int_0^\infty \left[e^{-\lambda x/k} \sum_{i=0}^{m-1} \left[\frac{\lambda p_c x}{k} \right]^i /i! \right] dx$$

$$= \sum_{i=0}^{m-1} \frac{\lambda^i p_c^i}{i! k^i} \int_0^\infty x^i \cdot e^{-\lambda x/k} dx$$

$$= \sum_{i=0}^{m-1} \frac{\lambda^i p_c^i}{i! k^i} \cdot \frac{x^i}{(\lambda/k)^{i+1}}$$

$$= \frac{k}{\lambda} \sum_{i=0}^{m-1} p_c^i \qquad (5.25)$$

Finally the system's computation availability is given by

$$AV_c(t) = \sum_{j=1}^m k_j P_j(t)$$

$$= \sum_{j=1}^m jk P_j(t) \qquad (5.26)$$

Where

$AV_c(t)$ is the computation availability of the gracefully degrading system.

For a two (independent and identical) module gracefully degrading system, reliability, computation reliability, computation availability, mean time to failure, and mean computation before failure are as follows [2]:

$$R_{gs}(t) = 2 p_c e^{-\lambda t} + (1 - 2p_c)e^{-2\lambda t} \qquad (5.27)$$

$$R_c(t,x) = e^{-\lambda(t+\frac{x}{k})} \left[2 p_c + e^{-\lambda t} \left(1 - 2p_c + \frac{p_c \lambda x}{k} \right) \right] \qquad (5.28)$$

$$AV_c(t) = [p_c + (1 - p_c)e^{-\lambda t}] \cdot 2ke^{-\lambda t} \qquad (5.29)$$

$$MTTF = \frac{1}{\lambda}(p_c + \tfrac{1}{2}) \qquad (5.30)$$

and

$$MCBF = \frac{k}{\lambda}(p_c + 1) \qquad (5.31)$$

Where

$R_{gs}(t)$ is the reliability of the system.
$R_c(t,x)$ is the computation reliability.
$AV_c(t)$ is the computation availability.
$MTTF$ is the mean time to failure.
$MCBF$ is the mean computation before failure.

5.6.3 Model III

This Markov model represents a multiprocessor system with repair. The system has two independent and identical active processors with computation capacity k [2]. The system fails when both the processors fail. The state–space diagram of the system is shown in Figure 5.3. This model is based on assumptions such as follows:

   i.   The system is composed of two independent, identical and active pro-
        cessors.
   ii. Failure times of each processor are exponentially distributed.
   iii. A repaired processor is as good as new.
   vi. Only one failed processor is repaired at a time.

v.   When the system has two processors operating normally, a certain proportion of failures are covered.

vi. The numeral in each box of Figure 5.3 denotes the state number and the number of failed processors in that state.

The following symbols are associated with this model:

i is the ith state of the system: $i = 0$ (both processors operating normally), $i = 1$ (one processor operating normally, other failed), $i = 2$ (system failed).

$P_i(t)$ is the probability that the system is in state i at time t, for $i = 0, 1, 2$.

λ is the constant failure rate of a processor.

μ is the constant repair rate of a processor.

Δt is the time interval.

k is the computation capacity.

P_c is the (coverage) probability that the system reconfigures given that a fault has been discovered.

The following differential equations are associated with this model:

$$\frac{dP_0(t)}{dt} = -2\lambda P_0(t) + \mu P_1(t) \tag{5.32}$$

$$\frac{dP_1(t)}{dt} = -(\lambda + \mu)P_1(t) + 2\lambda p_c P_0(t) + \mu P_2(t) \tag{5.33}$$

$$\frac{dP_2(t)}{dt} = -\mu P_2(t) + \lambda P_1(t) + 2\lambda(1 - p_c)P_0(t) \tag{5.34}$$

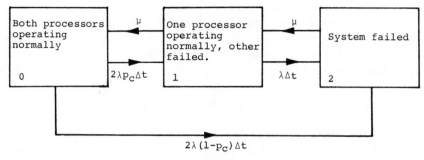

Figure 5.3   A Two-Processor System With Repair

At time $t = 0$, $P_0(0) = 1$ and other initial condition probabilities are equal to zero.

To obtain steady state probabilities we set the left hand sides of Eqs. (5.32) through (5.34) equal to zero:

$$\mu P_1 - 2\lambda P_0 = 0 \tag{5.35}$$

$$\mu P_2 + 2\lambda p_c P_0 - (\lambda + \mu)P_1 = 0 \tag{5.36}$$

$$\lambda P_1 + 2\lambda(1 - p_c)P_0 - \mu P_2 = 0 \tag{5.37}$$

In addition, to obtain expressions for probabilities P_0, P_1, and P_2 we solve the above system of equations with the aid of the following relationship:

$$P_0 + P_1 + P_2 = 1 \tag{5.38}$$

Thus from Eqs. (5.36) through (5.38), we get

$$A_{sp} = P_0 + P_1 = \mu(\mu + 2\lambda)/G \tag{5.39}$$

$$G \equiv \mu^2 + 2\lambda\mu(2 - p_c) + 2\lambda^2 \tag{5.40}$$

Where

A_{sp} is the steady state availability of the multiprocessor system.

The steady state computation availability is given by

$$A_{sc} = 2kP_0 + kP_1$$

$$= k\{2\mu(\mu + \lambda)\}/G \tag{5.41}$$

5.7   RELIABILITY ANALYSIS OF A REDUNDANT SYSTEM

In complex redundant systems the detection of a failed unit and switchover may or may not be perfect. Therefore, predicted reliability of such systems may be over-optimistic with the assumption of perfect (100% probability of success) detection and switchover. To overcome this shortcoming in a redundant system's reliability analysis, the concept of "coverage" was introduced in references [9,10]. The reliability of a redundant system with two non-identical modules is given by

$$R_{rs} = (1 - F_1) + p_c F_1(1 - F_2) \tag{5.42}$$

Where

R_{rs} is the two-module redundant system's reliability.
F_1 is the failure probability of module 1.
F_2 is the failure probability of module 2.
p_c is the conditional probability that a system recovers, given that
         a failure has occurred.

For $p_c = 1$, Eq. (5.42) becomes the same as for the two-module parallel system. For k identical modules, Eq. (5.42) can be generalized to the following form:

$$R_s = (1 - F) \sum_{j=0}^{k-1} F^j \cdot p_c^j \qquad (5.43)$$

Where

F is the failure probability of a module.
R_s is the system's reliability.

For $0 < y < 1$, the following relationship is valid [11]:

$$\sum_{j=0}^{k} y^j = (1 - y^{k+1})/(1 - y) \qquad (5.44)$$

With the aid of relationship (5.44), Eq. (5.43) simplifies to

$$R_s = (1 - F) [(1 - p_c^k \cdot F^k)/(1 - p_c F)] \qquad (5.45)$$

5.8 SUMMARY

This chapter addressed areas associated with computer hardware reliability. Important issues in computer system reliability were listed, and four distinct ways to achieve required reliability were described. These are standby redundancy, hybrid redundancy, massive redundancy, and gracefully degrading redundancy. Performance-related reliability measures for computer systems were presented and categorized into group I and group II. Group I includes measures such as system reliability, mean time to failure, mission time, and system availability. These measures are quite suitable for standby, hybrid and massive redundant systems. Group II includes measures such as computation reliability, mean computation before failure, capacity threshold, computation availability, and computation threshold. These measures are useful for gracefully degrading systems. Three practically inclined formulas to determine system availability and computing efficiency were presented. Finally, three Markov models representing gracefully degrading systems were developed.

5.9 EXERCISES

1. Define the following four terms:

   i. system availability
   ii. computation reliability
   iii. computation capacity
   iv. massive redundant system

2. What are the advantages and disadvantages of a gracefully degrading system?
3. Discuss at least three important issues concerning computer system reliability today.
4. What are the assumptions associated with Markov reliability modeling?
5. What are the benefits and drawbacks of Markov reliability and availability modeling?
6. Describe the concept of "coverage".
7. With the aid of Eqs. (5.32) through (5.34), obtain expressions for $P_0(t)$, $P_1(t)$, and $P_2(t)$. These probabilities are associated with model III.

5.10 REFERENCES

1. J. Goldberg, "A Survey of the Design and Analysis of Fault-Tolerant Computers", in *Reliability and Fault Tree Analysis* edited by R.E. Barlow, J.B. Fussell and N.D. Singpurwalla, published by Society for Industrial and Applied Mathematics, Philadelphia, 1975, pp. 667–685.

2. M.D. Beaudry, "Performance Related Reliability Measures for Computing Systems", IEEE Transactions on Computers, Vol. 27, June 1978, pp. 540–547.

3. W.G. Bouricius, W.C. Carter, and P.R. Schneider, "Reliability Modeling Techniques for Self-Repairing Computer Systems", Proceedings of 12th Association of Computing Machinery National Conference, August 1969, pp. 295–305.

4. F.P. Mathur and A. Avizienis, "Reliability Analysis and Architecture of a Highly Redundant Digital System: Generalized Triple Modular Redundancy with Self-Repair", Proceedings of the American Federation of Information Processing Societies (AFIPS), 1970, pp. 375–383.

5. J. Von Neumann, "Probabilistic Logics and the Synthesis of Reliable Organisms from Unreliable Components", in *Automata Studies* Edited by C.E. Shannon, J. McCarthy, Princeton University Press, Princeton, New Jersey, 1956, pp. 43–98.

6. J. Losq, "A Highly Efficient Redundancy Scheme: Self-Purging Redundancy", IEEE Transactions on Computers, Vol. 25, June 1976, pp. 569–578.

7. B.R. Borgerson and R.F. Freitas, "A Reliability Model for Gracefully Degrading Standby-Sparing Systems", IEEE Transactions on Computers, Vol. 24, 1975, pp. 517–525.

8. G.B. McCarter and J. Gold, "Large Digital Computer Dependability Measurement", Proceedings of the Fourth National Symposium on Reliability and Quality Control in Electronics, 1958, pp. 95–112.

9. H. Wyle and G.J. Burnett, "Some Relationships Between Failure Detection Probability and Computer System Reliability", Proceedings of the Fall Joint Computer Conference, American Federation of Information Processing Societies (AFIPS), Vol. 31, 1967, pp. 745–756.

10. D.P. Siewiorek and R.S. Swarz, *The Theory and Practice of Reliable System Design,* Digital Press, Digital Equipment Corporation, Bedford, Massachusetts, 1982.

6
RELIABILITY ANALYSIS OF COMPUTER SYSTEMS

6.1 INTRODUCTION

Computer systems are analyzed from various different angles with respect to reliability. Usually the objective of these analyses is to predict and/or improve reliability of computer systems under various conditions. Analyses may make use of simple or highly sophisticated mathematics. An example of the sophisticated mathematics used is the semi-Markovian theory [1,2]. Some examples of computer system reliability analyses conducted under diverse conditions are as follows:

  i. Reliability and availability models for maintained systems featuring hardware failures and design faults [1].
  ii. Reliability analysis of systems with concurrent error detection [3].
  iii. A reliability model for various switch designs in hybrid redundancy [4].
  iv. Reliability modeling of multiprocessor structures [5].
  v. Reliability Analysis of N-modular redundancy systems with intermittent and permanent faults [6].

This chapter is concerned with reliability analysis performed under various conditions. The different types of reliability analyses associated with computer systems are presented in the subsequent sections.

6.2 REDUNDANCY SCHEMES FOR COMPUTER SYSTEMS

The following redundancy schemes have been proposed to improve the reliability of computer systems [4,7].

6.2.1 Scheme Type I

Probably the most widely used scheme is triple-modular redundancy (TMR). This scheme was first proposed in reference [8] and calls for replicating each independent module thrice. The *TMR* scheme can tolerate failure of one module. In other words, the system only fails when more than one module fails or the voter fails. The voter forms a series configuration with the three independent module units. The purpose of the voter is to provide an output based upon its majority of input votes, e.g. if the majority of inputs indicate failures, the output of the voter will indicate a failure. The reliability of the *TMR* system with voter is expressed as follows:

$$R_{tr} = R_{vOt}(3R_m^2 - 2R_m^3) \tag{6.1}$$

Where

R_{tr} is the triple modular redundancy (TMR) system reliability with voter.

R_{vOt} is the voter reliability.

R_m is the module reliability.

6.2.2 Scheme Type II

This scheme is a logical extension of triple-modular redundancy and is known as *N*-modular redundancy (NMR). Obviously in this case the system contains *N* independent modules. The number *N* is any odd number. the *N*-modular redundancy system can tolerate a maximum of *k* modular failures if the value of *N* is equal to $(2k + 1)$. The entire system fails if the voter fails; the voter forms a series configuration with the *N*-module unit. The *N*-modular redundancy system reliability may be written as follows:

$$R_{Nr} = R_{vot} \cdot A \tag{6.2}$$

Where

$$A \equiv \sum_{j=0}^{k} \binom{N}{j} R_m^{N-j}(1 - R_m)^j \tag{6.3}$$

The following symbols are associated with Eq. (6.2):

R_{Nr} is the *N*-modular redundancy system reliability with voter.

R_{vot} is the voter reliability.

R_m is the module reliability.

The symbols *k* and *N* were defined earlier.

6.2.3 Scheme Type III

This is known as the hybrid redundancy scheme [9,10]. With the application of this scheme, it is possible to attain longer periods of fault free operation and reliability than achievable by schemes I (TMR) and II (NMR). The hybrid redundancy scheme with a triple modular redundancy core is shown in

Figure 6.1. This figure shows that the switch chooses three out of k modules whose outputs are to be voted on [4]. A *TMR* core is formed by these three modules. By comparing the voter output to the module outputs, the faulty modules are identified. After the identification of faulty modules, a faulty module belonging to the triple modular redundancy core is logically replaced by one of the unfailed spares. In this scheme, it is assumed that the hybrid redundancy system can fail if either voter or switch fails. More specifically, it is assumed that voter and switch units form a series configuration with the subsystem containing k modules. The hybrid system reliability is given by

$$R_{hd} = [1 - kR_m(1 - R_m)^{k-1} - (1 - R_m)^k] \cdot R_{vot} \cdot R_s \qquad (6.4)$$

Where

R_m	is the module reliability.
k	is the number of modules.
R_{vot}	is the voter reliability.
R_s	is the switch reliability.
R_{hd}	is the reliability of the hybrid system with a triple modular redundancy core and $k - 3$ spare modules.

If the failure times of module, voter and switch are described by an exponential distribution, the reliability of each of these items is given by

$$R_m(t) = e^{-\lambda_m t} \qquad (6.5)$$

$$R_{vot}(t) = e^{-\lambda_{vot} \cdot t} \qquad (6.6)$$

$$R_s(t) = e^{-\lambda_s t} \qquad (6.7)$$

Where

$R_m(t)$	is the module reliability at time t.
$R_{vot}(t)$	is the voter reliability at time t.
$R_s(t)$	is the switch reliability at time t.
λ_m	is the constant failure rate of a module.
λ_{vot}	is the constant failure rate of the voter.
λ_s	is the constant failure rate of the switch.

By substituting Eqs. (6.5) through (6.7) into Eq. (6.4), we get:

$$R_{hd}(t) = [1 - ke^{-\lambda_m t}(1 - e^{-\lambda_m t})^{k-1} - (1 - e^{-\lambda_m t})^k] \cdot e^{-(\lambda_{vot} + \lambda_s)t} \qquad (6.8)$$

Where

$R_{hd}(t)$	is the time-dependent reliability of the hybrid system with a *TMR* core and $(k - 3)$ spare modules.

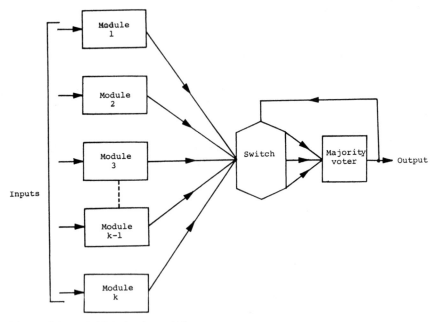

Figure 6.1 Hybrid Redundancy Scheme

The mean time to failure of the hybrid system can be obtained from the following relationship:

$$MTTF_{hd} = \int_0^\infty R_{hd}(t) \cdot dt \qquad (6.9)$$

Where

$MTTF_{hd}$ is the mean time to failure of the hybrid system.

6.2.4 Scheme Type IV

This scheme is known as the checker-redundant scheme [3,4] in which each module has a checker. Some assumptions associated with this scheme are as follows:

i.   The scheme has k identical and independent modules.
ii. If a checker associated with an active module detects a fault, the function of that module is immediately taken over by another module.
iii. When all the modules in the system fail, the system fails.
iv. The scheme has a switch acting in series (i.e., if the switch fails the entire checker-redundant system fails).

The reliability of the checker-redundant system is given by

$$R_{cd} = [1 - (1 - r)^k] \cdot R_s$$

Where

$r \equiv$ $R_m \cdot R_{ck}$
R_m is the module reliability.
R_{ck} is the checker reliability.
R_s is the switch reliability.
R_{cd} is the checker-redundant system reliability.
k is the number of modules.

6.2.5 Scheme Type V

This scheme is concerned with cascading of triple modular redundancy units as shown in Figure 6.2. This figure represents a situation where the *TMR* subsystem 1 output is fed to *TMR* subsystem 2 and in turn the *TMR* subsystem 2 output is fed to *TMR* subsystem 3. This process continues for M independent *TMR* subsystems. Each *TMR* subsystem contains three independent and identical modules in series with a voter. The reliability of the configuration shown in Figure 6.2 can be expressed as follows:

$$R_{cTMR} = \prod_{j=1}^{M} R_{votj} \cdot R_{TMRj} \qquad (6.11)$$

Where

$$R_{TMRj} = 3R_j^2 - 2R_j^3 \qquad (6.12)$$

The following symbols are associated with Eq. (6.11):

R_{cTMR} is the reliability of the system containing M *TMR* subsystems in series.
M is the number of *TMR* subsystems.
R_{votj} is the reliability of jth *TMR* subsystem's voter for $j = 1, 2, 3, \ldots, M$.
R_j is the reliability of a module in *TMR* subsystem j for $j = 1, 2, 3, \ldots, M$.

Example 6.1

A system is composed of two independent *TMR* subsystems in series. In subsystems 1 and 2 the reliabilities of each module are 0.9 and 0.95, respectively.

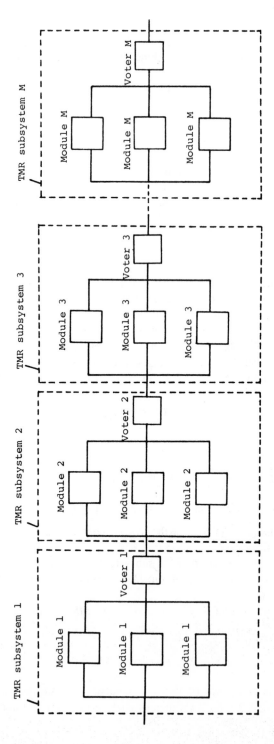

Figure 6.2 *M TMR* Subsystems in Series

Similarly reliabilities of voters associated with subsystems 1 and 2 are 0.8 and 0.85, respectively. Calculate the system reliability with the aid of Eq. (6.11).

With the aid of the specified data and Eq. (6.11), we get

$$R_{cTMR} = R_{vot1} \cdot R_{TMR1} \cdot R_{vot2} \cdot R_{TMR2}$$

$$= R_{vot1}\{3R_1^2 - 2R_1^3\}R_{vot2} \cdot \{3R_2^2 - 2R_2^3\}$$

$$= (0.8)\{3(0.9)^2 - 2(0.9)^3\} \cdot (0.85)\{3(0.95)^2 - 2(0.95)^3\}$$

$$= 0.6562$$

If the jth voter and jth TMR subsystem's module failure rates are constant, then their respective time-dependent reliabilities are

$$R_{votj}(t) = e^{-\lambda_{votj}t} \tag{6.13}$$

and

$$R_j(t) = e^{-\lambda_j t} \tag{6.14}$$

Where

t	is time.
$R_{votj}(t)$	is the time-dependent reliability of voter j associated with TMR subsystem j for $j = 1, 2, 3, \ldots, M$.
$R_j(t)$	is the time-dependent reliability of a module associated with TMR subsystem j.
λ_{votj}	is the constant failure rate of voter j associated with TMR subsystem j for $j = 1, 2, 3, \ldots, M$.
λ_j	is the constant failure rate of a module associated with TMR subsystem j for $j = 1, 2, 3, \ldots, M$.

By substituting Eqs. (6.13) through (6.14) into Eq. (6.11),

$$R_{cTMR}(t) = \prod_{j=1}^{M} R_{votj}(t) \cdot [3\{R_j(t)\}^2 - 2\{R_j(t)\}^3]$$

$$= \prod_{j=1}^{M} e^{-\lambda_{votj}t}[3e^{-2\lambda_j t} - 2e^{-3\lambda_j t}] \tag{6.15}$$

For identical TMR subsystems, the above equation becomes

$$R_{cTMR}(t) = [e^{-\lambda_{vot}t}\{3e^{-2\lambda t} - 2e^{-3\lambda t}\}]^M \tag{6.16}$$

The system mean time to failure can be obtained from the following relationship:

$$MTTF_{cTMR} = \int_0^\infty \prod_{j=1}^{M} e^{-\lambda_{votj}t}[3e^{-2\lambda_j t} - 2e^{-3\lambda_j t}]dt \qquad (6.17)$$

Where

    $MTTF_{cTMR}$ is the mean time to failure of system containing M independent *TMR* subsystems in series.

For $M = 2$, Eq. (6.17) becomes

$$MTTF_{cTMR} = \int_0^\infty \prod_{j=1}^{2} e^{-\lambda_{votj}t}[3e^{-2\lambda_j t} - 2e^{-3\lambda_j t}]dt$$

$$= \int_0^\infty [3e^{-(2\lambda_1 + \lambda_{vot1})t} - 2e^{-(3\lambda_1 + \lambda_{vot1})t}][3e^{-(2\lambda_2 + \lambda_{vot2})t}$$

$$- 2e^{-(3\lambda_2 + \lambda_{vot2})t}] \cdot dt$$

$$= \int_0^\infty [9e^{-(A_1 + A_3)t} - 6e^{-(A_2 + A_3)t} - 6e^{-(A_1 + A_4)t} + 4e^{-(A_2 + A_4)t}]dt$$

$$= \left[-\frac{9e^{-(A_1 + A_3)t}}{(A_1 + A_3)} + \frac{6e^{-(A_2 + A_3)t}}{(A_2 + A_3)} + \frac{6e^{-(A_1 + A_4)t}}{(A_1 + A_4)} - \frac{4e^{-(A_2 + A_4)t}}{(A_2 + A_4)} \right]_0^\infty$$

$$= \frac{9}{(A_1 + A_3)} - \frac{6}{(A_2 + A_3)} - \frac{6}{(A_1 + A_4)} + \frac{4}{(A_2 + A_4)} \qquad (6.18)$$

Where

$$A_1 \equiv 2\lambda_1 + \lambda_{vot1} \qquad (6.19)$$

$$A_2 \equiv 3\lambda_1 + \lambda_{vot1} \qquad (6.20)$$

$$A_3 \equiv 2\lambda_2 + \lambda_{vot2} \qquad (6.21)$$

$$A_4 \equiv 3\lambda_2 + \lambda_{vot2} \qquad (6.22)$$

For $M = 2$ and identical *TMR* subsystems, Eq. (6.17) reduces to

$$MTTF_{cTMR} = \int_0^\infty [3e^{-(\lambda_{vot} + 2\lambda)t} - 2e^{-(\lambda_{vot} + 3\lambda)t}]^2 \, dt$$

$$= \int_0^\infty [9e^{-2(\lambda_{vot} + 2\lambda)t} - 12e^{-(2\lambda_{vot} + 5\lambda)t} + 4e^{-2(\lambda_{vot} + 3\lambda)t}] \, dt$$

$$= \left[-\frac{9e^{-2(\lambda_{vot} + 2\lambda)t}}{2(\lambda_{vot} + 2\lambda)} + \frac{12e^{-(2\lambda_{vot} + 5\lambda)t}}{(2\lambda_{vot} + 5\lambda)} - \frac{4e^{-2(\lambda_{vot} + 3\lambda)t}}{2(\lambda_{vot} + 3\lambda)} \right]_0^\infty$$

$$= \frac{9}{2(\lambda_{vot} + 2\lambda)} - \frac{12}{(2\lambda_{vot} + 5\lambda)} + \frac{4}{2(\lambda_{vot} + 3\lambda)} \qquad (6.23)$$

Where

λ is the constant failure rate of a module associated with the *TMR* subsystem.

λ_{vot} is the constant failure rate of a voter associated with the *TMR* subsystem.

Example 6.2

In Eq. (6.23), the values of λ and λ_{vot} are 0.0005 failure/hour and 0.0001 failure/hour, respectively. Compute the value of $MTTF_{cTMR}$.

$$MTTF_{cTMR} = \frac{9}{2\{0.0001 + 2(0.0005)\}} - \frac{12}{2\{2(0.0001) + 5(0.0005)\}}$$

$$+ \frac{4}{2\{0.0001 + 3(0.0005)\}}$$

$$= 3,118.69 \text{ hours}$$

Thus the mean time to failure of system containing two identical and independent *TMR* subsystems in series is 3,118.69 hours.

6.2.6 Scheme Type VI

This scheme is a logical extension of scheme type V. In this case, in addition to triplicating modules, the voters are also triplicated as shown in Figure 6.3. This figure shows that the output of each triplicated module is fed into each of the triplicated voters. In turn the output of each voter is fed into a module. However, at the last stage of the system there is only a single voter.

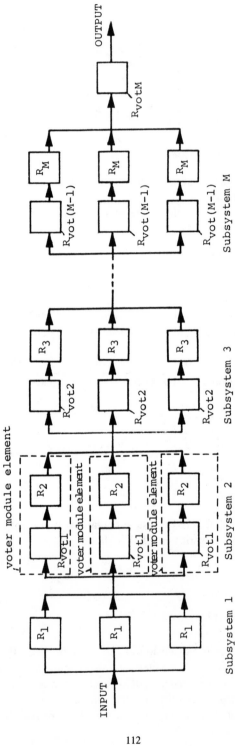

Figure 6.3 A System with Triplicated Modules and Voters

112

The outputs of all the three last stage modules are fed into this voter. The advantage of this configuration over the Figure 6.2 configuration is that all but one of the single points of failure can be eliminated. In Figure 6.3 it is to be noted that for the success of subsystem 1, at least two of the three modules must function normally. Similarly, for the success of subsystem 2 at least 2 units of voter–module element out of three must work normally. This goes on until subsystem M. The reliability of the system shown in Figure 6.3 is expressed as follows [7]:

$$R_s = [3R_1^2 - 2R_1^3] \cdot R_{votM} \prod_{j=2}^{M} [3\{R_j \cdot R_{vot(j-1)}\}^2 - 2\{R_j R_{vot(j-1)}\}^3] \qquad (6.24)$$

Where

R_1 is the reliability of a module contained in subsystem 1.

R_j is the reliability of a module contained in subsystem j for $j = 2, 3, \ldots, M$.

$R_{vot(j-1)}$ is the reliability of a voter contained in subsystem j for $j = 2, 3, \ldots, M$.

R_{votM} is the reliability of voter M.

M is the total number of subsystems.

For constant failure rates of modules and voters, Eq. (6.24) becomes

$$R_s(t) = [3\{R_1(t)\}^2 - 2\{R_1(t)\}^3]R_{votM}(t) \prod_{j=2}^{M} [3\{R_j(t) \cdot R_{vot(j-1)}(t)\}^2$$

$$- 2\{R_j(t) \cdot R_{vot(j-1)}(t)\}^3] \qquad (6.25)$$

Where

$$R_1(t) = e^{-\lambda_1 t} \qquad (6.26)$$

$$R_{votM}(t) = e^{-(\lambda_{votM})t} \qquad (6.27)$$

$$R_j(t) = e^{-\lambda_j t} \qquad (6.28)$$

$$R_{vot(j-1)}(t) = e^{-\{\lambda_{vot(j-1)}\}t} \qquad (6.29)$$

Symbols used in Eqs. (6.26) through (6.29) are:

t is time.

λ_1 is the constant failure rate of a module contained in subsystem 1.

λ_{votM} is the constant failure rate of voter M.

λ_j is the constant failure rate of a module contained in subsystem j for $j = 2, 3, \ldots, M$.

$\lambda_{vot(j-1)}$ is the constant failure rate of a voter contained in subsystem j for $j = 1, 2, 3, \ldots, M$.

The system mean time to failure $MTTF_s$ can be obtained from the following relationship:

$$MTTF_s = \int_0^\infty R_s(t)\, dt$$

$$= \int_0^\infty [3\{R_1(t)\}^2 - 2\{R_1(t)\}^3] R_{votM}(t) \prod_{j=2}^M [3\{R_j(t) \cdot R_{vot(j-1)}(t)\}^2$$

$$- 2\{R_j(t) \cdot R_{vot(j-1)}(t)\}^3]\, dt \qquad (6.30)$$

If the last voter with reliability R_{votM} in Figure 6.3 is also triplicated, then its reliability equation has to be replaced with one for a *TMR* subsystem. More clearly, R_{votM} is to be replaced with the following equation:

$$R_{tvotM} = [3R_{votM}^2 - 2R_{votM}^3] \qquad (6.31)$$

By replacing R_{votM} in Eq. (6.24) with the right hand side of Eq. (6.31), we get

$$R_s = [3R_1^2 - 2R_1^3][3R_{votM}^2 - 2R_{votM}^3] \prod_{j=2}^M [3\{R_j R_{vot(j-1)}\}^2$$

$$- 2\{R_j R_{vot(j-1)}\}^3] \qquad (6.32)$$

For the constant failure rates of modules and voters, Eq. (6.32) becomes

$$R_s(t) = Y(t) \cdot X(t) \cdot \prod_{j=2}^M [3\{R_j(t) \cdot R_{vot(j-1)}(t)\}^2 - 2\{R_j \cdot R_{vot(j-1)}(t)\}^3]$$

$$(6.33)$$

Where

$$Y(t) \equiv [3\{R_1(t)\}^2 - 2\{R_1(t)\}^3] \qquad (6.34)$$

$$X(t) \equiv [3\{R_{votM}(t)\}^2 - 2\{R_{votM}(t)\}^3] \qquad (6.35)$$

Equations (6.26) through (6.29) define $R_1(t)$, $R_{votM}(t)$, $R_j(t)$, and $R_{vot(j-1)}(t)$, respectively. To obtain system mean time to failure, integrate Eq. (6.33) over interval $[0,\infty]$.

6.3 RELIABILITY EVALUATION OF A MULTI-MINIPROCESSOR COMPUTER

This section presents a mathematical model to evaluate the reliability of a multi-miniprocessor computer [5,11]. In this model it is assumed that with the aid of a crosspoint switch, up to sixteen processors can communicate with up to an equal number of shared memory ports. The reliability of a multi-miniprocessor computer can be determined from the following equation:

$$R_{mmp} = R_{sw} \cdot A_1 \cdot A_2 \tag{6.36}$$

Where

$$A_1 \equiv \sum_{j=0}^{12} \binom{16}{j} R_{psr}^{16-j} \cdot F_{psr}^{j} \tag{6.37}$$

$$A_2 \equiv \sum_{j=0}^{12} \binom{16}{j} R_{mr}^{16-j} \cdot F_{mr}^{j} \tag{6.38}$$

$$\binom{16}{j} = \frac{16!}{j!(16-j)!} \tag{6.39}$$

The symbols used in Eqs. (6.36) through (6.38) are defined below:

R_{sw} is the switch reliability.
R_{psr} is the processor plus associated circuitry reliability.
F_{psr} is the processor plus associated circuitry failure probability.
R_{mr} is the memory plus associated circuitry reliability.
F_{mr} is the memory plus associated circuitry failure probability.
R_{mmp} is the reliability of multi-miniprocessor computer.

It is to be noted that Eq. (6.36) was developed specifically to evaluate reliability of a multi-miniprocessor computer with sixteen processors and an equal number of 64K memories, with a minimum of four processors and four memory ports needed for the task.

6.4 RELIABILITY ANALYSIS OF REPAIRABLE SYSTEMS

This section presents two Markov models representing repairable systems composed of identical redundant modules. In these models it is assumed that there are a certain amount of single faults from which a system with redundant modules cannot automatically recover. The reliability of a system with redundant modules may be reduced drastically even with a very small number of single faults [12].

6.4.1 Model I

This Markov model represents a system composed of two active identical modules. At least one of the modules must work normally for the system's success. The system is repaired when only one of the modules fails. The system state–space diagram is shown in Figure 6.4. The following assumptions are associated with model I:

i.   The failure rate of a module is constant.
ii.   The repair rate of a failed module is constant.
iii. There are a certain proportion, *p,* of faults from which the two-module redundant system can recover automatically.
iv.   There are a certain proportion $(1 - p)$ of faults from which the two-module redundant system cannot recover automatically.
v.   Numerals in boxes of Figure 6.4 denote the system's states.

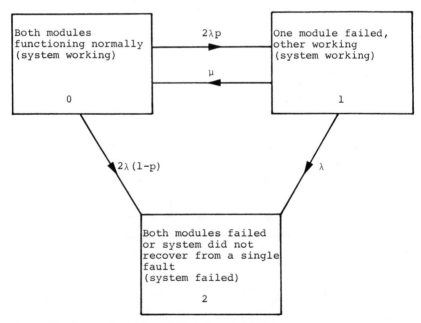

Figure 6.4   System Transition Diagram for Model I

The following symbols are associated with model I:

i is the ith state of the system: $i = 0$ (both modules functioning normally), $i = 1$ (one module failed, other working), $i = 2$ (both modules failed or system did not recover from a single fault).

$P_i(t)$ is the probability that the system is in state i at time t for $i = 0, 1, 2$.

λ is the constant failure rate of a module.

μ is the constant repair rate of a failed module.

p is the proportion of faults from which the two-module redundant system can recover automatically.

$1 - p$ is the proportion of faults from which the two-module redundant system cannot recover automatically.

The following system of differential equations [13] is associated with Figure 6.4:

$$\frac{dP_0(t)}{dt} + 2\lambda P_0(t) = \mu P_1(t) \tag{6.40}$$

$$\frac{dP_1(t)}{dt} + (\lambda + \mu)P_1(t) = 2\lambda p \cdot P_0(t) \tag{6.41}$$

$$\frac{dP_2(t)}{dt} = \lambda P_1(t) + 2\lambda(1 - p) \cdot P_0(t) \tag{6.42}$$

At time $t = 0$, $P_0(0) = 1$ and $P_1(0) = P_2(0) = 0$

With the aid of Laplace transforms, Eqs. (6.40) through (6.42) can be solved to find expressions for state probabilities $P_0(t)$, $P_1(t)$, and $P_2(t)$. By differentiating $P_2(t)$ with respect to time t, we get

$$\frac{dP_2(t)}{dt} = f_s(t) \tag{6.43}$$

Where

$f_s(t)$ is the failure density function of the system.

The system's mean time to failure $MTTF_s$ is given by

$$MTTF_s = \int_0^\infty t \cdot f_s(t) \cdot dt$$

$$= \frac{1 + \beta(5 - 3p)}{2\lambda\beta\{1 + \beta^{-1}(1 - p)\}} \tag{6.44}$$

Where

$$\beta = \lambda/\mu \tag{6.45}$$

For $p = 1$, the $MTTF_s$ becomes

$$MTTF_s \simeq \mu/2\lambda^2 \tag{6.46}$$

6.4.2 Model II

This Markov model represents a system with K number of active identical modules. At least $(K - 1)$ of the total modules must work normally for the system's success; the system has only one spare module. The system is repaired when only one of the modules fails. The system transition diagram is shown in Figure 6.5. Assumptions such as given below pertain to this model:

  i.   All the modules contained in the system are identical.
 ii.   The failure rate of a module is constant.

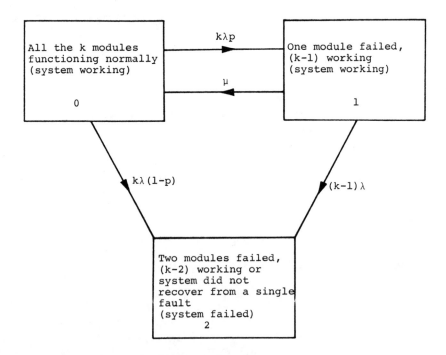

Figure 6.5   System Transition Diagram for Model II.

   iii.   The system contains K number of modules.

   vi.   Only one of the K modules is spare.

   v.   There are a certain proportion, $(1 - p)$, of faults from which the K active module system cannot automatically recover.

   vi.   The repair rate of a failed module is constant.

   vii.   There are a certain proportion p of faults from which the K active module system can automatically recover.

   viii.   Numerals in boxes of Figure 6.5 denote the system's states.

The following symbols were used to develop equations for model II:

j is the jth state of the system: $j = 0$ (all the K modules functioning normally), $j = 1$ (one module failed, $(K - 1)$ working), $j = 2$ (two modules failed, $(K - 2)$ working or system did not recover from a single fault).

K is the total number of modules in the system.

$P_j(t)$ is the probability that the system is in state j at time t for $j = 0, 1, 2$.

λ is the constant failure rate of a module.

μ is the constant repair rate of a failed module.

p is the proportion of faults from which the K good module system can automatically recover.

$(1 - p)$ is the proportion of faults from which the K good module system cannot automatically recover.

The following system of differential equations is associated with Figure 6.5:

$$\frac{dP_0(t)}{dt} + K\lambda\, P_0(t) = \mu \cdot P_1(t) \tag{6.47}$$

$$\frac{dP_1(t)}{dt} + (\mu + (K - 1)\lambda)P_1(t) = K\lambda p P_0(t) \tag{6.48}$$

$$\frac{dP_2(t)}{dt} = (K - 1)\lambda \cdot P_1(t) + K\lambda(1 - p) \cdot P_0(t) \tag{6.49}$$

At time $t = 0$, $P_0(0) = 1$ and $P_1(0) = P_2(0) = 0$.

    With the aid of Laplace transforms, Eqs. (6.47) through (6.49) can be solved to obtain expressions for state probabilities $P_0(t)$, $P_1(t)$, and $P_2(t)$. By differentiating $P_2(t)$ with respect to time t, we get

$$\frac{dP_2(t)}{dt} = f_{Ks}(t) \tag{6.50}$$

Where

$f_{Ks}(t)$ is the failure density function of the K module system.

The mean time to failure $MTTF_{Ks}$ of the K module system [12] is given by

$$MTTF_{Ks} = \int_0^\infty t \cdot f_{Ks}(t) \cdot dt$$

$$= \mu \left[1 + \frac{(1 - p)\theta}{(K - 1)} \right]^{-1} \cdot D^{-1}$$

(6.51)

Where

$$D \equiv K(K - 1)\lambda^2$$ (6.52)

$$\theta \equiv \frac{\mu}{\lambda}$$ (6.53)

6.5   RELIABILITY EVALUATION OF A COMPUTER SYSTEM

This section presents a reliability model of a total computer system [14]. The assumed block diagram of the entire computer system is shown in Figure 6.6. In this figure the computer system is composed of two subsystems A and B in series. Detailed assumed block diagrams of both these subsystems are shown in Figures 6.7 and 6.8, respectively.

In this model it is assumed that the computer system is composed of the following items:

  i.   one memory unit
  ii. one cardreader
  iii. one central processing unit

Figure 6.6   Subsystems of a Computer System (Detailed block diagrams of subsystems A and B are presented in Figures 6.7 and 6.8)

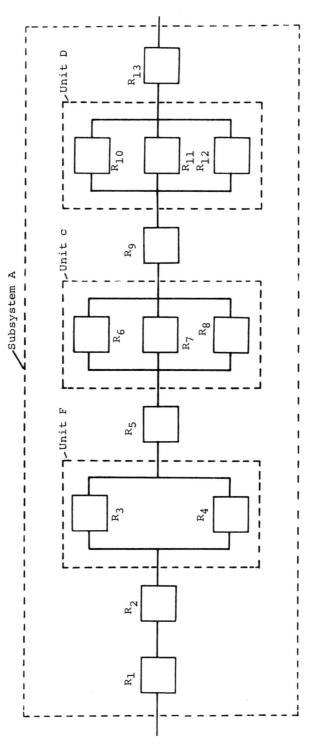

Figure 6.7 Block Diagram Representing Elements of Subsystem *A* of the Computer System

    iv.   two lineprinters in parallel
     v.   two channels in parallel
    vi.   one disk control unit
   vii.   two terminal control units (I and II)
  viii.   one communication controller
    ix.   three disks (at least two must work for successful operation)
     x.   one magnetic tape control unit
    xi.   two teletypes in parallel
   xii.   four terminals (at least two must work for successful operation)
  xiii.   three tapes (at least two must work for successful operation)
  xiv.   one slow speed input/output device controller.

In developing a reliability expression for the computer system, the following assumptions were made:

     i.   Elements of the computer fail independent.
    ii.   In Figure 6.7, at least two disks must work normally for the success of unit C. All three disks are identical.
   iii.   In Figure 6.7, at least two tapes must work normally for the success of unit D. All three tapes are identical.
   iv.   In Figure 6.8, at least two terminals must work normally for the success of unit D. All four terminals are identical.
    v.   In Figure 6.7, the two elements (channels) of unit F are identical.
   vi.   In Figure 6.8, the two elements (lineprinters) of unit G are identical.
   vii.   In Figure 6.8, the two elements (teletypes) of unit H are identical.

The reliability of the entire computer system is given by

$$R_{cs} = R_A \cdot R_B \qquad (6.54)$$

Where

R_A is the reliability of computer subsystem A shown in Figure 6.7.
R_B is the reliability of computer subsystem B shown in Figure 6.8.

The reliability of the computer subsystem A shown in Figure 6.7 is given by

$$R_A = R_1 \cdot R_2 \cdot [1 - (1 - R_{ch})^2] \cdot R_5 \cdot [3 R_d^2 - 2R_d^3] \cdot R_9 \cdot [3R_t^2 - 2R_t^3] \cdot R_{13} \qquad (6.55)$$

$$R_{ch} = R_3 = R_4 \qquad (6.56)$$

$$R_d = R_6 = R_7 = R_8 \qquad (6.57)$$

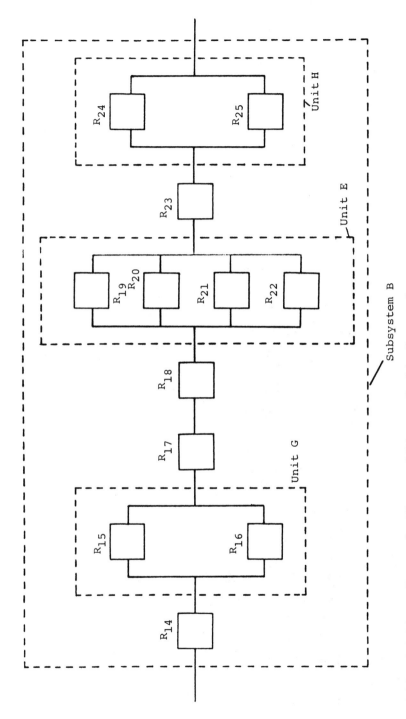

Figure 6.8 Block Diagram Representing Elements of Subsystem *B* of the Computer System

$$R_t = R_{10} = R_{11} = R_{12} \tag{6.58}$$

Where

R_1 is the reliability of the central processing unit (CPU).
R_2 is the reliability of the memory unit.
R_{ch} is the reliability of a channel.
R_5 is the reliability of the disk control unit.
R_d is the reliability of a disk.
R_9 is the reliability of the magnetic tape control unit.
R_t is the reliability of a tape.
R_{13} is the reliability of the slow speed input/output device controller.

Similarly, the reliability of the computer subsystem B shown in Figure 6.8 is given by

$$R_B = R_{14} \cdot [1 - (1 - (1 - R_{lp})^2]$$

$$\cdot R_{17} \cdot R_{18} [3R_{tm}^4 - 8R_{tm}^3 + 6R_{tm}^2] \cdot R_{23} \cdot [1 - (1 - R_{tt})^2] \tag{6.59}$$

$$R_{lp} = R_{15} = R_{16} \tag{6.60}$$

$$R_{tm} = R_{19} = R_{20} = R_{21} = R_{22} \tag{6.61}$$

$$R_{tt} = R_{24} = R_{25} \tag{6.62}$$

Where

R_{14} is the reliability of the cardreader.
R_{lp} is the reliability of a lineprinter.
R_{17} is the reliability of the communication controller.
R_{18} is the reliability of the terminal control unit for four terminals.
R_{tm} is the reliability of a terminal.
R_{23} is the reliability of the terminal control unit for two teletypes.
R_{tt} is the reliability of a teletype.

If the failure times of elements shown in Figures 6.7 and 6.8 are exponentially distributed, then the time t-dependent reliability of the computer system is given by

$$R_{cs}(t) = R_A(t) \cdot R_B(t) \tag{6.63}$$

Where

$$R_A(t) = R_1(t) \cdot R_2(t)[1 - (1 - R_{ch}(t))^2] \cdot R_5(t) \cdot [3\{R_d(t)\}^2$$
$$- 2\{R_d(t)\}^3] \cdot R_9(t)[3\{R_t(t)\}^2 - 2\{R_t(t)\}^3] \cdot R_{13}(t) \qquad (6.64)$$

$$R_B(t) = R_{14}(t)[1 - (1 - R_{lp}(t))^2] \cdot R_{17}(t) \cdot R_{18}(t)[3\{R_{tm}(t)\}^4$$
$$- 8\{R_{tm}(t)\}^3 + 6\{R_{tm}(t)\}^2] \cdot R_{23}(t) \cdot [1 - (1 - R_{tt}(t))^2] \qquad (6.65)$$

$$R_1(t) = e^{-\lambda_1 t} \qquad (6.66)$$

$$R_2(t) = e^{-\lambda_2 t} \qquad (6.67)$$

$$R_{ch}(t) = e^{-\lambda_{ch} \cdot t} \qquad (6.68)$$

$$R_5(t) = e^{-\lambda_5 t} \qquad (6.69)$$

$$R_d(t) = e^{-\lambda_d t} \qquad (6.70)$$

$$R_9(t) = e^{-\lambda_9 t} \qquad (6.71)$$

$$R_t(t) = e^{-\lambda_t t} \qquad (6.72)$$

$$R_{13}(t) = e^{-\lambda_{13} t} \qquad (6.73)$$

$$R_{14}(t) = e^{-\lambda_{14} t} \qquad (6.74)$$

$$R_{lp}(t) = e^{-\lambda_{lp} t} \qquad (6.75)$$

$$R_{17}(t) = e^{-\lambda_{17} t} \qquad (6.76)$$

$$R_{18}(t) = e^{-\lambda_{18} t} \qquad (6.77)$$

$$R_{tm}(t) = e^{-\lambda_{tm} t} \qquad (6.78)$$

$$R_{23}(t) = e^{-\lambda_{23} t} \qquad (6.79)$$

$$R_{tt}(t) = e^{-\lambda_{tt} t} \qquad (6.80)$$

Where

λ_1 is the constant failure rate of the central processing unit (CPU).
λ_2 is the constant failure rate of the memory unit.
λ_{ch} is the constant failure rate of a channel.
λ_5 is the constant failure rate of the disk control unit.
λ_d is the constant failure rate of a disk.

λ_9 is the constant failure rate of the magnetic tape control unit.

λ_t is the constant failure rate of a tape.

λ_{13} is the constant failure rate of the slow speed input/output device controller.

λ_{14} is the constant failure rate of the cardreader.

λ_{lp} is the constant failure rate of a lineprinter.

λ_{17} is the constant failure rate of the communication controller.

λ_{18} is the constant failure rate of the terminal control unit for four terminals.

λ_{tm} is the constant failure rate of a terminal.

λ_{23} is the constant failure rate of the terminal control unit for two teletypes.

λ_{tt} is the constant failure rate of a teletype.

The mean time to failure of the computer system can be obtained by integrating Eq. (6.63) over the interval $[0, \infty]$.

6.6 SUMMARY

This chapter presented several aspects of reliability analysis associated with computer systems. Six different types of redundancy schemes for use in computer systems were discussed. These schemes are as follows:

  i. hybrid redundancy
 ii. checker-redundant scheme
iii. triple-modular redundancy (TMR)
 iv. N-modular redundancy (NMR)
  v. cascading of triple-modular redundancy units
 vi. cascading of triple-modular redundancy units plus triplicated voters.

Reliability expressions for all these schemes were presented. For three of the above schemes, equations to determine mean time to failure were presented. A mathematical model to evaluate reliability of a multi-miniprocessor computer was discussed, and the reliability expressions for it was given.

Two Markov models (I and II) representing repairable systems composed of identical redundant modules were presented. In both models, it was assumed that there are a certain amount of single faults from which a system with redundant modules cannot recover automatically. Model I is concerned with two identical modules, whereas model II deals with K identical modules.

Finally, a mathematical model to evaluate the reliability of an entire specific computer system was presented and the reliability equation of the system was developed.

6.7 EXERCISES

1. Discuss in detail the following three terms:
   i.   Triple-modular redundancy
   ii. N-modular redundancy
   iii. Hybrid redundancy.
2. Obtain an expression for mean time to failure with the aid of Eq. (6.17) for $M = 3$.
3. What are the advantages and disadvantages of the hybrid redundancy scheme?
4. Make comparisons of the triple modular redundancy scheme with the hybrid redundancy approach. Which one is better?
5. With the aid of differential Eqs. (6.40) through (6.42), develop an expression for system reliability. Make use of the resulting reliability equation to prove that a system's mean time to failure is given by

$$MTTF_s = \frac{1 + \beta(5 - 3p)}{2\lambda\beta\{1 + \beta^{-1}(1 - p)\}} \qquad (6.81)$$

Where

$$\beta = \lambda/\mu$$

(Symbols λ, μ, and p are associated with Eqs. (6.40) through (6.42) and are defined in the chapter.)

6. In Figure 6.5, a transition diagram for a specific system is shown. With the aid of this diagram, develop an expression for probability that the system is in state 1 [i.e. one module failed, $(K - 1)$ working].

6.8 REFERENCES

1. A. Costes, C. Landrault, and J.C. Laprie, "Reliability and Availability Models for Maintained Systems Featuring Hardware Failures and Design Faults", IEEE Transactions on Computers, Vol. 27, June 1978, pp. 548–560.

2. S. Osaki and T. Nishio, *Reliability Evaluation of Some Fault-Tolerant Computer Architectures*, Springer-Verlag, Berlin, 1980.

3. C.V. Ramamoorthy and Y.W. Han, "Reliability Analysis of Systems with Concurrent Error Detection", IEEE Transactions on Computers, Vol. 24, September 1975, pp. 868–878.

4. A.D. Ingle and D.P. Siewiorek, "A Reliability Model for Various Switch Designs in Hybrid Redundancy", IEEE Transactions on Computers, Vol. 25, Feb. 1976, pp. 115–133.

5. A.D. Ingle and D.P. Siewiorek, "Reliability Modeling of Multiprocessor Structures", Proceedings of the IEEE Computer Society International Conference (COMPCON), San Francisco, Feb. 24–26, 1976, pp. 24–29.

6. I. Koren and S.Y.H. Su, "Reliability Analysis of N-Modular Redundancy Systems with Intermittent and Permanent Faults", IEEE Transactions on Computers, Vol. 28, 1979, pp. 514–520.

7. D.P. Siewiorek and R.S. Swarz, *The Theory and Practice of Reliable System Design*, Digital Press, Bedford, Massachusetts 01730, USA, 1982.

8. J. Von Neumann, "Probabilistic Logics and the Synthesis of Reliable Organisms from Unreliable Components", in *Automata Studies* (Annals of Mathematical Studies), C.E. Shannon and J. McCarthy, Editors, Princeton University Press, Princeton, NJ, 1956, pp. 43–98.

9. J. Goldberg, K.N. Levitt, and R.A. Short, "Techniques for the Realization of Ultrareliable Spaceborne Computers, Final Report–Phase I", Project 5580, Stanford Research Institute, Menlo Park, California, September 1966.

10. F.P. Mathur and A. Avizienis, "Reliability Analysis and Architecture of a Hybrid Redundant Digital System: Generalized Triple Modular Redundancy with Self-Repair", in 1970 Spring Joint Computer Conference, AFIPS Conf. Proceedings, Vol. 36, 1970, pp. 375–383.

11. W.A. Wulf and C.G. Bell, "C.mmp: A Multi-Mini-Processor", Proceedings of the Fall Joint Computer Conference, 1972, pp. 765–777. Published by American Federation of Information Processing Societies (AFIPS).

12. T.F. Arnold, "The Concept of Coverage and Its Effect on the Reliability Model of a Repairable System", IEEE Transactions on Computers, Vol. 22, 1973, pp. 251–254.

13. B.S. Dhillon, *Reliability Engineering In System Design and Operation*, Van Nostrand Reinhold Company, New York, 1983.

14. V.B. Patki and B.N. Chatterji, "Reliability Modeling of Computer Systems", Journal of Electronics Engineering (India), Vol. XXIV, 1983, pp. 683–694.

7

MICROCOMPUTER SYSTEM RELIABILITY ANALYSIS AND QUEUEING THEORY

7.1 INTRODUCTION

In our modern society, dependence on microcomputer systems has increased considerably. These systems are being used in various areas. The word "microcomputer" may have different meanings to different people [1]. Its usage depends upon one's personal point of view. For example, to some it may mean a few-chip computer, a single-chip processor, an 8-bit processor, or an MOS (Metal-Oxide Semiconductor) LSI (Large-Scale Integration) processor. Similarly, to others, it may mean an inexpensive computer, a small computer, a personal computer, or a dedicated computer. However, a microcomputer may be best understood by describing it basically as just an inexpensive computer [1], because the need for economy is the instrumental force behind the rapid growth in microcomputer technology. The reliability of a microcomputer system is in no way less important than that of a larger computer; therefore a discussion of this is included in this chapter.

The second part of the chapter is devoted to another important aspect of computer system engineering, i.e. queueing theory. The history of queueing theory goes back to the year 1913, when A.K. Erlang's contribution entitled "Solution of Some Problems in the Theory of Probabilities of Significance in Automatic Telephone Exchanges" was first published [2]. Today, queueing theory has progressed to a considerable level and finds applications in many areas. Computer systems is one of these application areas. In computer systems, queueing theory is quite useful to estimate the value of some computer performance measures. Two examples of such measures are buffer storage requirements at message switching centers, and waiting time to use an on-line terminal [3]. As the topics of microcomputer system reliability and queueing theory are related to computer system reliability, therefore intention of the author was to familiar readers with these two important areas as well. This is the reason why they are grouped together in this chapter.

7.2 MICROCOMPUTERS

7.2.1 Microcomputers and Related Products

In order to make the distinction between microcomputers and related products, this section briefly describes the following items [4]:

  i.   Minicomputers
 ii.   Microprocessors
iii.   Microcomputers
 iv.   Programmable pocket calculators
  v.   Microcomputer systems

Minicomputers appeared on the scene in the early part of the 1960's. In
relation to microcomputers, these computers were about five times as expen-
sive, about three times as fast, and had a typical word size of 16 bits rather
than the 8 bits of the microcomputers. The Digital Equipment Corporation's
PDP-8 and PDP-11 are two prime examples of minicomputers.

A large scale integrated (LSI) digital processing circuit on a single silicon
chip is known as a microprocessor. A microprocessor contains data paths,
registers, and control logic, but does not have memory for storing data or
programs or any access or display methods. (Examples of such methods are
keyboard light-emitting diodes.) The control logic defines the machine
language set. A microprocessor may cost somewhere from $3 to $50. There
are various kinds of products in which microprocessors are used, such as:

  i.   Household appliances
 ii.   Auto ignitions
iii.   Computers
 iv.   Calculators
  v.   Machine tools

A microcomputer is a module which may cost from $100 to $1200. It contains items such as:

  i.   A clock
 ii.   A microprocessor
iii.   Buffers
 iv.   Drivers
  v.   Random access memory (RAM)
 vi.   Input–output interface circuits

Some examples of well-known microcomputers are as follows:

    i.   Heathkit H-11
   ii.   Intel SBC80/10
  iii.   Altair 8800

Every programmable calculator consists of a microprocessor. This is probably why sometimes a calculator is referred to as a microcomputer. For straight-forward numerical calculations, programmable calculators are much simpler to use in comparison to microcomputers. However, on the other hand, micro-computers are more flexible than programmable calculators. A true computer can be loaded with any type of suitable program and data, whereas a calcula-tor is confined to numerical computations using a sealed control program. Two examples of a programmable calculator are Texas Instruments SR-59 and Hewlett-Packard HP-65.

Finally, a microcomputer system is composed of a microcomputer as well as various input–output and auxiliary storage devices attached to it. Two examples are Commodore PET 2001 and Radio Shack TRS-80 home comput-ers.

7.2.2   Reliability Analysis of Microcomputer Systems with Triple-Modular Redundancy

Redundancy can be used to increase reliability of a system. There are vari-ous redundant configurations used for such a purpose, for example, parallel, standby, and triple-modular redundancy. In the past, in computer industry triple-modular redundancy was restricted to critical systems only, due to economic reasons. Nowadays triple-modular redundancy is becoming more feasible for general systems too due to decreasing cost of computer processor and memory hardware.

When applying triple-modular-redundancy to microcomputer systems, one must give full consideration to concerns such as the following [5].

    i.   The reliability of semiconductor memory associated with microproces-sors.
   ii.   The danger in using the same unreliable technology to construct a single-chip microprocessor and the many voter chips needed for use in a system.
  iii.   The need for resynchronization of replicated microprocessors after the occurrence of a transient failure.

Basic Elements of a Typical Microcomputer System. A simple model of a microcomputer system may be described as consisting of a microprocessor and a memory with programs and data. The microprocessor is fed with the memory control outputs. Conversely, the microprocessor data, address and control outputs are fed to the memory. Each peripheral interface is composed of voters. The purpose of these voters is to monitor triplicated processor input/output commands. In the case when triple-modular redundancy is used, a typical microprocessor might have more than 39 lines to be voted upon [5].

Microcomputer System Reliability Analysis. The reliability of m independent and identical voters in series is given by

$$R_{vm} = (R_{sv})^m \tag{7.1}$$

Where

R_{vm} is the reliability of m voters in series arrangement (if there are m module inputs, then for each module m voters may be used).
R_{sv} is the reliability of a single voter.
m is the number of independent voters.

The reliability of the microprocessor/memory module-voter series system is given by

$$R_{mvs} = R_{mm} \cdot R_{vm}$$

$$= R_{mm} \cdot (R_{sv})^m \tag{7.2}$$

Where

R_{mvs} is the microprocessor/memory module-voter reliability.
R_{mm} is the microprocessor/memory module reliability.

Basically, the triple-modular redundancy (TMR) arrangement is same as the 2-out-of-3 unit parallel system configuration. More clearly, in a 2-out-of-3 unit parallel system, at least two units must function successfully for the system's success. With respect to microcomputer systems using triple-modular redundancy, it means there are three triplicated microprocessor/memory module-voter series systems functioning in parallel configuration. At least two of these systems must work normally for the overall system's success. Thus the TMR system reliability is

$$R_{TMR} = R_{mvs}^3 + 3R_{mvs}^2 (1 - R_{mvs}) \tag{7.3}$$

By substituting for R_{mvs} from Eq. (7.2) into Eq. (7.3) we get

$$R_{TMR} = [R_{mm}(R_{sv})^m]^3 + 3[R_{mm}(R_{sv})^m]^2[1 - R_{mm} \cdot (R_{sv})^m] \tag{7.4}$$

For constant failure rates, the reliability expressions for the microprocessor/memory module and the voter, respectively, become

$$R_{mm}(t) = e^{-\lambda_{mm}t} \tag{7.5}$$

and

$$R_{sv}(t) = e^{-\lambda_{sv}t} \tag{7.6}$$

Where

$R_{mm}(t)$ is the microprocessor/memory module reliability at time t.
$R_{sv}(t)$ is the single voter reliability at time t.
λ_{mm} is the constant failure rate of the microprocessor/memory module.
λ_{sv} is the constant failure rate of the single voter.

With the aid of Eqs. (7.4), (7.5) and (7.6), the time-dependent TMR system reliability, $R_{TMR}(t)$, is given by

$$R_{TMR}(t) = [e^{-(\lambda_{mm}+m\lambda_{sv})t}]^3 + 3[e^{-(\lambda_{mm}+m\lambda_{sv})t}]^2$$

$$[1 - e^{-(\lambda_{mm}+m\lambda_{sv})t}]$$

$$= 3[e^{-(\lambda_{mm}+m\lambda_{sv})t}]^2 - 2[e^{-(\lambda_{mm}+m\lambda_{sv})t}]^3 \tag{7.7}$$

In order to obtain TMR system mean time to failure $MTTF_{TMR}$ we integrate Eq. (7.7) as follows:

$$MTTF_{TMR} = \int_0^\infty R_{TMR}(t) \cdot dt$$

$$= \frac{3}{2(\lambda_{mm} + m\lambda_{sv})} - \frac{2}{3(\lambda_{mm} + m\lambda_{sv})} \tag{7.8}$$

Reliability Modeling of a Microcomputer Semiconductor Memory System. Microcomputer memory chip system reliability is expressed as follows:

$$R_{smc} = (R_{mc})^{pq} \tag{7.9}$$

Where

R_{smc} is the microcomputer memory chip system reliability.
R_{mc} is the memory chip reliability.
pq is the 1-bit by w-word memory chip (these chips are arranged in $p \times q$ matrix to form the p-bit by wq-word array).

The overall reliability of the microcomputer memory chip–common circuitry module is given by

$$R_{mcc} = R_{cc} \cdot R_{smc}$$

$$= R_{cc} \cdot (R_{mc})^{pq} \qquad (7.10)$$

Where

R_{mcc} is the microcomputer memory chip–common circuitry module reliability.

R_{cc} is the common circuitry reliability.

Thus the microcomputer triple-modular redundancy memory system reliability is given by

$$R_{ms} = 3R_{mcc}^2 - 2R_{mcc}^3$$

$$= 3[R_{cc}(R_{mc})^{pq}]^2 - 2[R_{cc}(R_{mc})^{pq}]^3 \qquad (7.11)$$

For constant failure rates of the memory chip and the common circuitry, respectively, the time t-dependent reliability may be expressed as follows:

$$R_{mc}(t) = e^{-\lambda_{mc}t} \qquad (7.12)$$

and

$$R_{cc}(t) = e^{-\lambda_{cc}t} \qquad (7.13)$$

Where

λ_{mc} is the constant failure rate of the memory chip.

λ_{cc} is the constant failure rate of the common circuitry.

$R_{mc}(t)$ is the reliability of the memory chip at time t.

$R_{cc}(t)$ is the reliability of the common circuitry at time t.

Substituting Eqs. (7.12) and (7.13) into Eq. (7.11) yields

$$R_{ms}(t) = 3[R_{cc}(t)(R_{mc}(t))^{pq}]^2 - 2[R_{cc}(t)(R_{mc}(t))^{pq}]^3$$

$$= 3[e^{-(\lambda_{cc} + pq\lambda_{mc})t}]^2 - 2[e^{-(\lambda_{cc} + pq\lambda_{mc})t}]^3 \qquad (7.14)$$

The microcomputer TMR memory system mean time to failure $MTTF_{ms}$ is given by

$$MTTF = \int_0^\infty R_{ms}(t)dt$$

$$= \int_0^\infty [3e^{-2(\lambda_{cc} + pq\lambda_{mc})t} - 2e^{-3(\lambda_{cc} + pq\lambda_{mc})t}] \cdot dt$$

$$= \frac{3}{2(\lambda_{cc} + pq\lambda_{mc})} - \frac{2}{3(\lambda_{cc} + pq\lambda_{mc})} \tag{7.15}$$

7.3 QUEUEING THEORY

Queues are also referred to as waiting lines where everyone may have experienced frustration of waiting to get served. In 1905, A.K. Erlang, a Danish telephone engineer was the first person to study queues. He developed telephone-traffic theory. In computers queueing theory has many applications and is somewhat related to reliability theory. That is why it is presented here.

7.3.1 Important Laws and Formulas

This section presents selective laws and formulas [6]. These laws and formulas become quite useful in computer system performance analysis.

Arrival Rate Formula. The arrival rate λ is defined by

$$\lambda = \frac{n_r}{t_0} \tag{7.16}$$

Where

n_r is the number of arrivals of requests.
t_0 is the observation time.

Example 7.1

During an observation period of 10 minutes, 30 random messages arrived at a switching center for a communication line. Calculate the value of the arrival rate.

With the aid of the above data and Eq. (7.16), we get

$$\lambda = \frac{30}{10} = 3 \text{ messages/minute}$$

Thus the value of the arrival rate $\lambda = 3$ messages/minute.

Utilization Formula. The utilization of the resource is expressed as follows:

$$z = \frac{T_b}{t_0} \tag{7.17}$$

Where

z is the utilization of the resource.
T_b is the busy time of the resource during the observation period.

Example 7.2

During the observation time of 20 minutes, it was observed that the resource was busy for 15 minutes. Compute the value of z, the utilization of the resource.

Substituting the given data into Eq. (7.17) yields:

$$z = \frac{15}{20} = 0.75 \text{ or } 75\%.$$

Thus, the utilization of the resource is 75%.

Throughput Formula. The throughput is defined as

$$TH_p = \frac{R_c}{t_0} \tag{7.18}$$

Where

TH_p is the throughput.
R_c is the number of requests completed during the observation interval.

Example 7.3

Assume that during the observation period of 30 minutes, 90 requests were completed. Calculate the value of the throughput.

By substituting the above data into Eq. (7.18), we get

$$TH_p = \frac{90}{30} = 3 \text{ requests/minute}$$

Thus the value of the throughput is 3 requests/minute.

Service Requirement Formula. The mean service requirement per request is expressed as follows:

$$\alpha_{ms} = \frac{T_b}{R_c} \tag{7.19}$$

The symbols T_b and R_c are already defined.

Example 7.4

In an interval of time it was observed that 16 requests were completed. During the observation interval the resource was busy for 4 minutes. Calculate the mean service requirement time to handle one request.

With the aid of the above data and Eq. (7.19), we get

$$\alpha_{ms} = \frac{4}{16} = 0.25 \text{ minutes}$$

Thus the value of the mean service requirement time per request is 0.25 minutes.

The Utilization Law. Algebraically, it is expressed as

$$\frac{T_b}{T_0} = \frac{R_c}{t_0} \cdot \frac{T_b}{R_c} \tag{7.20}$$

With the aid of Eqs. (7.17), (7.18), and (7.19) we may express the utilization law as follows:

$$z = TH_p \cdot \alpha_{ms}$$

$$= (\text{throughput}) \cdot (\text{mean service requirement time per request}) \tag{7.21}$$

Residence Time Formula. The residence time is the mean system residence time per request. Algebraically

$$T_r = \frac{T_a}{R_c} \tag{7.22}$$

Where

T_r is the mean system residence time per request.
T_a is the accumulated time in system.

Example 7.5

During an observation period 10 requests were completed and 5 request-minutes of residence time were accumulated. Compute the value of the mean system residence time per request.

Substituting the above data into Eq. (7.22) results in

$$T_r = \frac{5}{10} = 0.5 \text{ minutes}$$

Mean Number of Requests Formula. The mean number of requests in the system can be expressed as follows:

$$r_m = \frac{T_a}{t_0} \tag{7.23}$$

Where

r_m is the mean number of requests in the system.

Example 7.6

During a 10 minute observation period, 4 request-minutes of residence time were accumulated. Determine the value of the mean number of requests in the system. With the aid of the given data and Eq. (7.23) we get

$$r_m = \frac{4}{10} = 0.4$$

Thus the value of the mean number of requests in the system is 0.4.

Little's Law. This is expressed as follows:

$$\frac{T_a}{t_0} = \frac{R_c}{t_0} \cdot \frac{T_a}{R_c}$$

With the aid of Eqs. (7.18), (7.22) and (7.23), Little's law may be expressed as follows:

$$r_m = TH_p \cdot T_r$$

$$= \text{(the throughput)} \cdot \text{(mean system residence time per request)} \tag{7.24}$$

The Response Time Law. This is defined as follows:

$$T_r = \frac{(\text{mean number of requests in the system})}{(\text{the throughput})} - (\text{mean think time})$$

$$= \frac{r_m}{TH_p} - T_{th} \tag{7.25}$$

Where

T_{th} is the mean think time.

Example 7.7

A system is used by 140 interactive users. The value of the system throughput is 4 interactions/second. If the mean think time is 32 seconds, compute the response time.

Utilizing the above data in Eq. (7.25) yields

$$T_r = \frac{140}{4} - 32$$

$$= 3 \text{ seconds}$$

Thus the value of the response time is 3 seconds.

7.3.2   Selective Queueing Theory Models

This section presents some of the well-known queueing theory models. One should note here that the derivation of equations associated with each of these models is omitted and can be found in standard queueing theory texts; references [2,3,7,8] provide useful background to readers.

Model I. This model is known as the single-channel, single-phase structure. An example of such a model is a single-facility computer equipment unit repair shop. The model is subject to the following assumptions:

i.   Poisson arrivals (failed computer equipment units) and exponential service (repair) times.
ii. Unlimited source of arrivals.
iii. Infinite queue.
iv. The waiting line (queue) discipline is first come, first served.
v.   The failed computer equipment unit arrival rate is less than its repair or service rate.

Thus, the probability of having k units of failed computer equipment (i.e. waiting units plus those in service) in the system is given by:

$$P_k = \left[1 - \frac{\alpha}{\theta} \right] (\alpha/\theta)^k = (1 - \mu)(\mu)^k \qquad (7.26)$$

Where

$\mu \equiv (\alpha/\theta)$ is the repair (service) facility utilization factor.
P_k is the probability of having k units of failed computer equipment in the system.
k is the number of units of failed computer equipment in the system. This includes waiting units plus inservice units.
α is the average arrival rate of failed computer equipment units.
θ is the average service (repair) rate of failed computer equipment units.

From Eq. (7.26) the probability of having no failed computer equipment (i.e. $k = 0$) units in the system is

$$P_0 = \left[1 - \frac{\alpha}{\theta} \right]$$

$$= (1 - \mu) \qquad (7.27)$$

Similarly, the probability of having m or more failed computer equipment units in the system is

$$P_{k \geqslant m} = \left[\frac{\alpha}{\theta} \right]^m$$

$$= \mu^m \qquad (7.28)$$

The mean time T_m in the system and the average waiting time, T_{mw}, respectively, are given by

$$T_m = (\theta - \alpha)^{-1} \qquad (7.29)$$

and

$$T_{mw} = \alpha/\theta(\theta - \alpha) \qquad (7.30)$$

The average number of failed computer equipment units in the waiting line is given by

$$U_{ac} = \frac{\mu^2}{1 - \mu} \tag{7.31}$$

Where

$\mu \equiv \alpha/\theta$

U_{ac} is the average number of failed computer equipment units in the waiting line.

The average number of failed computer equipment units in the system is

$$U_{as} = \frac{\mu}{1 - \mu} \tag{7.32}$$

Example 7.8

A single-channel, single-phase computer equipment repair facility has Poisson arrivals and exponential service (repair) times. The mean arrival rate and the mean service (repair) rate are $\alpha = 4$/day and $\theta = 10$/day, respectively. Calculate the probability of having no failed computer equipment unit in the system and the average number of failed computer equipment units in the queue, if

   i. the waiting line is unlimited.
  ii. the arrival source population is unlimited.
 iii. the queue discipline is first come, first served.

By substituting the above data into Eq. (7.27) we get

$$P_0 = \left[1 - \frac{4}{10} \right] = 0.6$$

Thus the probability of having no failed computer equipment unit in the system is 0.6 or 60%.

Again, substituting the given data into Eq. (7.31) yields

$$U_{ac} = \frac{0.4}{1 - 0.4}$$

$$= 0.67$$

It means that there will be an average of 0.67 failed computer equipment units waiting in the queue.

Model II. This model is basically same as model I but with one exception, i.e. the presence of finite or truncated queue. More clearly, in this case, the queue cannot have an unlimited length. One practical example of a limited queue is the length of the driveway preceding a drive-in bank teller window. Such a driveway can only practically accommodate a handful of vehicles. Similar limitations can be found in computer systems. In model II, the assumption of arrival rate being less than the service (repair) rate is no longer required.

Thus the probability of having k units in the system [2]] is given by

$$P_k = \mu^k \cdot \frac{(1 - \mu)}{1 - \mu^{z+1}} \qquad \text{for } k \leqslant z \tag{7.33}$$

Where

$\mu \equiv \alpha/\theta$

z \qquad is the maximum number of units in the system.

The probability of having zero units in the system is

$$P_0 = \frac{1 - \mu}{1 - \mu^{z+1}} \tag{7.34}$$

The average number of units in the system is expressed as follows:

$$U_{as} = \frac{\mu}{1 - \mu} - \frac{y\mu^y}{(1 - \mu^y)} \tag{7.35}$$

Where

$y \equiv z + 1$

Similarly, the average number of units in the waiting line is

$$U_{ac} = U_{as} - \mu(1 - P_z) \tag{7.36}$$

Finally, the average time in the system and the mean waiting time, respectively, are expressed as follows:

$$T_m = U_{as}/(\alpha - \alpha P_z) \tag{7.37}$$

and

$$T_{mw} = \frac{U_{as}}{(\alpha - \alpha P_z)} - \frac{1}{\theta} \tag{7.38}$$

Model III. Again, this model is basically same as model I but with one exception, i.e. the presence of undefined service times. In this model it is assumed that the service (repair) times are described by a probability distribution with a known mean value $1/\theta$ and a standard deviation s. In addition, it is assumed that service or repair times are independent. The following equations are associated with this model [2]:

$$U_{ac} = (\alpha^2 s^2 + \mu^2)/2(1 - \mu) \qquad (7.39)$$

Where

$$\mu \equiv \alpha/\theta$$

$$U_{as} = \mu + \frac{(\alpha^2 s^2 + \mu^2)}{2(1 - \mu)} \qquad (7.40)$$

$$P_0 = 1 - \mu \qquad (7.41)$$

$$T_{mw} = \frac{(\alpha^2 s^2 + \mu^2)}{2\alpha(1 - \mu)} \qquad (7.42)$$

$$T_m = \frac{U_{ac}}{\alpha} + \theta^{-1} \qquad (7.43)$$

Model IV. This model is known as the multiple-channel, single-phase structure. More clearly, instead of having only a single-channel service or repair as in the case of Models I through III, this model has n number of such repair or service channels. The following assumptions are associated with this model:

i.   The repair or service channels are identical.
ii. The arrival source population and the queue are infinite.
iii. Poisson arrivals (failed computer equipment units) and exponential service or repair times.
iv. The failed computer equipment units' arrival rate is less than the mean repair (service) rate for the overall system (the overall system service rate is given by $n \cdot \theta$).
v.   The queue discipline is first come, first served.

The probability of having k units of failed computer equipment (i.e. waiting units plus inservice units) in the system is given by

$$P_k = \frac{\mu^k}{k!} \left[\sum_{k=0}^{n-1} \frac{\mu^k}{k!} + \frac{\mu^n}{n! \left[1 - \frac{\mu}{n} \right]} \right]^{-1} , \text{ for } k \leqslant n \qquad (7.44)$$

and

$$P_k = \left\{ \frac{\mu^k}{n!\, n^{k-n}} \right\} \cdot \left[\sum_{k=0}^{n-1} \frac{\mu^k}{k!} + \frac{\mu^n}{n! \left[1 - \frac{\mu}{n} \right]} \right]^{-1} , \text{ for } k > n \qquad (7.45)$$

The probability of having zero units of failed computer equipment in the system is

$$P_0 = \left[\sum_{k=0}^{n-1} \frac{\mu^k}{k!} + \frac{\mu^n}{n! \left[1 - \frac{\mu}{n} \right]} \right]^{-1} \qquad (7.46)$$

The average number of failed computer equipment units in the waiting line is

$$U_{ac} = \frac{\mu^{n+1} \cdot P_0}{n!n \left[1 - \frac{\mu}{n} \right]^2} \qquad (7.47)$$

Similarly, the average number of failed computer equipment units in the system is given by

$$U_{as} = \mu + \frac{\mu^{n+1} \cdot P_0}{n!n \left[1 - \frac{\mu}{n} \right]^2} \qquad (7.48)$$

Finally, the mean time in the system and the average waiting time, respectively, are given by

$$T_m = \frac{1}{\theta} + \frac{1}{\alpha} \cdot \frac{\mu^{n+1} \cdot P_0}{n!n\left(1 - \frac{\mu}{n}\right)^2} \qquad (7.49)$$

and

$$T_{mw} = U_{ac}/\alpha \qquad (7.50)$$

7.4 SUMMARY

This chapter presented both microcomputer system reliability analysis and queueing theory.

To make the distinction between microcomputers and related products, items such as minicomputers, microprocessors, microcomputers, programmable pocket calculators, and microcomputer systems were briefly described. The reliability analysis of a microcomputer system with triple-modular redundancy was presented. This analysis included development of equations for microcomputer system reliability and mean time to failure. In addition, equations were developed for microcomputer semiconductor memory system reliability and mean time to failure.

Important laws and formulas related to queueing theory were presented. The three laws described were the utilization law, Little's law, and the response time law. The formulas were concerned with the following items:

   i.   arrival rate
   ii. utilization
  iii. throughput
  vi. service requirement
   v. residence time
  vi. mean number of requests

Four selective queueing theory models were presented. Three of these belong to the family of single-channel, single-phase models.

The structure of the fourth model is known as multiple-channel, single-phase. For all four models, equations to calculate the value of measures such as the probability of having no failed units in the system, the mean number of failed units in the queue, the average number of units in the system, the mean time in the system, and the average waiting time were presented.

7.5 EXERCISES

1. Describe the difference between a microprocessor and a microcomputer.
2. Write an essay on the applications of microcomputers.
3. Discuss the history of queueing theory.
4. Discuss the applications of queueing theory in computer systems.
5. Prove that the reliability of a voter (or a single unit) is given by

$$R(t) \; = \; e^{-\lambda_{sv}t} \qquad\qquad (7.51)$$

Where

    t is time.
    λ_{sv} is the single voter (or a single unit) constant failure rate.

6. Prove the following reliability expression [labeled as Eq. (7.3)]:

$$R_{TMR} \; = \; R_{mvs}^3 \; + \; 3R_{mvs}^2(1 \; - \; R_{mvs}) \qquad\qquad (7.52)$$

7. Prove the following formula:

$$MTTF \; = \; \int_0^\infty R(t)\, dt \qquad\qquad (7.53)$$

Where

    $MTTF$ is the microcomputer system mean time to failure.
    t is time.
    $R(t)$ is the microcomputer system reliability at time t.

8. A single-channel, single-phase computer equipment repair facility has Poisson arrivals and exponential service (repair) times. The mean arrival rate and the mean service (repair) rate are $\alpha = 3$/day and $\theta = 16$/day, respectively. Compute the average number of failed computer equipment units in the system and the probability of having 2 or more failed computer equipment units in the system, if

    i.   the queue discipline is first come, first served.
   ii.   the waiting line is unlimited.
  iii.   the arrival source population is unlimited.

7.6 REFERENCES

1. J.F. Wakerly and E.J. McCluskey, "Microcomputers in the Computer Engineering Curriculum", Computer, Vol. 10, 1977, pp. 32–38.

2. S.M. Lee, L.J. Moore, and B.W. Taylor, *Management Science,* Wm.C. Brown Company, Dubuque, Iowa, 1981.

3. A.O. Allen, "Elements of Queueing Theory for System Design", IBM Systems Journal, Vol. 14, 1975, pp. 161–187.

4. R.W. Berger, "Microcomputers and Software Quality Control", Proceedings of the Annual American Society for Quality Control Conference, Chicago, 1978, pp. 328–332.

5. J.F. Wakerly, "Microcomputer Reliability Improvement Using Triple-Modular Redundancy", Proceedings of the IEEE, Vol. 64, 1976, pp. 889–895.

6. E.D. Lazowska, J. Zahorjan, G. Scott-Graham, and K.C. Sevcik, *Quantitative System Performance*, Prentice-Hall, Inc., Englewood Cliffs, New Jersey, 1984.

7. K.S. Trivedi, *Probability and Statistics with Reliability, Queueing and Computer Science Applications*, Prentice-Hall, Inc., Englewood Cliffs, New Jersey, 1982.

8. T.L. Saaty, *Elements of Queueing Theory*, McGraw-Hill Book Company, New York, 1961.

8
ADDITIONAL TOPICS IN COMPUTER HARDWARE RELIABILITY

8.1 INTRODUCTION

Over the past number of years, research work in computer hardware reliability has been progressing in many directions. As a result of this ongoing effort, many publications have appeared. The objective of this chapter is to cover only those topics which generally have not been discussed in previous chapters, such as the following:

    i.   Reliability analysis of computer systems with common-cause failures.
   ii.   Life cycle costing.
  iii.   Integrated circuit defects.
   iv.   Reliability analysis of space computers.
    v.   Computer memory reliability modeling.

The above topics were selected from the published literature because of their special usefulness to computer system reliability engineers. A *common-cause failure* is defined as any instance where multiple units or components fail due to a single cause [1]. A redundant computer system may fail due to the occurrence of a common-cause failure. Reasons for the occurrence of common-cause failures may be operations and maintenance errors, vibrations, temperature, dust, humidity, fire, design deficiencies, and so on. The *life cycle cost* is the total cost of a system from its birth to death. Just as in any other engineering system, the concept of life cycle costing is applicable to computer systems. Integrated circuits are widely used in computer systems. Since the study of their defects is important to the overall reliability of computer systems, this topic is explored briefly. In spacecrafts, computers perform various functions. Their reliability is of utmost importance because of mission criticality, high investment, and so on.

Finally, memory reliability is as important as the reliability of any other critical computer part. The single-bit error correction scheme can be used to improve memory reliability and is explored briefly.

8.2 RELIABILITY ANALYSIS OF COMPUTER SYSTEMS WITH COMMON-CAUSE FAILURES

The subject of common-cause failures has been receiving increasing attention for the past few years. In the general reliability analysis of redundant computers or other engineering systems, the occurrence of common-cause failures is not considered because of the assumption of independent failures. However, in practice this assumption is easily violated [2]. Common-cause failures in redundant systems may occur due to causes such as shown in Figure 8.1. Most of these causes should be self-explanatory; only two are described below.

The normal external environment includes common-cause factors such as temperature, vibration, humidity, dust, and so on. Natural external phenomena such as fire, flood, tornado, and earthquake are included in the external catastrophe category.

In order to predict the realistic reliability of redundant computer systems, one must take into consideration the occurrence of common-cause failure.

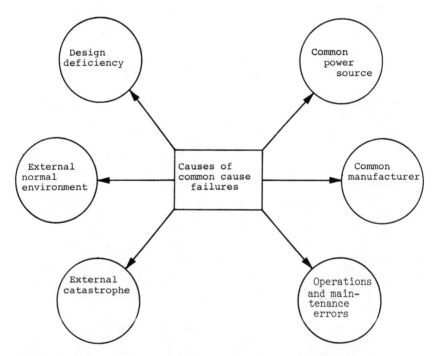

Figure 8.1   Some Causes of Common-Cause Failures in Redundant Systems

Because due to a common-cause failure, redundant computers may fail simultaneously or near simultaneously. This section presents two mathematical models representing redundant computer systems with common-cause failures. In both the cases the Markov method is utilized.

Model I. This model represents two redundant computers with common-cause failures. At least one computer must function normally for the system's success. The system fails only when both computers are in the nonoperational state. In addition, both computers may fail due to a common-cause failure. The system state–space diagram is shown in Figure 8.2. The following assumptions are associated with this model:

i.   the computer failure rate is constant.
ii. The computer system common-cause failure rate is constant.
iii. The failed computer system (both computers failed) is never repaired.
iv. Common-cause and other failures are statistically independent.
v.   Both computers are identical and active (at time $t = 0$).
vi. The common-cause failure can only occur with more than one computer.

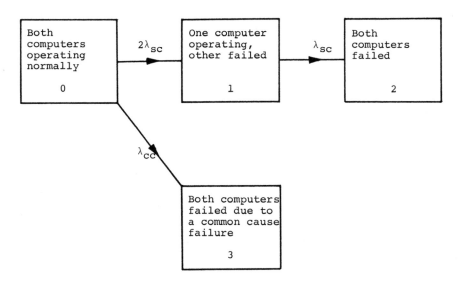

Figure 8.2   Transition Diagram of Two Redundant Computers with Common-Cause Failures. (The number in the box denotes the state of the computer system.)

The following symbols are associated with the model:

i is the ith state of the computer system: $i = 0$ (both computers operating normally), $i = 1$ (one computer operating, other failed), $i = 2$ (both computers failed), $i = 3$ (both computers failed due to a common-cause failure).

$P_i(t)$ is the probability that the computer system is in state i at time t, $i = 0, 1, 2, 3$.

s is the Laplace transform variable.

λ_{sc} is the single computer constant failure rate.

λ_{cc} is the computer system common-cause failure rate.

With the aid of Markov method [3], we obtained the following differential equations associated with Figure 8.2:

$$\frac{dP_0(t)}{dt} + (2\lambda_{sc} + \lambda_{cc})P_0(t) = 0 \tag{8.1}$$

$$\frac{dP_1(t)}{dt} + \lambda_{sc}P_1(t) = 2\lambda_{sc} \cdot P_0(t) \tag{8.2}$$

$$\frac{dP_2(t)}{dt} = \lambda_{sc} \cdot P_1(t) \tag{8.3}$$

$$\frac{dP_3(t)}{dt} = \lambda_{cc} \cdot P_0(t) \tag{8.4}$$

At time $t = 0$, $P_0(0) = 1$ and $P_1(0) = P_2(0) = P_3(0) = 0$

With the aid of Eqs. (8.1) through (8.4), the Laplace transforms of the solution are

$$P_0(s) = \frac{1}{s + 2\lambda_{sc} + \lambda_{cc}} \tag{8.5}$$

$$P_1(s) = \frac{2\lambda_{sc}}{(s + 2\lambda_{sc} + \lambda_{cc})(s + \lambda_{sc})} \tag{8.6}$$

$$P_2(s) = \frac{2\lambda_{sc}^2}{s(s + 2\lambda_{sc} + \lambda_{cc})(s + \lambda_{sc})} \tag{8.7}$$

$$P_3(s) = \frac{\lambda_{cc}}{s(s + 2\lambda_{sc} + \lambda_{cc})} \tag{8.8}$$

Where

$P_i(s)$ is the Laplace transform of the ith state probability; $i = 0$, 1, 2, 3.

Taking the inverse Laplace transform of the above four equations, we get:

$$P_0(t) = e^{-(2\lambda_{sc}+\lambda_{cc})t} \tag{8.9}$$

$$P_1(t) = A\{e^{-\lambda_{sc}t} - e^{-(2\lambda_{sc}+\lambda_{cc})t}\} \tag{8.10}$$

Where

$$A \equiv 2\lambda_{sc}/(2\lambda_{sc} + \lambda_{cc} - \lambda_{sc})$$

$$P_2(t) = B + A\left[\frac{\lambda_{sc}}{2\lambda_{sc} + \lambda_{cc}}\cdot e^{-(2\lambda_{sc}+\lambda_{cc})t} - e^{-\lambda_{sc}t}\right] \tag{8.11}$$

$$B \equiv 2\lambda_{sc}/(2\lambda_{sc} + \lambda_{cc})$$

$$P_3(t) = \frac{\lambda_{cc}}{2\lambda_{sc} + \lambda_{cc}}\{1 - e^{-(2\lambda_{sc}+\lambda_{cc})t}\} \tag{8.12}$$

The redundant computer system reliability is given by

$$R_{cs}(t) = P_0(t) + P_1(t)$$

$$= e^{-(2\lambda_{sc}+\lambda_{cc})t} + A\{e^{-\lambda_{sc}t} - e^{-(2\lambda_{sc}+\lambda_{cc})t}\} \tag{8.13}$$

Where

$R_{cs}(t)$ is the computer system reliability at time t.

The Laplace transform of the computer system reliability is

$$R_{cs}(s) = \frac{1}{(s + 2\lambda_{sc} + \lambda_{cc})} + \frac{2\lambda_{sc}}{(s + 2\lambda_{sc} + \lambda_{cc})(s + \lambda_{sc})} \tag{8.14}$$

The computer system mean time to failure $MTTF_{cs}$ is expressed as follows:

$$MTTF_{cs} = \lim_{s\to 0} R_{cs}(s) \tag{8.15}$$

Using Eq. (8.14) in Eq. (8.15) yields

$$MTTF_{cs} = \lim_{s \to 0} \left[\frac{1}{(s + 2\lambda_{sc} + \lambda_{cc})} + \frac{2\lambda_{sc}}{(s + 2\lambda_{sc} + \lambda_{cc})(s + \lambda_{sc})} \right]$$

$$= \frac{1}{2\lambda_{sc} + \lambda_{cc}} + \frac{2\lambda_{sc}}{(2\lambda_{sc} + \lambda_{cc})\lambda_{sc}}$$

$$= \frac{3}{(2\lambda_{sc} + \lambda cc)} \tag{8.16}$$

Model II. This model is the same as model I with one exception, i.e., when a computer fails it is immediately repaired. To handle this situation the diagram in Figure 8.2 is modified as shown in Figure 8.3. This figure shows a new transition from state 1 to state 0. The symbol θ in Figure 8.3 denotes the constant repair rate of a computer. The symbols and assumptions used to develop equations for model I are also applicable for model II.

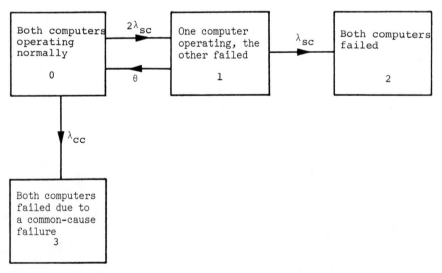

Figure 8.3 Transition Diagram of a Redundant Computer System with Repair and Common-Cause Failures. (The number in the box denotes the state of the computer system.)

With the aid of Markov technique, we write down the following differential equations associated with Figure 8.3:

$$\frac{dP_0(t)}{dt} + (2\lambda_{sc} + \lambda_{cc})P_0(t) = P_1(t)\cdot\theta \qquad (8.17)$$

$$\frac{dP_1(t)}{dt} + (\lambda_{sc} + \theta)\cdot P_1(t) = 2\lambda_{sc}\cdot P_0(t) \qquad (8.18)$$

$$\frac{dP_2(t)}{dt} = \lambda_{sc}\cdot P_1(t) \qquad (8.19)$$

$$\frac{dP_3(t)}{dt} = \lambda_{cc}\cdot P_0(t) \qquad (8.20)$$

At time $t = 0$, $P_0(0) = 1$ and other initial condition probabilities are equal to zero.

With the aid of Eqs. (8.17) through (8.20), the Laplace transforms of the solution are

$$P_0(s) = \frac{s + \lambda_{sc} + \theta}{c} \qquad (8.21)$$

Where

$$c \equiv (s + 2\lambda_{sc} + \lambda_{cc})(s + \lambda_{sc} + \theta) - 2\lambda_{sc}\cdot\theta$$

$$P_1(s) = 2\lambda_{sc}/c \qquad (8.22)$$

$$P_2(s) = 2\lambda_{sc}^2/sc \qquad (8.23)$$

$$P_3(s) = \lambda_{cc}(s + \lambda_{sc} + \theta)/sc \qquad (8.24)$$

Where

$P_i(s)$ is the Laplace transform of the ith state probability; $i = 0$, 1, 2, 3.

By adding Eqs. (8.21) and (8.22), we get the Laplace transform of the computer system reliability as follows:

$$R_{sc}(s) = P_0(s) + P_1(s)$$

$$= \frac{(s + \lambda_{sc} + \theta)}{c} + \frac{2\lambda_{sc}}{c} \qquad (8.25)$$

Using Eq. (8.25) in Eq. (8.15) yields the repairable computer system mean time to failure

$$MTTF_{csr} = \lim_{s \to 0} \left[\frac{s + \lambda_{sc} + 2\lambda_{sc} + \theta}{c} \right]$$

$$= \frac{\lambda_{sc} + 2\lambda_{sc} + \theta}{(2\lambda_{sc} + \lambda_{cc})(\lambda_{sc} + \theta) - 2\lambda_{sc}\theta}$$

$$= \frac{3\lambda_{sc} + \theta}{2\lambda_{sc}^2 + \lambda_{cc} \cdot \lambda_{sc} + \lambda_{cc}\theta} \qquad (8.26)$$

Where

$MTTF_{csr}$ is the repairable computer system mean time to failure.

8.3   COMPUTER SYSTEM LIFE CYCLE COSTING

The life cycle cost of a computer may be described as the total of all costs to the buyer in procurement and ownership of that product (computer) over its entire life span. There are various needs and uses of life cycle costing. Some of these are as follows:

    i.   To make sound decisions for computer replacement.
    ii.   To select a manufacturer of a computer out of competing manufacturers.
   iii.   To make comparison of the costs of alternative methods to fulfil a requirement.

This section presents four cost models concerned with computer systems.

Model I. This model is concerned with estimating the life cycle cost of a computer. The life cycle cost of a computer may simply be defined as follows:

$$LCC_c = C_{cp} + C_{co} \qquad (8.27)$$

Where

LCC_c is the life cycle cost of a computer.
C_{cp} is the computer procurement cost.
C_{co} is the computer ownership cost.

Alternatively, the life cycle cost may be expressed as follows:

$$LCC_c = C_{cnc} + C_{crc} \qquad (8.28)$$

Where

C_{cnc} is the non-recurring costs of the computer.
C_{crc} is the recurring costs of the computer.

Model II. This mathematical model can be used to estimate the monthly maintenance cost of computer hardware [4]. Thus, the computer hardware maintenance cost C_{mc} per month is expressed as follows:

$$C_{mc} = \sum_{i=1}^{3} C_i \qquad (8.29)$$

Where

C_1 is the corrective maintenance cost.
C_2 is the preventive maintenance cost.
C_3 is the cost of inventory.

The costs C_1, C_2 and C_3 are defined as follows:

$$C_1 = E_r E_h \{MTTR + T_{cm}\}/MTBF \qquad (8.30)$$

$$C_2 = S_{iv} \cdot R_c \qquad (8.31)$$

and

$$C_2 = E_r E_h \{E_{st} + E_{tm}\}/T_{pm} \qquad (8.32)$$

Where

E_r is the rate per hour of the customer engineer.
E_h is the monthly operating hours of the equipment.
$MTTR$ is the mean time to repair.
T_{cm} is the travel time of the customer engineer for corrective maintenance.
$MTBF$ is the mean time between failures.
S_{iv} is the maintenance spare parts original manufacturing cost (i.e. inventory value).
R_c is the inventory cost rate per month. (This includes handling costs and spares' depreciative charges per month.)
E_{st} is the customer engineer's scheduled time for preventive maintenance.

E_{tm} is the travel time of the customer engineer for preventive maintenance.

T_{pm} is the scheduled preventive maintenance interval.

The customer engineer's hourly rate is given by

$$E_r = C_p + [p_h(1 + i)]/t_f \qquad (8.33)$$

Where

C_p is the hourly cost of parts.

p_h is the hourly pay of the customer engineer.

t_f is the fraction of total time customer engineer spends for the maintenance purpose.

i is the overhead rate.

Model III. This model is concerned with estimating the expected cost associated with the hardware–software system [5]. The following three cost components are considered in this model:

  i.   the system downtime cost.
 ii.   the cost of a failure.
iii.   the maintenance activity cost.

The hardware–software system expected total cost is expressed as follows:

$$K_e(t) = A + K_{fh} \cdot F_{hf}(t) + K_{vh} \cdot \mu t + K_{fs} F_{sf}(t) + K_{vs} \cdot t\theta_s \qquad (8.34)$$

Where

$A \equiv K_s \int_0^t [1 - AV_s(y)] dy$

K_s is the system downtime cost per unit time.

t is time.

$AV_s(t)$ is the time-dependent system availability.

K_{fh} is the fixed cost of a hardware failure.

$F_{hf}(t)$ is the number of hardware failures expected by time t.

K_{vh} is the variable cost of a hardware repair per unit time.

μ is the constant hardware repair rate.

K_{fs} is the fixed cost of a software failure.

$F_{sf}(t)$ is the number of software failures expected by time t.

K_{vs} is the variable cost of a software repair per unit time.

θ_s is the constant software error removal rate when there are j number of errors present in the system.

Model IV. This model is used to estimate yearly labor expense associated with servicing a computer system. Thus the yearly labor cost is expressed as follows:

$$C_{ta} = H \cdot C_l[\alpha + \beta] \qquad (8.35)$$

Where

$$\alpha \equiv (MTTR + T)/MTBF$$
$$\beta \equiv (T_{mp} + T_t)/T_{mbp}$$

The symbols used in the above equations are defined below.

C_l is the hourly cost for labor.
$MTBF$ is the mean time between failures.
$MTTR$ is the mean time to repair.
T is the travel time associated with a repair call.
T_{mbp} is the average time between preventive maintenance.
T_t is the travel time associated with a preventive maintenance call.
T_{mp} is the average time to carry out preventive maintenance.
H is the number of hours in one year (i.e. 8760 hours).

8.4 INTEGRATED CIRCUIT DEFECTS

This section is specifically concerned with the modeling of pinhole defects associated with integrated circuits. These kinds of defects occur in dielectric insulators. Examples of such insulators are oxidized polysilicon, and thick and thin silicon oxides [6]. The size of pinhole defects is normally much less than a micrometer. The consequence of pinhole defect occurrence is a short circuit; this can happen between conductors produced at various photolithographic levels.

Thus the mean number of failures due to pinhole defects is expressed as follows:

$$\lambda_m = Y_c \alpha \qquad (8.36)$$

Where

Y_c is the critical area where the two conductors overlap, or that area where pinhole defects can cause a short circuit.
α is the defect density per unit area.

The critical area Y_c is given by

$$Y_c = Y\beta \qquad (8.37)$$

Where

Y is the chip area.
β is the fraction of Y that is sensitive to pinholes.

8.5   RELIABILITY ANALYSIS OF SPACE COMPUTERS

In spacecrafts, various functions are performed by computers. The reliability
of space computers is of utmost importance because a computer failure may
lead to a catastrophe. This section presents two mathematical models concerned with space computers.

Model I. This model is concerned with reliability analysis of a redundant
flight computer system [7]. The computer system is composed of m number of
identical computers. One of these m computers is labeled as prime and the
leftover $(m - 1)$ are labeled as spares. The computer failure is detected
irrespective of whether it involves the prime or spares. When the prime computer fails, the new prime computer is chosen out of the normally functioning
spare computers. The computer system failure criteria are expressed as follows:

   i.   Failure of all the computers.
  ii.   Designation of a failed spare computer as the prime computer when
      the failure of that spare computer was not detected.
 iii.   Failure of the prime computer without being detected.

For this model it is assumed that the completion of the spacecraft mission
will be attempted irrespective of the number of computer failures detected.
The probability of a computer failure is given by

$$P_c(t) = 1 - \exp[-\lambda_c t] \qquad (8.38)$$

Where

$P_c(t)$ is the probability of a computer failure.
λ_c is the constant failure rate of a computer.
t is time.

The probability of the total computer system failure before the completion
of the spacecraft mission is:

$$P_s = P_c^m P_{cd}^{m-1} + P_c(1 - P_{cd}) \sum_{i=0}^{m-1} (P_c \cdot P_{cd})^i \qquad (8.39)$$

Where

P_s is the probability of the total computer system failure before the completion of the spacecraft mission (this probability is equal to the mission failure probability and to the spacecraft loss probability).

P_c is the probability of a computer failure.

P_{cd} is the probability that a computer failure is detected.

m is the number of identical computers.

Model II. This is concerned with determining the expected cost contribution, K_e, of failure of a spacecraft (satellite) due to failure of its computer. The assumptions given below are associated with this model [8,9]:

i.   The space satellite is designed for a certain wear-out period of time.

ii.   The survival probability of the satellite equipment other than the computer decreases with time.

iii.   A computer failure occurring just after the spacecraft launch will be costlier than one occurring at a later stage.

iv.   A computer failure occurring after the specified wear-out time of the satellite will have zero cost.

The expected cost contribution, K_e, of failure of a spacecraft (satellite) due to failure of its computer is expressed as follows:

$$K_e = C_{sr} \int_0^{T_{sw}} \left[1 - \frac{t}{T_{sw}} \right] \cdot R_{se}(t) \, \{dP_c(t)/dt\} dt \qquad (8.40)$$

Where

t is time.

$R_{se}(t)$ is the spacecraft reliability, at time t, excluding the computer system.

$P_c(t)$ is the probability of computer failure at time t.

T_{sw} is the spacecraft wear-out life.

C_{sr} is the spacecraft replacement cost.

Example 8.1

The spacecraft equipment (other than the computer) failure rate λ_s is constant and the computer failure times are exponentially distributed. Thus the reliabilities of the spacecraft equipment (other than the computer) and the computer are expressed, respectively, as follows.

$$R_{se}(t) = e^{-\lambda_s t} \qquad (8.41)$$

and

$$R_c(t) = e^{-\lambda_c t} \tag{8.42}$$

Where

t is time.
λ_c is the constant failure rate of a computer.
$R_{se}(t)$ is the spacecraft equipment (other than the computer) reliability.
$R_c(t)$ is the spacecraft computer reliability.

Obtain an expression for K_e with the aid of Eq. (8.40).
By differentiating Eq. (8.42) with respect to time t, we get

$$\frac{dR_c(t)}{dt} = -\frac{dP_c(t)}{dt} = -\lambda_c e^{-\lambda_c t} \tag{8.43}$$

Thus from Eq. (8.43) we get

$$\frac{dP_c(t)}{dt} = \lambda_c e^{-\lambda_c t} \tag{8.44}$$

Substituting Eqs. (8.41) and (8.44) into Eq. (8.40) results in

$$
\begin{aligned}
K_e &= C_{sr} \int_0^{T_{sw}} \left[1 - \frac{t}{T_{sw}} \right] \cdot e^{-\lambda_s t} (\lambda_c e^{-\lambda_c t}) \cdot dt \\
&= \lambda_c C_{sr} \int_0^{T_{sw}} \left[1 - \frac{t}{T_{sw}} \right] e^{-(\lambda_s + \lambda_c)t} \cdot dt \\
&= \frac{\lambda_c C_{sr}}{\lambda_c + \lambda_s} \left\{ 1 + \frac{e^{-T_{sw}(\lambda_s + \lambda_c)} - 1}{T_{sw}(\lambda_s + \lambda_c)} \right\}
\end{aligned}
\tag{8.45}
$$

In Example 8.1 it was assumed the spacecraft has only one computer. However, if we assume that the spacecraft has two identical and independent computers and at least one must function normally for the overall system's success, the redundant computer system reliability is

$$R_c(t) = 2e^{-\lambda_c t} - e^{-2\lambda_c t} \tag{8.46}$$

By differentiating Eq. (8.46) with respect to time t, we get

$$\frac{dR_c(t)}{dt} = -\frac{dP_c(t)}{dt} = -2\lambda_c e^{-\lambda_c t} + 2\lambda_c e^{-2\lambda_c t} \tag{8.47}$$

Thus from Eq. (8.47) we get

$$\frac{dP_c(t)}{dt} = 2\lambda_c e^{-\lambda_c t} - 2\lambda_c e^{-2\lambda_c t} \tag{8.48}$$

Where

$P_c(t)$ is the redundant computer system probability of failure.

Substituting Eqs. (8.41) and (8.48) into Eq. (8.40) yields:

$$K_e = C_{sr} \int_0^{T_{sw}} \left[1 - \frac{t}{T_{sw}} \right] e^{-\lambda_s t} (2\lambda_c e^{-\lambda_c t} - 2\lambda_c e^{-2\lambda_c t}) \cdot dt$$

$$= C_{sr} \cdot 2\lambda_c \int_0^{T_{sw}} \left[1 - \frac{t}{T_{sw}} \right] \{ e^{-(\lambda_s + \lambda_c)t} - e^{-(2\lambda_c + \lambda_s)t} \} \cdot dt$$

$$\tag{8.49}$$

8.6 COMPUTER MEMORY RELIABILITY MODELING

The use of appropriate error correction schemes leads to improvement in the reliability of semiconductor memory systems. The Hamming code for single-bit error correction is one of such schemes. This scheme has received a wide acceptance. However, the chip failure mode distributions are the factors on which the degree of reliability improvement depends [10]. The analyses presented in this section are specifically concerned with a 4K word system. In these analyses, it is assumed that a semiconductor memory device has four major types of failures. These are entire-chip failure, single-bit failure, full-column failure and half-column failure.

A 4K Random Access Memory (RAM) is composed of 64 columns. The term half-column failure means there are 32 inoperative bits. Similarly, the term full-column failure implies that there are 64 inoperative bits. With the implementation of the error-correction scheme, 22 total bits are required for a 16-bit word in memory. Furthermore, it takes 22 RAMs to keep 4K words.

The failure rate λ_1 of an individual bit is given by

$$\lambda_1 = \frac{\alpha_1 \lambda_d}{(100)(4096)} \tag{8.50}$$

Where

α_1 is the percentage of single-bit failure.
λ_d is the device constant failure rate.

The individual full-column failure rate λ_2 is expressed as follows:

$$\lambda_2 = \frac{\alpha_2 \lambda_d}{(100)(64)} \tag{8.51}$$

Where

α_2 is the percentage of full-column failure.

The failure rate λ_3 of an individual entire chip is given by

$$\lambda_3 = \frac{\alpha_3 \cdot \lambda_d}{(100)} \tag{8.52}$$

Where

α_3 is the percentage of entire-chip failure.

The individual half-column failure rate, λ_4, is defined as

$$\lambda_4 = \frac{\alpha_4 \cdot \lambda_d}{(100)(128)} \tag{8.53}$$

Where

α_4 is the percentage of half-column failure.

With the aid of equations (8.50) through (8.53), the 4K word system reliability $R_{4K}(t)$ at time t is expressed as follows:

$$R_{4K}(t) = A_1 + e^{-22\lambda_3 t}[A_2 + e^{-22\lambda_2 t}\{A_3 + e^{-22\lambda_4 t}A_4\}^2]^{64} \tag{8.54}$$

Where

$$A_1 \equiv 22(1 - e^{-\lambda_3 t})e^{-21\lambda_d t} \tag{8.55}$$

$$A_2 \equiv 22(1 - e^{-\lambda_2 t})e^{-21\lambda_2 t}\{e^{-(64\lambda_1 + 2\lambda_4)t}\}^{21} \tag{8.56}$$

$$A_3 \equiv 22(1 - e^{-\lambda_4 t})(e^{-\lambda_4 t - 32\lambda_1 t})^{21} \tag{8.57}$$

$$A_4 \equiv \{e^{-22\lambda_1 t} + 22e^{-21\lambda_1 t}(1 - e^{-\lambda_1 t})\}^{32} \tag{8.58}$$

The reliability $R_s(t)$ of a 4MK word system containing identical M 4K word systems is given by

$$R_s(t) = \{R_4 K(t)\}^M \tag{8.59}$$

In the absence of error correction, the $4K$ word system reliability $R_{4Ka}(t)$ at time t simply is

$$R_{4Ka}(t) = \{e^{-\lambda_d t}\}^b \qquad (8.60)$$

Where

b is the number of bits in a word. (In this case the value of b is equal to 17.)

8.7 SUMMARY

This chapter presented five miscellaneous topics in computer hardware reliability. The reliability analysis of computer systems with common-cause failures was presented and six causes of common-cause failures were presented with the aid of a diagram. These causes are design deficiency, normal external environment, operations and maintenance errors, common manufacturer, external catastrophe, and common power source. Two Markov models were presented to perform reliability analysis of redundant computers with and without repair. Mean time to failure ($MTTF$) formulas were developed for both models. A life cycle cost model was presented to estimate the total cost of a computer system over its life span. In addition, two cost models were presented to estimate the monthly maintenance cost of computer hardware and the expected cost associated with the hardware–software system.

A model to determine the average number of failures due to pinhole defects was presented along with reliability analysis of space computers. A formula to calculate the probability of the total computer system failure before the completion of a spacecraft mission was developed. The expected contributed cost of failure of a spacecraft (satellite) due to failure of its computer was expressed mathematically. Finally, a mathematical model to determine the reliability of a $4K$ word system (memory) was presented.

8.8 EXERCISES

1. What are the causes for the occurrence of common-cause failures?
2. Define the term "the life cycle cost of a computer".
3. Discuss the history of the life cycle costing concept.
4. In Figure 8.3, assume that the computer system is also repaired at a constant rate μ from state 3 to state 0 and from state 2 to state 0. Develop an expression for the computer system steady-state availability.
5. What is a pinhole defect?

6. What are the major differences and similarities between computers for use on ground and in outer space?

7. With the aid of Eq. (8.54), develop an expression for the $4K$ word system mean time to failure $MTTF$.

8.9 REFERENCES

1. W.C. Gangloff, "Common-Mode Failure Analysis", IEEE Transactions on Power Apparatus and Systems, Vol. 94, 1975, pp. 27–30.

2. B.S. Dhillon, "On Common-Cause Failures—Bibliography", Microelectronics and Reliability, Vol. 18, 1978, pp. 533–534.

3. B.S. Dhillon, *Reliability Engineering in System Design and Operation,* Van Nostrand Reinhold Company, New York, 1983.

4. M. Phister, *Data Processing Technology and Economics,* Santa Monica Publishing Company, Santa Monica, California, 1979.

5. A.L. Goel and J.B. Soenjoto, "Hardware–Software Availability: A Cost Based Trade-off Study", Proceedings of the Annual Reliability and Maintainability Symposium, 1983, pp. 303–309.

6. C.H. Stapper, "Modeling of Integrated Circuit Defect Sensitivities", IBM Journal of Research and Development, Vol. 27, 1983, pp. 549–557.

7. R.J. Filene and W.M. Daly, "The Reliability Impact of Mission Abort Strategies on Redundant Flight Computer Systems", IEEE Transactions on Computers, Vol. 23, 1974, pp. 739–743.

8. H. Hecht, "Economics of Reliability for Spacecraft Computers", Proceedings of the Annual Reliability and Maintainability Symposium, 1972, pp. 554–564.

9. H. Hecht, "Figure of Merit for Fault-Tolerant Space Computers", IEEE Transactions on Computers, Vol. 22, 1973, pp. 246–251.

10. S.Q. Wang and K. Lovelace, "Improvement of Memory Reliability by Single-Bit-Error Correction", Proceedings of the IEEE Computer Society International Conference, San Francisco, 1977, pp. 175–178.

9

SOFTWARE QUALITY MANAGEMENT

9.1 INTRODUCTION

The quality and reliability of computer software is as important as that of computer hardware. Computer programs are no longer short and simple. It is not uncommon to find computer programs with over a million instructions. What is even more alarming is that in the U.S. Government fiscal year 1980 out of the approximately $57 billion expenditure on computer systems, $32 billion was spent on software. According to a report released by the U.S. Air Force in 1972, software cost may rise to as high as approximately 80% of the total computer hardware and software costs.

Obviously, the increase in computer programs' size will increase the problem of software quality assurance. The main objective of a quality assurance program is to assure that the end software items are of good quality, through planned and systematic activities to achieve, maintain, and determine that quality [1]. To produce good quality software products, the commitment from top management is essential. Otherwise, there can only be good intentions but no effective software quality assurance program. The management commitment involves setting organizational goals for software quality, allocating necessary resources, and so on. This chapter describes various important areas of software quality management.

9.2 THE SOFTWARE QUALITY ASSURANCE PROGRAM

To achieve a program's quality goal effectively, software quality assurance concepts have to be understood very clearly. However, many software quality assurance programs do not have this understanding. There are various factors which give rise to this problem:

i. Treating software quality assurance requirements as secondary requirements.
ii. Defining software quality assurance requirements in an unclear manner.
iii. Making use of individuals with secondary quality interests.
iv. Lacking a fully developed methodology.

This section discusses some selected aspects related to a software quality assurance program.

9.2.1 Functions of Software Quality Assurance

These may vary from one project to another and from one company to another. However, generally they can be classified into eight distinct categories [2] as shown in Figure 9.1. Each of these categories is discussed below.

Performing Quality Assurance Audits and Reviews. Quality assurance audits and reviews are conducted on software products to make certain that procedures, policies, and software standards established and identified in the

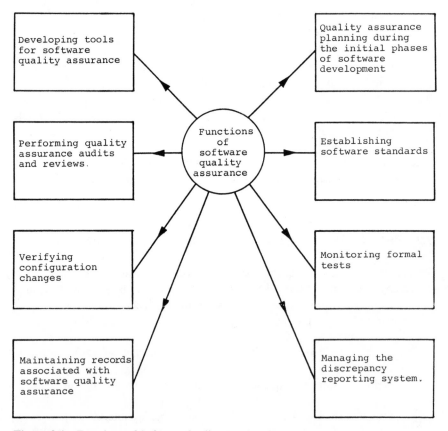

Figure 9.1 Functions of Software Quality Assurance

appropriate documents are practiced. The documents are reviewed with respect to technical content, objective clarity, interdocument consistency, traceability to upper level specifications, adherence to format, and so on. There are various kinds of audits conducted on software projects. Some of them are as follows:

i. *Software test audits:* These audits are performed at the end of each test phase. One of their objectives is to assure that the test team makes use of current approved versions of test specifications.

ii. *Software design audits:* These audits are concerned with design documentation content and format as well as those of the test plans.

iii. *Audit of requirements:* This audit reviews the project plan, software specifications, etc. and is performed before the system design review.

iv. *Predelivery software audit:* The purpose of this audit is to determine the adequacy of unit testing. This audit is conducted before software delivery to the test team.

v. *Periodic audits:* These audits are performed during the unit and code test phases to allow software developers time to implement corrective measures.

vi. *Interface verification audit:* The objective of this audit is to identify and rectify potential interface difficulties. This audit involves auditing of programming specifications, interface requirements, and so on.

Establishing Software Standards. To improve software product maintainability and readability, various kinds of software standards are used. There are basically two factors responsible for the success of these standards. One is that they serve as a useful tool against which to examine the software. By auditing themselves, programmers can avoid surprises at turnover time.

The other factor is that software standards are developed through close links between test, quality assurance, project, design, and development offices, rather than representing only the directives of the project office, quality assurance, or executive offices.

Developing Tools for Software Quality Assurance. Various kinds of software quality assurance tools are used to find solutions to problems in technical areas. In areas such as code verification, file management, and data base generation, these tools perform various kinds of functions, usually software tools are used to perform difficult, repetitive, tedious, costly, or error prone tasks. So far software tools are found to be a component of a software quality assurance program essential for its successful implementation. Generally one can say that the reason for their importance is that they provide a cost effective technique for correctly examining large and complex software products in a short time frame.

Some important examples of software quality assurance tools are the FOR-TRAN code auditor, structure programming auditor, and product assurance confidence evaluator.

The FORTRAN code auditor is concerned with auditing software standards automatically. On the other hand the structured programming auditor is used for the verification purposes, for example, to verify compliance with a structure programming standard. To determine quantitatively the thoroughness and rigorousness of a test on a program, the software quality assurance tool known as the product assurance confidence evaluator is used.

Maintaining Records Associated With Software Quality Assurance. Establishment of an effective system is necessary to keep software quality assurance related records. Only by having such a system in the early stage of a project's life cycle can one retain and control quality assurance records effectively. The quality assurance records may be grouped into the following six categories:

    i.   Software quality assurance plans and procedures.
    ii. Software quality assurance reviews.
   iii. Discrepancy and design problem reports.
   iv. Deviations and waivers.
    v.   Software quality assurance audits.
   vi. Test data packages.

Quality Assurance Planning During the Initial Phases of Software Development. This is another important function of software quality assurance. During the initial phases of the software development life cycle, the quality assurance program implementation success largely depends on software quality assurance planning. A quality assurance plan is only established after the review of the project plan, work contract statement, system specifications, and so on. The plan covers areas such as the following:

    i.   Effective quality assurance tools required to assure appropriate software quality with respect to factors such as reliability, maintainability, testability, accountability, and usability.
    ii. Tasks, functions, and responsibilities of software quality assurance.

Usually, the quality assurance plan is approved by the program manager and the customer after review by concerned project organizations.

Verifying Configuration Changes. This is an important function of software quality assurance and is concerned with configuration tests on the controlled master libraries of each version. The purpose of these tests is to make sure that no inadvertent or unauthorized code changes have taken place.

Normally new versions of programs are only released after the application of formal configuration control procedures.

Monitoring Formal Tests. This function is as important as any of the other seven functions of software quality assurance. This test monitoring function is concerned with on-site inspection and test surveillance during program testing by quality assurance personnel. The tasks performed by quality assurance personnel are certification of correctness of the test output analysis, comparing the hardware/software components configuration used in testing with one specified in the test procedure, monitoring the actual tests to find out if they are being performed according to specifications in test procedures, ascertaining effective recording of potential discrepancies, and so on.

Managing and Discrepancy Reporting System. Usually this function is also performed by the software quality assurance organization. The reporting system is concerned with tracking, correctly recording and reporting all project discrepancies. Various kinds of analysis can be performed with the data obtained from the discrepancy reporting system. For example, periodic error trend analyses of the error rate for various programs can be generated.

9.2.2   Ten Components of a Successful Software Quality Assurance Program

The following procedures are important to the success of a software quality assurance program [3]:

i. Develop a quality assurance activity and ensure that it is independent.
ii. Ensure that the quality assurance activity starts at an early stage of the software development cycle.
iii. Perform a detailed verification analysis of the requirements and design.
iv. Perform analysis of the code in addition to testing it.
v. Make sure that prior to the start of testing, the development testing is well planned.
vi. Ensure that documentation is controlled and cannot be modified without proper controls.
vii. Keep track of the computer resources needed by the end program.
viii. Carefully evaluate interfaces between any two elements in the system and resolve, if any, ambiguities, misunderstandings, and incompatabilities.
ix. Remain skeptical of errors in software received from the developer.
x. Always try to perform some kind of quality assurance activity or activities in a situation where you cannot perform the ideal maximum of activities.

9.2.3 Software Design Reviews and Reasons for High Software Costs

The main purpose of software design review is to produce cost effective, high quality, and reliable software. The majority of errors in the large software systems are introduced during the early stages of the development process [4]. Furthermore, about 60% of total software errors are introduced before the start of coding. Many of these errors can be rectified during the design review before the beginning of coding. Software design reviews can be grouped as follows [5]:

i.   *System design review:* In this review, the technically related requirements allocated to software are examined.
ii. *Preliminary design review:* Once the computer program component software level is defined, this review is performed, which carefully examines the selected software design approach prior to the detail design as well as the functional interfaces.
iii. *Critical design review:* This review is conducted before the coding to evaluate the finished detail design.

There are various kinds of difficulties associated with modern software development programs. For example, high development and maintenance costs, too many errors, and slippage of schedules. One U.S. Air Force study indicated that to develop Air Force Avionics, the software costs about $75 per instruction; however, to maintain it costs up to $4000 per instruction [6]. There are various factors responsible for the high cost of software. Some of them are shown in Figure 9.2.

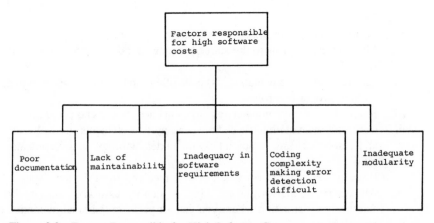

Figure 9.2   Factors Responsible for High Software Costs

9.2.4 Factors Responsible for the Software Development Problem

   i. Inadequate knowledge of requirements put forward by the user.
  ii. Poorly defined requirements.
 iii. Poor test planning and test techniques.
 iv. Poor management planning, control, and organization.
  v. Poor programming, design, and documentation methods.
 vi. Poor communication among involved individuals or groups.
vii. Poor verification of requirements and design.

9.3 SOFTWARE QUALITY ASSURANCE ORGANIZATION

To produce reliable software, the establishment of a software quality assurance organization is important. The existence of a software quality assurance organization alone will not be enough, but its status within the overall organizational structure will determine its effectiveness. The software quality assurance group must have enough authority to perform its required functions without any difficulty, especially when it comes to dealing with other groups or departments. Furthermore, it must be placed at a level where its access to top management is on the same footing as that of other competitive groups it deals with. This section discusses various aspects of the software quality assurance organization.

9.3.1 Responsibilities and Qualifications of a Software Quality Assurance Manager

Some of the duties of a software quality assurance manager are as follows [7]:

   i. Establishing the software quality control organization, practices and procedures.
  ii. Preparing a software quality program on an annual basis with respect to manpower, budgets, goals, and so on.
 iii. Interfacing with customers.
 iv. Liaison with regulatory and standardization bodies.
  v. Developing new concepts and procedures.
 vi. Formation of a software quality advisory committee.
 vii. Dissemination of new software quality related information to concerned individuals and groups.
viii. Keeping abreast of current software quality matters.
 ix. Auditing conformance to the software quality policy.

    x.   Maintaining membership in professional societies and industry asso-
         ciations.
   xi.   Participating in software design reviews.
  xii.   Providing consulting services to others.
 xiii.   Keeping the management informed with matters related to software
         quality.
 xiv.   Recruiting and training software quality personnel.

Similarly, a software quality assurance manager should possess qualifications such as follows:

     i.   Bachelor's or advanced degree in computer science, engineering or
         natural sciences.
    ii.   More than ten years of experience in various aspects of computer
         programming. At least five of these years should be in a supervisory
         function.
   iii.   Active participant in one or more professional societies such as
         American Society for Quality Control (ASQC), Institution of Electri-
         cal and Electronics Engineers (IEEE) Computer Society, Society of
         Reliability Engineers, etc.
   iv.   Possesses comprehensive and advanced knowledge of software
         engineering.
    v.   Possesses appropriate skills in oral and written communication.
   vi.   Competent in statistical analysis.
  vii.   Possesses knowledge of finance and marketing functions.
 viii.   Enthusiasm, patience, and persistence.
   ix.   Ability to think, listen, utilize time, plan, delegate, motivate, sell and
         organize effectively.
    x.   Ability to make decisions.
   xi.   Creative, fair, and honest.
  xii.   Possesses negotiating skill.

9.3.2   Attributes of a Good Software Quality Assurance Engineer

There are many characteristics that a good software quality assurance engineer should possess. Some of them are as follows:

     i.   Good communication skills.
    ii.   A degree in computer science, mathematics, natural sciences, or
         engineering.
   iii.   Experience in software design and development approaches and
         methods, and in programming.
   iv.   Very possessive of his or her work.

    v. Ability to improve software development methodologies.
   vi. Ability to deal with people.
  vii. Ability to learn to effectively manage and report on projects concerned with software development.
 viii. Capable of assuming a leadership role in a short time period.
   ix. Well motivated and organized.
    x. Ability to sort and sift facts.

9.4 SOFTWARE CONFIGURATION MANAGEMENT

Configuration management is a tool which assures both the manufacturer and the user that the end product fully satisfies the requirements in the specification. In the development of the configuration discipline, the United States armed forces have played an important role. For example, it was the U.S. Air Force who prepared a document entitled "Configuration Management During the Development and Acquisition Phases" as early as June, 1962.

With respect to computers, a set of computer software characteristics explained in documentation and realized in code are referred to as a configuration. Software configuration management is the management of changes associated with the configuration of software. There are various specific reasons for the application of the configuration management tool. Some of them are the realization of economy in terms of time and money, increasing project efficiency, and so on. The functions of software configuration management are as follows [9,10]:

    i. *Identification:* The identification of a software product is obtained by simply asking a question, i.e., what is the configuration of the system?
   ii. *Control:* Changes to software configuration by simply saying "how are the configuration changes to be or being controlled?"
  iii. *Auditing:* The software product being developed is audited by saying "Does the software product being developed fully meet the specified requirements?"
  iv. *Status accounting:* The changes made to the software product are determined by simply saying "What changes were made to the software product?"

Another term which is frequently used in configuration management is "baseline". This may be described as an approved point of reference for control of future changes to software product design, development and performance.

9.4.1   Advantages of Software Configuration Management

There are several advantages of software configuration management. Some of them are as follows:

    i.   Goals are established in a formal manner.
    ii. The overall cost is reduced.
    iii. The end software product is precisely identified.
    iv. Redundant effort is reduced.
    v.   It is equally applicable to small or large projects.
    vi. The resulting product is better.
    vii. Resources are channeled in an effective manner.

9.5   SOFTWARE QUALITY ASSURANCE STANDARDS

There are various types of published quality assurance standards currently in use to develop software products. Some of the reasons for having several software quality standards are as follows:

    i.   Great diversity in the types of software product being developed.
    ii. Great diversity in the technological methods, approaches, and procedures being used.
    iii. Great diversity in the types of software being maintained.
    iv. Great diversity in the management methods, approaches, and procedures being used.

Therefore, by keeping the above factors in mind, it is fair to say that there can be no single set of standards or policies for all the purposes. However, the overall end purpose of any software quality assurance standard is to produce a good quality, cost effective product. A customer may expect manufacturers to develop their software products according to one or more of the published software quality assurance standards. Therefore, customers and top level management expect that the software quality assurance management and personnel are fully aware of and thoroughly understand the importance of these standards.

Some of the published standards associated with software quality assurance are as follows [11,12].

    i.   MIL-S-52779: Software Quality Assurance Requirements, prepared by the U.S. Department of Defense. This document is approved for use by all the three services, namely, Navy, Air Force and Army.

The document presents a software quality assurance specification for purchase by all the three services.

ii.   MIL-HDBK-334: Evaluation of Contractor's Software Quality Assurance Program, prepared by the U.S. Department of Defense. This document is used by the government procurement agency to evaluate the final software quality assurance program in a situation when MIL-S-52779 is applicable to a contract.

iii. MIL-STD-1679: Weapon System Software Development, prepared by the U.S. Navy. This standard basically is concerned with the total acquisition of software. However, quality assurance as a crucial management function is also addressed in this document.

iv.   FAA-STD-018: This standard was developed by the U.S. Federal Aviation Administration (FAA). The document is concerned with software quality assurance in FAA systems.

v.   IEEE-P730: This document was prepared by the Institute of Electrical and Electronic Engineers (IEEE), USA. For software quality assurance plans, this document serves as a trial use standard.

vi.   AQAP-13: This Allied Quality Assurance Publication (AQAP)-13 was developed by the North Atlantic Treaty Organization (NATO). This document is used for software quality assurance of NATO procurements. It is the equivalent of MIL-S-52779.

vii. DLAM-8200.1: This Defense Logistics Agency Manual (DLAM) is a product of the U.S. Department of Defense. This document directs representatives of Contract Administration Services in auditing of software quality assurance activities of defense contractors.

viii. AQAP-14: This is the NATO equivalent of MIL-HDBK-334. This handbook is useful in evaluating the software quality control system of NATO contractors.

9.6   SOFTWARE QUALITY ASSURANCE BENEFITS

Software quality assurance has many advantages [2]. Some of them are as follows:

i.   Helpful to enhance mangement's visibility into the software development process because of audits and reviews.
ii.   The quality assurance records are centralized.
iii. The software tools' development and maintenance are centralized.
iv.   Reduces project risk because of thorough testing and better requirements traceability.
v.   Useful to enforce software standards.

   vi.   Fulfilment of deliverable items' contractual requirements is assured by an independent body.

9.7 SUMMARY

This chapter discussed various aspects of software quality management. Eight functions of software quality assurance were described. These are quality assurance reviews and audits, developing software standards, developing software quality assurance tools, maintaining records, quality assurance planning during the initial phases of the software development, verifying configuration changes, monitoring formal tests, and managing the discrepancy reporting system. Ten components of a successful software quality assurance program were presented along with software design reviews and reasons for high software costs. Factors responsible for the software development problem are discussed.

Various areas of software quality assurance organization were discussed. Qualifications and responsibilities of a software quality assurance manager were listed. In addition, attributes of a good software quality assurance engineer were presented. The topic of software configuration management was briefly described. Finally, eight of the published software quality assurance standards were briefly discussed and advantages of software quality assurance were listed.

9.8 EXERCISES

1. What are the functions of a software quality assurance group?
2. What is the difference between hardware quality assurance and software quality assurance?
3. List at least seven questions that you may ask the developer of software during the software design review.
4. What are the factors contributing to high software costs?
5. Discuss the duties of a software quality assurance engineer.
6. Describe the following terms associated with software configuration management:

      i.   Configuration
     ii.   Baseline
    iii.   Configuration item
    vi.   Configuration control
     v.   Configuration identification

7. Describe the four most important published software quality assurance standards.
8. What are the advantages of having a software quality assurance program?
9. What are the benefits of configuration management?

9.9 REFERENCES

1. K.S. Mendis, "A Software Quality Assurance Program for the 80's", Proceedings of the Annual Conference of the American Society for Quality Control, Atlanta, 1980, pp. 379–388.

2. K.F. Fischer, "A Program for Software Quality Assurance", Proceedings of the Annual Conference of the American Society for Quality Control, Chicago, 1978, pp. 333–340.

3. R.J. Rubey, "Planning for Software Reliability", Proceedings of the Annual Reliability and Maintainability Symposium, USA, 1977, pp. 495–499.

4. B.W. Boehm, "Software Engineering", IEEE Transactions on Computers, Vol. 25, 1976, pp. 1226–1241.

5. J. McKissick, "Quality Control of Computer Software", Proceedings of the Annual American Society for Quality Control Technical Conference, 1977, pp. 391–398.

6. R.R. Prudhomme, "New Software Methodologies and Quality Software", Proceedings of the Annual American Society for Quality Control Conference, Houston, 1979, pp. 357–363.

7. G.D. Tice, "Management Policy and Practices for Quality Software", Proceedings of the Annual American Society for Quality Control Conference, Boston, 1983, pp. 369–372.

8. K.S. Mendis, "Software Quality Assurance Staffing Problems", Proceedings of the Annual American Society for Quality Control Conference, Boston, 1983, pp. 108–112.

9. R.L. Glass, *Software Reliability Guidebook,* Prentice-Hall, Inc., Englewood Cliffs, New Jersey, 1979.

10. E.H. Bersoff, V.D. Henderson, and S.G. Siegel, *Software Configuration Management,* Prentice-Hall, Inc., Englewood Cliffs, New Jersey, 1980.

11. M.J. Fisher, "Software Quality Assurance Standards—The Coming Revolution", The Journal of Systems and Software, Vol. 2, 1981, pp. 357–362.

12. R. Dunn and R. Ullman, *Quality Assurance for Computer Software,* McGraw-Hill Book Company, New York, 1982.

10

SOFTWARE DESIGN AND TESTING

10.1 INTRODUCTION

Both design and testing are components of software development. Design may be described as a thought-intensive task which is the pivotal point of any fair size engineering project. The design phase is very crucial to the quality and reliability of the product that will emerge out of it; and for software construction, design is a make-or-break phase. In the software life cycle, requirements definitions and specification preparation precede the design phase [1]. Usually it is expected that a software designer should have a well-defined problem definition to work with, but in real life this may not be so. Therefore, the designer must be not only a good thinker but flexible, with a high degree of tolerance and an awareness of the various kinds of tools and procedures needed to develop the software product. This chapter presents a number of such design tools and procedures.

The other component of software development is testing. It may be described as the process of executing a program with the objective of discovering software errors. In many companies, as high as 50% of program development budgets is spent on testing software [2]. In testing, the purpose of the software tester is to make the program under consideration fail. In order to fulfil this objective, the tester makes use of many methods and procedures. In addition, there are several types of testing performed, for example module testing, acceptance testing, and top-down testing.

This chapter explores various aspects of software design and testing.

10.2 SOFTWARE LIFE CYCLE

This simply refers to the process of software development and use. This process is composed of several phases. The names and the number of these phases are not universally agreed upon. For example in references [3,4] the software life cycle is divided into six distinct phases:

   i.   requirement definition
  ii.   preliminary design
 iii.   detail design
 iv.   coding

    v.   integration and testing
   vi.   maintenance

and

    i.   concept and analysis
   ii.   requirements definition
  iii.   design
  iv.   code, debug and test
    v.   installation and evaluation
   vi.   operation and maintenance

On the other hand, in references [1,5] the software life cycle is expressed as having five and seven distinct phases:

    i.   requirements/specifications
   ii.   design
  iii.   implementation
  iv.   checkout
    v.   maintenance

and

    i.   system requirements
   ii.   software requirements
  iii.   preliminary design
  iv.   detailed design
    v.   code and debug
   vi.   test
  vii.   maintenance

The number of phases or their labeled names do not really matter because their objective is the same, i.e. to have a good quality and cost effective product. The life cycle phases, *requirements/specifications, design, implementation, checkout,* and *maintenance* of reference [1] are briefly discussed below.

The requirements/specifications phase is concerned with understanding and defining the problem. The needs of the user/customer are communicated through the requirements specification document. Erroneous requirements are the cause of 15% of the errors in software systems [6]. The design phase is probably the most crucial phase of the software life cycle, being concerned with translating the problem and its associated specifications into solution blueprints. The implementation phase is concerned with translating the end result of the earlier phase into a computer processable and readable form.

This is the phase where the software becomes an executable entity. The next phase, known as the checkout phase, is concerned with detecting design errors, finding programming errors, interrogating doubtful requirements, and so on. Maintenance is the last phase of the software life cycle. This is concerned with rectifying errors, making modifications required by the user, etc.

10.3   TOOLS OF THE PROGRAMMING TRADE

In the programming trade one makes use of various kinds of software tools. It is not the intention of the author to present here a complete list of tools. A detailed list of programming tools may be found in reference [6]. For our purpose we have divided selected tools into three categories, i.e. development; test and evaluation; and operations and maintenance. Many of the tools are common to at least two of these three categories.

10.3.1   Development Tools

Some of these tools are as follows:

  i.   Top-down programming
  ii.   Modular programming
  iii. Structured programming
  iv.   Linkage editor
  v.   Data base analyzer
  vi.   Analyzer
  vii. Compiler
  viii. Consistency checker
  ix.   Overlay program
  x.   Timing analyzer
  xi.   Trace program
  xii. Cross-assembler
  xiii. Language processor

10.3.2   Test and Evaluation Tools

There are many kinds of tools used for the purpose of test and evaluation. Some of these are as follows:

  i.   Structure analyzer
  ii.   Snap generator
  iii. Program flow analyzer
  iv.   Modular programming
  v.   Structure programming

   vi. Comparator
  vii. Automated test generator
 viii. Accuracy study processor
   ix. Compiler
    x. Consistency checker
   xi. Cross-reference program
  xii. Decompiler
 xiii. Standards enforcer
  xiv. Trace program
   xv. Program sequencer
  xvi. Diagnostics/debug aids
 xvii. Editor
xviii. Interface checker
  xix. Logic-equation generator
   xx. Interrupt analyzer.

10.3.3 Operations and Maintenance Tools

During the operations and maintenance phase of software, there are also various kinds of tools used. Examples of such tools are listed below:

    i. Timing analyzer
   ii. Restructuring program
  iii. Modular programming
   iv. Structured programming
    v. Snap generator
   vi. Test beds
  vii. Program sequencer
 viii. Decompiler
   ix. Data base analyzer
    x. Automated test generator
   xi. Translator
  xii. Editor
 xiii. Cross-reference program

10.4 SOFTWARE DESIGN METHODS

There are various techniques used during the software design phase. Directly or indirectly, the objective of these methods is to produce a good software design because almost 45% of software system's errors tend to be design errors [7].

10.4.1 Design Quality Measures

Some of these measures are as follows [7]:

   i. Cohesion
  ii. Coupling
 iii. Hiding
 iv. Factoring

Cohesion may be described as the extent to which module elements versus the data and logical steps are conceptually related. There are several types of cohesion such as logical, sequential, procedural, functional, coincidental, temporal, and communicational. Some of the advantages of a highly cohesive module are as follows:

   i. It simplifies debugging in the event of error.
  ii. It is easy and straightforward to use.
 iii. It is easy to change in the event when there is a change in functional requirements.

Coupling is another measure of design quality and may be described as a measure of a module's dependency on the modules it communicates with. There are various types of coupling known as common, data, stamp, control, and content. In a case when there is tight coupling, a strong dependence will exist. Some of the disadvantages of a tightly coupled module are as follows:

   i. The changes made in the module under consideration may also require changes in the dependent modules.
  ii. There may be a difficulty in understanding the action of module under consideration.
 iii. Chances are greater that if there is an error in the module under consideration, it will affect its dependent modules as well.

The most beneficial coupling is considered to be that through data items passed as parameters.

Hiding is concerned with hiding a system level decision in only a small number of modules. This way if there is any need for change in the future, then that change will only be confined to those few modules. The hiding of design decisions is frequently practiced in well-designed software systems.

To increase the usability of modules, factoring of a module into small cohesive modules is practiced. This way the duplication of work is reduced. Normally, it may not be possible to factor the action of a single module into more than seven cohesive modules. The reason for this is that the human mind finds it rather cumbersome to handle more than seven things at a time.

10.4.2 Design Representation Tools

There are several types of design representation schemes used in software design, but there is no single commonly used scheme [8]. Several of these schemes are presented in references [9,10]. Some of these schemes are as follows:

    i.   *Hierarchy plus input-process-output (HIPO) diagram:* This is a documentation technique and becomes quite useful with structured and top-down design programming. Some of the disadvantages of this scheme are that the technique can only be mastered through practice, the method needs a significant amount of space for the total design implementation, and structural changes can only be laboriously accomplished.

    ii. *Data structure chart:* This is a technique which defines relationships among data only.

    iii. *Code listing:* This method is also used for design representation purposes and is available universally.

    iv. *Chapin charts:* Hierarchy plus input-process-output (HIPO) diagrams and conventional flowcharts are considered to be bridged by this method.

    v. *Flowchart:* This probably is the most widely used method and is also the most controversial one. Various symbols are used to construct a flow chart. The method has advantages because pictorial representation is easily understood by individuals without formal programming training, and the flowchart is universally familiar. On the other hand, it is clumsy for showing interrupts and subroutines, and needs a large space.

    vi. *Structured flowchart:* This is simply a flowchart modified for structured programming.

    vii. *Warnier-Orr diagram:* This method has been gaining popularity in recent years. To show the system structure, the method makes use of logic symbols, nested sets of braces, and some pseudo-code. The method is standardized, straightforward, and easy to understand. The prime disadvantage of the method is its not being pictorial [8].

    viii. *Pseudo-code:* Sometimes this is also known as the metacode. It may be simply described as a shorthand version of a language used for programming. This method has many advantages because it is easy to update, easy to learn, flexible, and can be stored in a computer with ease. The disadvantages of this method are that it is neither standardized nor pictorial.

10.4.3 Design Techniques

This section discusses three popular software design techniques used to help produce better software products:

i.   *Structured programming:* defines the internal structure of a module.
ii. *Top-down programming:* defines the overall structure among the modules of a program.
iii. *Modular design:* defines the module size.

Structured Programming. Along the high-level language and subroutine concepts, structured programming may be regarded as one of the most important steps forward in the technology of programming. Since the late 1960s, the method has been receiving widespread attention [11]. It was Dijkstra [12] who pointed out that a program's text and its execution flow must have a close correspondence. In addition, the careless use of GO TO statements is harmful. However, the absence or presents of GO TO statements in a program is not necessarily a good measure of whether the program is good or bad [13].

In the published literature there are many overlapping definitions of structured programming. For example in reference [14], it is stated as coding that avoids use of GO TO statements as well as program design that is modular and top down. On the other hand, the author of a well-known text [11] simply defines structured programming as the attitude of writing code with the purpose of communicating with human beings instead of machines. For an average programmer the following selected easy to use rules associated with structured programming are [15]:

i.   Restrict the use of GO TO statements in the module.
ii. Make sure that for each module there is only one entry and one exit.
iii. Make use of a language and compiler having structured programming capabilities for the implementation purpose.
iv. Make sure that all statements, including subroutine calls, are commented. This way the program will be more readable.

Some of the benefits of structured programming are as follows:

i.   It helps to increase the productivity of programmers with respect to instructions coded per man-hour.
ii. It serves as a useful tool in localizing an error.
iii. It maximizes the amount of code that can be reused in redesign work.
iv. It serves as an effective tool in understanding of the program design by the designer and others.
v.   Its clarity normally provides a significant advantage during the design process.

Similarly, the drawbacks of structured programming are as follows:

i.   In some situations, it requires more memory relative to a nonstructured program.

ii. Necessity of many unwilling supervisory personnel and programmers to learn new methods which they consider to be unproven.

iii. In some situations, it requires more running time than its counterpart, nonstructured programming.

iv. It requires extra effort because many programming languages lack certain control concepts necessary to implement the structured programming purpose.

Top-Down Programming. The top-down design is also known as hierarchic decomposition. The reason for the usage of this term is the cascading nature of the process [16]. Therefore, top-down design may be simply described as a decomposition process concerned with directing attention to the program control structure or to the program flow of control. In addition, it also concerns itself with the production of code at a later stage.

The top-down design method starts with a module representing the entire program. In the next step the module is decomposed into subroutines. Each of the subroutines is further broken down and this process continues until the broken down elements are in easy comprehensible form and straightforward to work with. These elements consist of basic computer language statements such as PL/1 statements and FORTRAN statements [15]. The analogy of the program structure may be drawn with a tree. The module representing the entire program is equivalent to the trunk of the tree and ultimately its leaves are equivalent to the computer language statements.

Some of the advantages associated with top-down structured programming are as follows [17]:

i.   It helps to produce better quality software.

ii. It helps to produce software in a more readable form.

iii. It helps to lower the cost of testing.

iv. It helps to minimize surprises because it is a systematic and disciplined approach.

v.   It helps to reduce the cost of software maintenance and ultimately the life cycle cost.

vi. It helps to increase confidence in the software.

vii. It forces the designer to understand, at each level, the functional and data requirements before progressing to the next design level.

Modular Design. In software work a module may be described basically as a self-contained, modest-sized subprogram performing independently on one specific function. If it is removed from the system, it will only disable its unique function; nothing else will be disabled. Programmers normally decompose a complex software development job into various distinct modules. The following two main criteria are associated with modular design:

i.   *Module size restriction:* This is concerned with defining the physical size of a module (i.e. maximum and minimum number of program language statements). This restriction is not difficult to define. Normally, the module size may vary from one project to another, however, in reference [15] the suggested maximum and minimum statements are 50 and 5, respectively.

ii. *Functional independence restriction:* This is concerned with defining the logic scope that a distinct module may cover. This functional restriction is not so simple to define. In this aspect the good judgement of programmers plays a useful role.

Some of the advantages and disadvantages of modular programming are as follows:

Advantages:
i.   Results in better software program design.
ii.   Software program writing, debugging and testing become easier.
iii. The top-down design approach fits quite well with this method.
iv.   A complex software development task can be decomposed into a number of manageable modules.
v.   After the deployment, changes are cheaper in cost. In addition, error corrections are also cheaper and easier.
vi.   Helps to produce more reliable programs.
vii. Helps to increase productivity of programmers.
viii. Allows one to assign difficult modules to more experienced programmers.

Disadvantages:
i.   May need more memory space.
ii.   Requires more effort during design.
iii. Requires a lot of effort to learn because of the limited number of formal design methods.
iv.   May require more run time.

10.5   SOFTWARE TESTING

A major portion of the program development budget is spent in many companies on software testing. Testing is performed to find out whether or not the newly developed softwares satisfy design specifications. It is quite likely that a newly developed program will still contain some bugs even if the best available software design techniques were used to develop it. this section presents various aspects of software testing.

10.5.1 Elements of a Good Test Plan

During the software system development, a test plan can be very effective. The purpose of the test plan is to define functions and the extent to which they are required to be tested during the test phases. A good test plan should contain information on items such as follows [18]:

     i.   The test phase planned duration.
    ii.   Functions that need to be tested.
   iii.   Documentation of test results.
   iv.   Scheme for classification of errors.
    v.   The test strategy to be employed.
   vi.   Performance requirements associated with the system and its elements; for example, response time and central processing unit time.
  vii.   Required level of error rate before the system can be classified as a deliverable item.
 viii.   The testing criteria to be satisfied; for example, the range of variables and percentage of branches and control paths.
   ix.   Errors the system is required to detect. In addition, the procedure to introduce these errors during testing and the consequences associated with each of these errors.

10.5.2 Characteristics of Simple and Super Complex Programs

There are significant differences in the procedure to test programs of various sizes. Programs may be classified into the following five categories [19]

    i.   Simple
   ii.   Intermediate complexity
  iii.   Complex
  iv.   Very complex
    v.   Super complex

In order to demonstrate the differences among the classifications, the first and the last categories are discussed. The detailed description of the remaining three categories may be found in reference [19].

A project with the following characteristics falls under the first category (i.e., simple):

    i.   It contains fewer than 1000 source statements and normally is developed by a single programmer within a time frame of six months.
   ii.   Usually it does not have any interactions with other systems or programs.

The main concerns associated with this type of simple program are its non-criticality, and that one individual serves as programmer–tester and the resulting quality is dependent on the ability of one individual. Similarly, a project with the following characteristics is known as super complex:

    i.   It has instructions numbering between one and ten million.

   ii.   Over one thousand programmers participate during its development time of several years.

  iii.   Frequently, it involves critical processes such as air defense or air traffic control.

  iv.   Often it has a very high reliability requirement.

   v.   Almost always, it involves telecommunications, real-time processing, etc.

The main concern associated with this type of program is that the final result largely depends upon the application of design and management formal and modern methods because of the mixture of programmer skills.

10.5.3 Types of testing

This section briefly discusses various types of testing. These are as follows [8,11,18]:

    i.   Performance testing
   ii.   Module testing
  iii.   Integration testing
  iv.   Top-down testing
   v.   Bottom-up testing
  vi.   Big bang testing
 vii.   Sandwich testing
viii.   Modified top-down testing
  ix.   Modified sandwich testing
   x.   Regression testing

One should note here that some of these may have certain overlap. Each is described below.

Performance Testing. This type of testing is concerned with finding out whether the actual system performance (e.g. central processing unit loading, response time) meets the specified values. This kind of comparison is useful to detect disguised development software errors.

Module Testing. Module testing is concerned with testing each module, usually in isolation from the rest of the system but under the environments to be experienced in the total system. Normally every effort is made to develop a generalized module test program instead of writing a totally new test program for each module tested. Module testing should be thoroughly executed because of reasons such as follows [18]:

  i.   Usually errors discovered can be corrected without any difficulty.
  ii. Usually consequences of errors discovered at a later time will be more grave.

Integration Testing. Integration testing is concerned with verification of the interfaces among the elements of the system (subsystems, modules, and parts). It is not possible to detect certain errors associated with the interaction of different program modules through unit testing; these can only be discovered through integration testing. All in all, the purpose of integration testing is to detect interface defects.

Top-down Testing. This form of testing is concerned with merging and testing the program from the top to the bottom. It is important to note that in the program structure, the top module is the only module that is unit tested in isolation. Once the testing of the top module is over, one by one the modules called directly by this module are merged with the top module. The resulting combination is tested [11].

This goes on until the combining and testing of all the modules is completed.

Bottom-up Testing. In this case, the merging and testing of the program takes place from the bottom to the top. The terminal modules are module (unit) tested in isolation. These are only those modules which do not call any other modules. After testing the terminal modules, the modules that directly call these tested terminal modules are the ones in line for testing. One should note here that these modules are not tested in isolation, rather, the testing is performed together with the previously tested lower level modules [11]. This goes on until the top of the program is reached.

Big Bang Testing. Big bang testing is concerned initially with unit testing each and every module in isolation from other modules. After such testing, the entire number of modules is integrated. This probably is the most commonly used method for the integration purpose. Relative to other software test approaches, the big-bang testing method has few benefits and many drawbacks. Therefore it is not always a desirable method and should be restricted to those programs which are well-designed and small.

Sandwich Testing. This method was developed from the combination of top-down and bottom-up test techniques, in order to extract benefits from both of them. This approach also attempts to banish some of the drawbacks of the parent methods. In this method, both bottom-up testing and top-down testing are used simultaneously. This way the program is integrated from both sides (i.e. bottom and top). The final meeting point from both the sides depends upon the program under consideration and can be predetermined by reviewing the program structure. Some of the advantages of this approach are presented in reference [11].

Modified Top-down Testing. In top-down design, problems involving critical modules have to wait for the completion of the control structure before testing can start. To overcome this difficulty, modified top-down testing is practiced. In this kind of testing, one is concerned with exercising the critical module with a test program during the control structure integration testing. Furthermore, in modified top-down testing each and every module is unit tested in isolation prior to its integration into the program. For each module, the modified top-down testing requires module drivers and stubs.

Modified Sandwich Testing. This method was developed from a compromise between modified top-down testing and bottom-up testing to overcome the difficulty of not being able to test specific modules within the program by the use of the sandwich testing method. This problem stems from the top-down part of sandwich testing, since there is a possibility of this problem existing for modules in the lower half of the program top part. This kind of problem is not experienced with the bottom-up part of sandwich testing. Thus in modified sandwich testing, prior to integration using top-down testing, the program top part modules are unit tested in isolation. No such change is necessary for the program lower part modules, as bottom-up testing is quite satisfactory for lower levels.

Regression Testing. In situations where software errors are detected, changes have to be made to the software to correct them. The testing involved under such conditions is referred to as regression testing. Broadly speaking, this type of testing is conducted to verify that the earlier tested software performance has not been altered because of changes.

10.5.4   Program Automated Testing Tools

There are various types of automated tools used for program testing. Almost since the birth of the computer industry, automated tools have been with us. Examples of automated tools are assemblers, compilers, editors, and source-code control programs. The function of compilers and assemblers is to convert programs from one representation to another. Editors and source-code control programs are useful to keep large size software systems within control.

The primary two reasons for the use of automated tools are cost-effectiveness and comprehensivity. With respect to cost-effectiveness, the human analyser's capability is significantly augmented with the use of automated tools. Similarly, with respect to comprehensivity, a specific feature may be missed through the manual process but with the automated tools this possibility is eliminated. On top of that, automated tools do not get tired.

Some of the program automated testing tools are as follows [20]:

    i.   Code auditors
   ii.   Automated execution verifiers
  iii.   Assertion processors
  iv.   Test file generators
   v.   Static analysers
  vi.   Test data generators
 vii.   Self-metric instrumentors
viii.   Output comparators

Two of the above tools are discussed below. Detailed descriptions of the remaining ones may be found in references [20,21].

Code Auditors. The purpose of a code auditor is to enforce specified standards for programming practice. Usually, these standards involve matters concerning program style and content. The code auditor becomes very useful in situations where specific requirements on the actual format of programs have to be satisfied or the generated program text will turn out to be large. The processing involved with a code auditor is basically interactive on the statement level. The code auditor is provided with two things, i.e., the user-generated instructions controlling the checks to be performed with the source program, and the source program file. Furthermore, each and every statement is applied with active rules by the code auditor. The program text is passed through by the auditor only once and the generated output report presents each violation type and location.

Output Comparators. The output comparator is a useful tool to determine differences between old and new outputs of a program. When programs are converted from one to another computer system, the comparators are found quite useful for verification analysis of program functional properties. In software work, output comparison approaches are frequently used. The two commercially available systems for comparison purposes are series-J/ comparator and logical file comparator [20]. Both these systems were developed for their intended use on IBM 360/370 series computers.

10.6 SOFTWARE PROBLEM SYMPTOMS AND CAUSES

This section lists many of the symptoms and causes of software problems. Some of these symptoms are as follows [3]:

    i.   Customers are dissatisfied with the end software product.
   ii.   Slipping schedules and overrunning costs.
  iii.   Operational systems are prone to errors.

   iv.   Difficulties with testing are experienced.

    v.   Problems with system maintenance are experienced.

   vi.   Many errors are discovered late in the development process.

  vii.   Disagreements over interpretations of requirements.

Similarly, some of the causes of the software problem are as follows:

    i.   Poor design methods.

   ii.   Inadequate test techniques.

  iii.   Ineffective programming methods.

  iv.   Specifying requirements in a poor manner.

    v.   Unsuitable languages used for programming.

   vi.   Inadequate knowledge of customer requirements.

  vii.   Ineffective methods used for documentation.

 viii.   Poor test planning.

   ix.   Inadequate intercommunication among working groups.

    x.   Inadequate verification of requirements and design.

   xi.   Inadequate management planning and control

  xii.   Unsuitable computer systems.

10.7 SUMMARY

This chapter presented various aspects of software design and testing. Phases of the software life cycle were briefly discussed and tools of the programming trade were presented under three distinct classifications. These classifications are development tools; test and evaluation tools; and operations and maintenance tools. Four kinds of design quality measures were discussed: cohesion, coupling, hiding, and factoring.

Design representation tools such as hierarchy plus input-process-output (HIPO) diagrams, data-structure charts, code listing, Chapin charts, flow chart, structured flowcharts, Warnier-Orr diagrams, and pseudo-code were covered under this topic. Three popular software design techniques were described: structured programming, top-down programming, and modular design.

Elements of a good test plan were presented along with characteristics of simple and super complex programs. Ten types of software testing were described: performance testing, module testing, integration testing, top-down testing, bottom-up testing, big bang testing, sandwich testing, modified top-down testing, modified sandwich testing, and regression testing. The topic of program automated testing tools was covered, listing eight types of test tools. Finally, the chapter listed software problem symptoms and causes.

10.8 EXERCISES

1. What is the difference (if any) between the structured programming and top-down programming?
2. Describe four of the following items:

   i. Assertion processors
   ii. Test file generators
   iii. Static analysers
   iv. Self-metric instrumentors
   v. Automated execution verifiers
   vi. Test data generators

3. What is the difference between the test file generator and test data generator?
4. What are the most commonly known phases of the software life cycle?
5. Describe the following three terms associated with software:

   i. Cohesion
   ii. Coupling
   iii. Hiding

6. Explain in detail the following five tools:

   i. Timing analyzer
   ii. Linkage editor
   iii. Snap generator
   iv. Interrupt analyzer
   v. Cross-assembler

7. Discuss in detail the hierarchy plus input-process-output diagrams.
8. What are the advantages and disadvantages of structured programming?
9. List the characteristics of a simple software program.
10. Describe the following three terms associated with software:

    i. Functional testing
    ii. Acceptance testing
    iii. Structural testing

11. What are the differences between software big bang testing and bottom-up testing?

10.9 REFERENCES

1. R.L. Glass, *Software Reliability Guidebook,* Prentice-Hall, Inc., Englewood Cliffs, New Jersey, 1979.

2. G.J. Myers, *Software Reliability Principles and Practices,* John Wiley & Sons, New York, 1976.

3. K.F. Fischer, "A Methodology for Developing Quality Software", Proceedings of the Annual American Society for Quality Control Conference, 1979, pp. 364–371.

4. R. Dunn and R. Ullman, *Quality Assurance for Computer Software,* McGraw-Hill Book Company, New York, 1982.

5. B.W. Boem, "Software Engineering", IEEE Transactions on Computers, Vol. 25, Dec. 1976, pp. 1226–1241.

6. W. Rauch-Hindin, "Software Tools: New Ways to Chip Software into Shape", Data Communications, April 1982, pp. 83–113.

7. R.D. Joshi, "Software Development for Reliable Software Systems", The Journal of Systems and Software, Vol. 3, 1983, pp. 107–121.

8. M.L. Shooman, Software Engineering: *Design, Reliability, and Management,* McGraw-Hill Book Company, New York, 1983.

9. R.E. Fairly, "Modern Software Design Technique", Proceedings of the Symposium on Computer Software Engineering, Polytechnic Press, New York, 1976, pp. 111–131.

10. L.J. Peters and L.L. Tripp, "Software Design Representation Schemes", Proceedings of the Symposium on Computer Software Engineering, Polytechnic Press, New York, 1976, pp. 31–56.

11. G.J. Myers, *Software Reliability: Principles and Practices,* John Wiley & Sons, New York, 1976.

12. E.W. Dijkstra, "GO TO Statement Considered Harmful", Communications of the Association for Computing Machinery, Vol. 11, 1968, 147–148.

13. D.E. Knuth, "Structured Programming with GO TO Statements", Computing Surveys, Vol. 6, 1974, pp. 261–301.

14. R. Rustin, *Debugging Techniques in Large Systems,* Prentice-Hall, Inc., Englewood Cliffs, New Jersey, 1971.

15. R.S. Wang, "Program with Measurable Structure", Proceedings of American Society for Quality Control, 1980, pp. 389–396.

16. A. Koestler, *The Ghost in the Machine,* Macmillan, New York, 1967.

17. R.R. Prudhomme, "New Software Methodologies and Quality Software", Proceedings of the Annual Conference of the American Society for Quality Control (ASQC), 1979, pp. 357–363.

18. H. Kopetz, *Software Reliability,* The Macmillan Press Ltd., London, 1979.

19. E. Yourdon, *Techniques of Program Structure and Design,* Prentice-Hall, Inc., Englewood Cliffs, New Jersey, 1975.

20. E.F. Miller, "Program Testing Tools and Their Use", in *Infotech State of the Art Report: Software Reliability,* Published by Infotech International Limited, Nicholson House, Maindenhead, Berkshire, England, 1977, pp. 183–216.

21. D.J. Reifer and R.L. Ettenger, "Test Tools: Are They A Cure-All?", Proceedings of the Annual Reliability and Maintainability Symposium, 1975, pp. 492–497.

11

SOFTWARE RELIABILITY MODELING

11.1 INTRODUCTION

Since the 1960s software reliability mathematical modeling has been receiving increasing attention. There are a number of reasons for the quantification of software reliability. Some of them are as follows:

i. In the engineering of software products, software reliability is a vital parameter.
ii. In the evaluation of the effectiveness of software engineering methodologies, software reliability plays a critical role.
iii. In scheduling and monitoring a software development effort, software reliability evaluation can help both the concerned engineers and managers.

The theories used to quantify software reliability can be classified [1] into four basic categories as shown in Figure 11.1. These are error seeding, empirical estimation, reliability estimation modeling, and complexity theories. Firstly, error seeding theory makes use of statistical maximum likelihood estimation. On the basis of seeded and intrinsic errors uncovered during the test period, the number of errors in the program are determined. Secondly, the empirical estimation theory is concerned with finding a best-fit statistical distribution for accumulated failure data. Thirdly, reliability estimation modeling theory deals with estimating standard reliability metrics. One example of such metrics is the reliability of a software program for a specified period. Fourthly, the complexity theory is established on several metrics. These are related to human cognition and software complexity. Examples of such metrics are the program size, the program development group size, and the number of elementary mental discriminations in a software program. On the basis of these metrics errors are predicted prior to software testing.

This chapter presents various aspects of software reliability modeling.

11.2 A BRIEF HISTORY OF SOFTWARE RELIABILITY MODELS

The history of software reliability models is not old in comparison to the history of hardware reliability models. The first paper concerned with software reliability models, appearing in 1967 [2], presented a Markov birth–death model. The next major step in the history of software reliability models took place in 1972 when Jelinski and Moranda [3] published their model. In this model they made an assumption that a hazard rate for failures is a piecewise constant and proportional to the faults remaining. In addition, the hazard rate decreases in steps with respect to time. Another mathematical model was developed during the same time span by M.L. Shooman [4]. Similarly, he assumed in his model that the hazard rate is proportional to remaining faults. Other contributions of the early 1970s were published in references [5–6]. In reference [5] Schick and Wolverton assumed that the hazard rate is proportional to the product of remaining faults and the time spent in debugging errors. On the other hand in reference [6] Schneidewind suggested the modeling of software reliability from an empirical angle.

An important milestone in software reliability modeling took place in 1975. This was due to the effort of Musa [7]. In his paper he suggested that the most important practical measure of failure-inducing stress on the program is execution time [8].

Some other models concerned with software reliability are given in references [9–11].

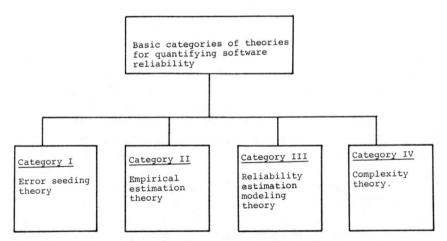

Figure 11.1 Basic Theories for Quantifying Software Reliability

11.3   CLASSIFICATION OF SOFTWARE RELIABILITY MODELS

Over the last number of years, there has been a significant growth in software reliability models. Most of these models may be classified into the five categories [1] shown in Figure 11.2.

Classification type I is concerned with Bayesian models. These models assume that the failure rate is a random process with regard to the failures occurred. Bayesian models are not simple to understand. Execution time models, in which program execution time is the driving force, fall under classification type II. The third classification is concerned with input space models. These models require one to enumerate all sets of inputs for a computer program and determine the proportion which leads to an error free operation. In a broader sense, input space models have little practical use because of their theoretical inclination.

Classification IV is composed of semi-Markov models, which assume fault correction as a semi-Markov process and focus attention on introducing new

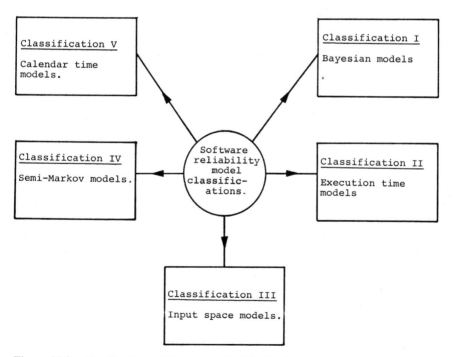

Figure 11.2   Classifications of Software Reliability Models

faults when rectifying the one already found. Classification V is composed of calendar time models. These are based on the assumption that the mechanism which causes computer programs to fail is close related to calendar time. The calendar time models were the initial attempt in the quantitative software reliability field.

11.4 SOFTWARE RELIABILITY MODELS

This section presents selective mathematical models used in software reliability work. Many of the competing software reliability models are presented in references [8,12–15].

11.4.1 Model I

This is known as the Jelinski-Moranda model [3]. In this model an exponential density function is assumed for software errors. The additional assumptions associated with this model are as follows:

    i.   The debugging time between software error occurrences has a hazard function which is proportional to the remaining software errors.

    ii. The occurrence rate between software errors is free of time dependency.

    iii. Each detected error is corrected without any delay.

The hazard function is expressed as follows:

$$\lambda(t_j) = C[E_i - (j - 1)] \tag{11.1}$$

Where

    C is the constant of proportionality.
    E_i is the number of initial software errors.
    t_j is the time between detection of the jth and $(j - 1)$st software errors.

In reliability theory [15] the reliability of an item can be defined as follows:

$$R(t) = \exp\left[-\int_0^t \lambda(z) \cdot dz\right] \tag{11.2}$$

Where

    $R(t)$ is the item reliability at time t.
    $\lambda(t)$ is the item hazard rate.

By substituting Eq. (11.1) into Eq. (11.2) we get

$$R(t_j) = \exp[-C\{E_i - (j - 1)\}t_j]$$ (11.3)

In reliability theory [15] the mean time to failure *MTTF* of an item is expressed as follows:

$$MTTF = \int_0^\infty R(t) \cdot dt$$ (11.4)

Thus substituting Eq. (11.3) into (11.4), we derive

$$MTTF = \int_0^\infty R(t_j)\,dt_j = \int_0^\infty \exp[-C\{E_i - (j - 1)\}t_j] \cdot dt_j$$

$$= \left[\frac{-1}{C\{E_i - (j - 1)\}} \cdot \exp[-C\{E_i - (j - 1)\}t_j] \right]_0^\infty$$

$$= \frac{1}{C\{E_i - (j - 1)\}}$$ (11.5)

With the aid of maximum likelihood estimation method [3] the values of parameters E_i and C can be estimated. Differentiating Eq. (11.3) with respect to t_j results in

$$\frac{dR(t_j)}{dt_j} = -f(t_j) = -C\{E_i - (j - 1)\}\exp[-C\{E_i - (j - 1)\}t_j]$$

(11.6)

Thus from Eq. (11.6), the density function $f(t_j)$ is

$$f(t_j) = C\{E_i - (j - 1)\}\exp[-C\{E_i - (j - 1)\}t_j]$$ (11.7)

With the aid of Eq. (11.7), the likelihood function [16] is given by

$$L(t_1, t_2, \ldots, t_k) = \prod_{j=1}^{k} C\{E_i - (j - 1)\}\exp[-C\{E_i - (j - 1)\}t_j]$$

(11.8)

Where

$t_1, t_2, \ldots, t_k$ is the sample of intervals of time between successive software errors.

By taking logarithms of Eq. (11.8), the expression becomes

$$\log L = \sum_{j=1}^{k} \log\{E_i - (j-1)\} + k \log C - \sum_{j=1}^{k} \{E_i - (j-1)\}t_j \cdot C$$

$$(11.9)$$

Taking a partial derivative of Eq. (11.9) with respect to C and E_i and setting the resulting expressions equal to zero, we obtain:

$$\frac{\partial \log L}{\partial C} = \frac{k}{C} - \sum_{j=1}^{k} \{E_i - (j-1)\} t_j = 0 \qquad (11.10)$$

$$\frac{\partial \log L}{\partial E_i} = \sum_{j=1}^{k} \frac{1}{E_i - (j-1)} - \sum_{j=1}^{k} C t_j = 0 \qquad (11.11)$$

Solving Eq. (11.10) for C results in

$$C = \frac{k}{\displaystyle\sum_{j=1}^{k} \{E_i - (j-1)\}t_j} \qquad (11.12)$$

Similarly, from Eq. (11.11) we get

$$\sum_{j=1}^{k} \frac{1}{\{E_i - (j-1)\}} = \sum_{j=1}^{k} t_j \cdot C \qquad (11.13)$$

By substituting Eq. (11.12) into Eq. (11.13) we get

$$\sum_{j=1}^{k} \frac{1}{\{E_i - (j-1)\}} = \frac{k \displaystyle\sum_{j=1}^{k} t_j}{\displaystyle\sum_{j=1}^{k} \{E_i - (j-1)\}t_j} \qquad (11.14)$$

The above equation is free of the proportionality constant C. Therefore the value of E_i can be estimated from this equation. In order to obtain the estimate for C, the estimated value of E_i has to be used in Eq. (11.12).

11.4.2 Model II

This software reliability model is known as the Shooman model [4]. The following assumptions are associated with this model:

 i. The total number of machine instructions remains constant.

ii.   At the beginning of integration testing, the total number of software errors in the program remains constant. Their number decreases directly as errors are rectified.
iii. No new software errors are added during the process of debugging.
iv.   The residual errors are given by the total number of errors initially present minus the cumulative errors rectified.
v.   The hazard function is proportional to the remaining number of errors (i.e. residual errors).

The hazard rate function is defined by

$$\lambda(t) = \alpha \cdot E_t(y) \tag{11.15}$$

Where

t is the system operating time.
$\lambda(t)$ is the hazard rate.
α is the proportionality constant.
y is the debugging time since the beginning of system integration.
$E_t(y)$ is the total software errors remaining in the program at time y.

The total software errors $E_t(y)$ remaining in the program at time y is given by

$$E_t(y) = \frac{E_{ti}}{I_m} - E_{cu}(y) \tag{11.16}$$

Where

E_{ti} is the total number of initial errors at time $y = 0$.
I_m is the total number of machine language instructions.
$E_{cu}(y)$ is the cumulative number of software errors rectified in interval y.

By substituting Eq. (11.16) into Eq. (11.15) we get

$$\lambda(t) = \alpha \left\{ \frac{E_{ti}}{I_m} - E_{cu}(y) \right\} \tag{11.17}$$

After substituting Eq. (11.17) into Eq. (11.2) the resulting expression becomes

$$R(t) = \exp\left[-\int_0^t \alpha \left\{ \frac{E_{ti}}{I_m} - E_{cu}(y) \right\} dz \right]$$

$$= \exp\left[-\alpha \left\{ \frac{E_{ti}}{I_m} - E_{cu}(y) \right\} t \right] \tag{11.18}$$

By substituting the above equation into Eq. (11.4) we get

$$MTTF = \int_0^\infty \exp \left[-\alpha \left\{ \frac{E_{ti}}{I_m} - E_{cu}(y) \right\} t \right] dt$$

$$= \frac{1}{\alpha \left\{ \dfrac{E_{ti}}{I_m} - E_{cu}(y) \right\}} \tag{11.19}$$

In the above equation there are two unknowns, i.e., E_{ti} and α. The values of these two parameters may be estimated with the aid of the moment matching method [17]. Considering two software error debugging periods y_1 and y_2 such that y_2 is greater than y_1,

$$\frac{\tau_1}{\theta_1} = \left[\alpha \left\{ \frac{E_{ti}}{I_m} - E_{cu}(y_1) \right\} \right]^{-1} \tag{11.20}$$

and

$$\frac{\tau_2}{\theta_2} = \left[\alpha \left\{ \frac{E_{ti}}{I_m} - E_{cu}(y_2) \right\} \right]^{-1} \tag{11.21}$$

Where

θ_1 is the total number of errors during the debugging period y_1.
θ_2 is the total number of errors during the debugging period y_2.
τ_1 is the operating time of the system corresponding to debugging period y_1.
τ_2 is the operating time of the system corresponding to debugging period y_2.

With the aid of Eqs. (11.20) and (11.21) we get

$$E_{ti} = \frac{I_m [\beta E_{cu}(y_1) - E_{cu}(y_2)]}{\beta - 1} \tag{11.22}$$

Where

$$\beta = (\theta_2 \cdot \tau_1)/(\theta_1 \cdot \tau_2)$$

$$= (MTTF_1)/MTTF_2 \tag{11.23}$$

Where

$$MTTF_1 = \frac{\tau_1}{\theta_1}$$

$$MTTF_2 = \frac{\tau_2}{\theta_2}$$

$MTTF_1$ is the mean time to software failure corresponding to period y_1.

$MTTF_2$ is the mean time to software failure corresponding to period y_2.

Substituting for E_{ti} from Eq. (11.22) into Eq. (11.20) yields the following expression:

$$\alpha = \theta_1 / \left[\tau_1 \left\{ \frac{E_{ti}}{I_m} - E_{cu}(y_1) \right\} \right] \tag{11.24}$$

Thus the values of E_{ti} and α can be estimated from Eqs. (11.22) and (11.24), respectively.

11.4.3 Model III

This is known as the Schick-Wolverton software reliability model [18]. This model is quite similar to the one developed by Jelinski and Moranda. The basic assumptions associated with Schick-Wolverton model are as follows:

   i.   Each error detected is corrected immediately without any delay.
  ii.   The Rayleigh probability density function describes the debugging time between error occurrences.
 iii.   The hazard rate is proportional to the debugging time and the remaining errors.

The hazard rate is defined by

$$\lambda(t_j) = \alpha[E_i - (j - 1)]t_j \tag{11.25}$$

Where

E_i is the total number of initial software errors.
t_j is the time between detection of the jth and $(j - 1)$st software errors.
α is the constant of proportionality.

Substituting Eq. (11.25) into Eq. (11.2) results in

$$R(t_j) = \exp\left[-\int_0^{t_j} \alpha[E_i - (j - 1)] t_j \cdot dt_j \right]$$

$$= \exp[-\alpha\{E_i - (j - 1)\}t_j^2/2] \tag{11.26}$$

With the aid of Eqs. (11.4) and (11.26) we get

$$MTTF = \int_0^\infty \exp[-\alpha\{E_i - (j - 1)\}t_j^2/2] \cdot dt_j$$

$$= [\pi/2\alpha\{E_i - (j - 1)\}]^{1/2} \tag{11.27}$$

After differentiating Eq. (11.26) with respect to t_j we get

$$\frac{dR(t_j)}{dt_j} = -f(t_j) = \alpha\{E_i - (j - 1)\}t_j \exp[-\alpha\{E_i - (j - 1)\}t_j^2/2] \tag{11.28}$$

From the above equation, the density function $f(t_j)$ is given by

$$f(t_j) = \alpha\{E_i - (j - 1)\}t_j \exp[-\alpha\{E_i - (j - 1)\}t_j^2/2] \tag{11.29}$$

In the above equation, to estimate the values of unknowns E_i and α, the maximum likelihood estimation technique [16] can be utilized. Thus with the aid of Eq. (11.29) and the likelihood estimation method, the resulting estimate expressions for E_i and α are

$$\hat{E}_i = \left[\frac{2k}{\alpha} + \sum_{j=1}^{k} (j - 1)t_j^2 \right] / T \tag{11.30}$$

Where

$$T \equiv \sum_{j=1}^{k} t_j^2$$

k is the total number of time intervals.
$\hat{E}_i$ is the maximum likelihood estimate of E_i.

and

$$\hat{\alpha} = 2 \sum_{j=1}^{k} \{E_i - (j - 1)\}^{-1} \cdot T^{-1} \tag{11.31}$$

Where

$\hat{\alpha}$ is the maximum likelihood estimate of α.

11.4.4   Model IV

This is known as the Musa model [19], which makes use of the execution time or the central processor time used in program testing as opposed to calendar development time. The basic assumptions associated with this model are as follows [1,14]:

i.   Program errors are statistically independent.
ii. The execution time between software failures is described by an exponential distribution. In other words, the piecewise failure rate is constant.
iii. The failure rate is proportional to residual software errors.
iv. The average instruction time is smaller than the execution time between software failures.
v.   The errors are rectified before software testing continues.
vi. The error rectification process is perfect. In other words, it does not introduce any new errors.

The hazard rate is defined as follows:

$$\lambda(t) = \alpha_0 \alpha_1 E_r \tag{11.32}$$

Where

t is the cumulative execution time used by the running program.
α_0 is the proportionality constant given by the mean instruction execution rate over the total number of instructions in the program.
α_1 is the constant of proportionality. This constant relates error exposure frequency to instruction execution frequency.
E_r is the number of residual software error.

The residual software errors are given by

$$E_r = E_i - E_c \tag{11.33}$$

Where

E_i is the total number of initial errors in the program.
E_c is the net number of errors removed.

Substituting Eq. (11.33) into Eq. (11.32) we get

$$\lambda(t) = \alpha_0 \cdot \alpha_1 (E_i - E_c) \tag{11.34}$$

The error correction rate is same as the hazard rate and is given by

$$\frac{dE_c}{dt} = \lambda(t) = \alpha_0 \alpha_1 (E_i - E_c) \tag{11.35}$$

By solving differential Eq. (11.35) for E_c, we get

$$E_c = E_i\{1 - \exp(-\alpha_0\alpha_1 t)\} \tag{11.36}$$

By definition, the mean time to failure MTTF is given by

$$MTTF = \frac{1}{\lambda(t)} = \frac{1}{\alpha_0 \cdot \alpha_1 E_i - \alpha_0\alpha_1 E_c} \tag{11.37}$$

Substituting for E_c from Eq. (11.36) into Eq. (11.37) yields

$$MTTF = \frac{1}{\alpha_0\alpha_1 E_i - \alpha_0\alpha_1 E_i\{1 - \exp(-\alpha_0\alpha_1 t)\}}$$

$$= \{\exp(\alpha_0\alpha_1 t)\}/\alpha_0\alpha_1 E_i \tag{11.38}$$

To make this model more effective, Eq. (11.35) is redefined as follows:

$$\frac{dE_c}{dt} = \mu_r \cdot \mu_c \lambda(t) \tag{11.39}$$

Where

μ_r is known as the error reduction factor and is given by the rate of reduction of errors divided by the error occurrence rate.

μ_c is known as the testing compression factor and is given by the error detection rate during testing divided by the error detection rate during operational use.

The number of failures N experienced in rectifying E_c amount of errors is defined as

$$N = E_c/\mu_r \tag{11.40}$$

Similarly, the initial number of failures M necessary to expose and correct E_i software errors is defined as

$$M = E_i/\mu_r \tag{11.41}$$

Therefore,

$$\mu_r = E_i/M \tag{11.42}$$

Substituting the above equation into Eq. (11.40) yields

$$N = E_c \cdot M/E_i \tag{11.43}$$

Solving differential equation (11.39) we get

$$E_c = E_i\{1 - \exp(-\alpha_0 \cdot \alpha_1 \mu_r \mu_c t)\} \tag{11.44}$$

With the aid of Eq. (11.43) and (11.44) we get

$$N = M\{1 - \exp(-\alpha_0 \alpha_1 \mu_r \mu_c t)\} \tag{11.45}$$

By substituting Eq. (11.44) into Eq. (11.37), the latter becomes

$$MTTF = \frac{1}{\alpha_0 \alpha_1 E_i - \alpha_0 \alpha_1 E_i\{1 - \exp(-\alpha_0 \alpha_1 \mu_r \mu_c t)\}}$$

$$= \{\exp(\alpha_0 \alpha_1 \mu_r \mu_c\, t)\}/\alpha_0 \alpha_1 E_i \tag{11.46}$$

Substituting for E_i from Eq. (11.41) into Eq. (11.46) yields the following expression:

$$MTTF = \{\exp(\alpha_0 \alpha_1 \mu_r \mu_c t)\}/(\alpha_0 \alpha_1 \mu_r M) \tag{11.47}$$

In the case when a mean time to failure objective of T_1 is specified for the program, the additional execution time needed to fulfill this objective (i.e. to increase $MTTF$ say, from T_0 to value T_1) is as follows:

$$\Delta t = \frac{M T_s}{\mu_c} \ln \left(\frac{T_1}{T_0} \right) \tag{11.48}$$

Where

T_s is the mean time to failure at the start of the test.

Similarly, the number of failures that must be experienced to increase $MTTF$ from T_0 to T_1 is given by

$$\Delta N = M \cdot T_s \left\{ \frac{1}{T_0} - \frac{1}{T_1} \right\} \tag{11.49}$$

11.4.5 Model V

This is known as the Weibull model and its application in software work was demonstrated by W.L. Wagoner [20]. His application of the Weibull model was concerned with the failure incidence of a 4000-statement software program.

The Weibull hazard function is defined by

$$\lambda(t) = \frac{\theta}{\mu} \left[\frac{t}{\mu} \right]^{\theta-1} \qquad (11.50)$$

Where

t   is time.
μ is the scale parameter.
θ is the shape parameter.

By substituting Eq. (11.50) into Eq. (11.2) we get the following expression for reliability

$$R(t) = \exp \left[-\int_0^t \frac{\theta}{\mu} \left[\frac{z}{\mu} \right]^{\theta-1} dz \right]$$

$$= \exp \left[- \left[\frac{t}{\mu} \right]^{\theta} \right] \qquad (11.51)$$

With the aid of Eqs. (11.4) and (11.51), the mean time to failure is given by

$$MTTF = \int_0^\infty \exp \left[- \left[\frac{t}{\mu} \right]^{\theta} \right] dt$$

$$= \left[\mu \Gamma \left[\frac{1}{\theta} \right] \right] / \theta$$

Where

$$\Gamma(\beta) = \int_0^\infty x^{(\beta-1)} \cdot e^{-x} dx \qquad (11.52)$$

$$\beta \equiv \frac{1}{\theta} \qquad (11.53)$$

Eq. (11.52) is known as the gamma function.

11.4.6 Model VI

This is known as the geometric model [21]. Quite similar to the Jelinski-Moranda model, this model is based on the assumption that the hazard rate between successive software errors reflects a geometric progression. Other assumptions associated with this model are similar to the ones for Jelinski-

Moranda model. The hazard function of the geometric model for the jth interval is described by

$$\lambda(t) = AB^{j-1} \qquad (11.54)$$

Where

A is a constant corresponding to the initial failure rate.

B is a constant corresponding to the failure rate step ratio.

The values of A and B can be estimated from the collected data. With the aid of Eqs. (11.2) and (11.54) we get

$$R(t_j) = \exp[-AB^\alpha t_j] \qquad (11.55)$$

Where

$\alpha\ [i.e.\ (j-1)]$ is the total number of time intervals.

t_j is the jth interval elapsed time.

Substituting Eq. (11.55) into Eq. (11.4) yields the following expression for mean time to failure:

$$MTTF = \int_0^\infty \exp[-AB^\alpha t_j]dt_j$$

$$= [AB^\alpha]^{-1} \qquad (11.56)$$

After differentiating Eq. (11.55) with respect to t_j, we get

$$\frac{dR(t_j)}{dt_j} = -f(t_j) = -AB^{j-1}\exp[-AB^{j-1}t_j] \qquad (11.57)$$

The unknowns A and B can be estimated with the aid of maximum likelihood estimation technique [21]. Thus with the aid of Eq. (11.58), the likelihood function becomes

$$L(t_1, t_2, \ldots, t_m) = \prod_{j=1}^m \{AB^{j-1}\exp[-AB^{j-1}t_j]\} \qquad (11.59)$$

Where

$t_1, t_2, \ldots, t_m$ is the sample of intervals of time between successive software errors.

Taking the logarithms of Eq. (11.59), the resulting expression becomes

$$\log L = m \log A + \sum_{j=1}^m \log B^{j-1} - \sum_{j=1}^m AB^{j-1}t_j \qquad (11.60)$$

Taking a partial derivative of Eq. (11.60) with respect to A and B and setting the resulting expressions equal to zero, we get

$$\frac{\partial \log L}{\partial A} = \frac{m}{A} - \sum_{j=1}^{m} B^{j-1} t_j = 0 \qquad (11.61)$$

$$\frac{\partial \log L}{\partial B} = \frac{1}{B} \sum_{j=1}^{m} (j - 1) - A \sum_{j=1}^{m} (j - 1) B^{j-2} t_j = 0 \qquad (11.62)$$

Solving Eq. (11.61) for A results in

$$A = \frac{m}{\sum_{j=1}^{m} B^{j-1} t_j} \qquad (11.63)$$

Substituting Eq. (11.63) into Eq. (11.62) yields

$$\frac{m + 1}{2} = \left[\sum_{j=1}^{m} j B^j t_j \right] / \sum_{j=1}^{m} B^j t_j \qquad (11.64)$$

The value of B can be estimated from the above equation. In order to obtain an estimate for A, one has to use the estimated value of B in Eq. (11.63).

11.5 SUMMARY

This chapter discussed various aspects of software reliability modeling. The theories used to quantify software reliability were grouped into four basic categories: empirical estimation, complexity, reliability estimation modeling, and error seeding. The history of software reliability models was briefly discussed, and software reliability models were classified into five distinct categories: input space models, calendar time models, Bayesian models, semi-Markov models, and execution time models. Each of these categories was briefly described.

Six selected software reliability models were presented. These are the Jelinski-Moranda model, the Shooman model, the Schick-Wolverton model, the Musa model, the Weibull model, and the geometric model. For Jelinski-Moranda, Shooman, Schick-Wolverton, Weibull, and geometric models, the hazard rate, reliability, and mean time to failure equations were presented. The maximum likelihood estimated method was used to estimate the values of unknowns associated with Jelinski-Moranda, Schick-Wolverton, and geometric models. In the case of the Shooman model, the moment matching method was used to estimate the values of its unknowns.

11.6 EXERCISES

1. Discuss in detail the history of software reliability models.
2. What are the theories used to quantify software reliability?
3. Describe in detail the following terms concerned with software reliability:

    i. Semi-Markov models
    ii. Execution time models
    iii. Bayesian models
    iv. Calendar time models

4. List the assumptions associated with the Weibull software reliability model.
5. Discuss the differences and similarities between Jelinski-Moranda and Schick-Wolverton reliability models.
6. What are the advantages and disadvantages of the Musa software reliability model?
7. Make comparisons between the execution time models and the Bayesian models used in software reliability work.

11.7 REFERENCES

1. T.E. Konchan, "Software Reliability and the Musa Model", Proceedings of the Annual American Society for Quality Control Conference, 1983, pp. 101–107.
2. G.R. Hudson, "Program Errors as a Birth-and-Death Process", Report No. SP-3011, System Development Corporation, December 1967.
3. Z. Jelinski and P.B. Moranda, "Software Reliability Research", in *Statistical Computer Performance Evaluation,* Edited by W. Freiberger, Academic Press, New York, 1972, pp. 465–484.
4. M.L. Shooman, "Probablistic Models for Software Reliability Prediction", in *Statistical Computer Performance Evaluation,* Edited by W. Freiberger, Academic Press, New York, 1972, pp. 485–502.
5. G.J. Schick and R.W. Wolverton, "Assessment of Software Reliability", presented at 11th Annual Meeting of German Operations Research Society, Hamburg, Germany, Sept. 6–8, 1972; in Proceedings of the Operations Research, Physica-Verlag, Wurzburg-Wien, 1973, pp. 395–422.
6. N.F. Schneidewind, "An Approach to Software in Reliability Prediction and Quality Control", Proceedings of the AFIPS Fall Conference, Published by AFIPS Press, Montvale, New Jersey, 1972, pp. 837–847.
7. J.D. Musa, "A Theory of Software Reliability and its Applications", IEEE Transactions on Software Engineering, Vol. 1, 1975, pp. 312–327.
8. J.D. Musa, "The Measurement and Management of Software Reliability", Proceedings of the Institute of Electrical and Electronics Engineers (IEEE), Vol. 68, 1980, pp. 1131–1143.

9. B. Littlewood and J.L. Verrall, "A Bayesian Reliability Growth Model for Computer Software", Journal of Royal Statistical Society—Series C, Vol. 22, 1972, pp. 70–77.

10. A.L. Goel and K. Okumoto, "Bayesian Software Prediction Models, Report No. RADC-TR-78-155" (5 Volumes), 1978. Available from Rome Air Development Center, Rome, New York.

11. A.L. Goel and K. Okumoto, "Time Dependent Error-Detection Rate Model for Software Reliability and Other Performance Measures", IEEE Transactions on Reliability, Vol. 28, 1979, pp. 206–211.

12. A.N. Sukert, "An Investigation of Software Reliability Models", Proceedings of the Annual Reliability and Maintainability Symposium, 1977, pp. 478–484.

13. G.J. Schick and R.W. Wolverton, "An Analysis of Competing Software Reliability Models", IEEE Transactions on Software Engineering, Vol. 4, 1978, pp. 104–120.

14. R. Dunn and R. Ullman, *Quality Assurance for Computer Software,* McGraw-Hill Book Company, New York, 1982.

15. B.S. Dhillon and C. Singh, *Engineering Reliability: New Techniques and Applications,* John Wiley & Sons, New York, 1981.

16. B.S. Dhillon, *Reliability Engineering in System Design and Operation,* Van Nostrand Reinhold Company, New York, 1983.

17. M.L. Shooman, *Probabilistic Reliability: An Engineering Approach,* McGraw-Hill Book Company, New York, 1968.

18. R.W. Wolverton and G.J. Schick, "Assessment of Software Reliability", TRW Systems Group, Report No. TRW-SS-72-04, September, 1972.

19. J.D. Musa, "A Theory of Software Reliability and Its Application", IEEE Transactions on Software Engineering, Vol. 1, September 1975, pp. 312–327.

20. W.L. Wagoner, "The Final Report on Software Reliability Study", The Aerospace Corporation, Report No. TOR-0074(4112)-1, August 15, 1973.

21. P.B. Moranda "Prediction of Software Reliability During Debugging", Proceedings of the Annual Reliability and Maintainability Symposium, 1975, pp. 327–332.

12
MODELS FOR SOFTWARE

12.1 INTRODUCTION

Just as in many other established disciplines, mathematical models are used in software work. These models make use of symbols to represent an entity. In computer software work, various kinds of models are developed to find solutions to problems in many diverse areas. Some of these areas are as follows:

- i.   Software costing
- ii.   Software manpower
- iii. Software reliability
- iv.   Predicting the course and consequences of software development
- v.   Software maintenance
- vi.   Software testing

Therefore, it is not wrong to state that mathematical models are also an important tool of software specialists, and understanding of such models is important to these professionals to produce better software products. In this chapter, each and every published mathematical model in software work is not presented; only selected ones considered to be relatively simple, practical, or easy to understand are included. The models covered address several diverse areas in software work, for example, software costing, software testing, and software manpower. The mathematical models related to software reliability were presented in Chapter 11.

12.2 SELECTED MATHEMATICAL MODELS

This section presents several mathematical models and formulas considered to be useful in making decisions related to software work.

12.2.1 Model I

This model was developed to estimate software development cost in the U.S. Air Force [1,2]. The software development cost is expressed as follows:

$$k_{sd} = \alpha_m \cdot k(1 + \mu) \tag{12.1}$$

Where

k_{sd}	is the software development cost.
k	is the mean labor rate (\$/man–month). This rate includes costs of administration, overhead, fees, and so on.
μ	is the ratio of secondary to primary costs (costs associated with documentation production, computer time, and travel are known as the secondary costs).
α_m	is the man–months of the total manpower required. This includes design, analysis, code, test, and so on.

The value of α_m may be estimated from the following expression:

$$\alpha_m = \mu_1 s^{\mu_2} \tag{12.2}$$

Where

s	is the program size (i.e. number of delivered instructions given in either source or object code in thousands).
μ_1	is the factor whose value depends on application and code type. For example, in the case of general application and object code, the value of μ_1 is 4.790. On the other hand, in the case of general application and source code, the value of μ_1 is 5.258.
μ_2	is the factor whose value depends on application and code type. For example, in the case of general application and object code, the value of μ_2 is 0.991. On the other hand, in the case of general application and source code, the value of μ_2 is 1.057.

12.2.2 Model II

This model is used to estimate software life cycle cost. In this model, the total life cycle cost of the software is composed of seven components. These components are as follows:

    i.   Design cost
   ii.   Analysis cost
  iii.   Code and checkout cost
  iv.   Test and integration cost
   v.   Documentation cost
  vi.   Installation cost
 vii.   Operating and support cost

Thus, the software life cycle cost is given by

$$c_L = c_1 + c_2 + c_3 + c_4 + c_5 + c_6 + c_7 \tag{12.3}$$

Where

c_1 is the design cost.
c_2 is the analysis cost.
c_3 is the code and checkout cost.
c_4 is the test and integration cost.
c_5 is the documentation cost.
c_6 is the installation cost.
c_7 is the operating and support cost.

Each of the above categories is described in detail in reference [3].

12.2.3 Model III

This model belongs to the family of test-related software reliability models. The model can be used to approximate the number of tests required for a defined value of reliability. In this model, the probability that an error occurs in the field is expressed as follows:

$$F_{ef} = F_{tm} \cdot F_{ue} \qquad (12.4)$$

Where

F_{ef} is the probability that an error occurs in the field.
F_{tm} is the probability of the program tester missing the error.
F_{ue} is the probability of the user exciting the error.

The value of F_{ue} can be obtained from the following expression:

$$F_{ue} = \frac{\theta}{\theta_1} \qquad (12.5)$$

Where

θ_1 is the number of possible equally likely input values of the module.
θ is the number of possible equally likely input values (of the module) causing errors.

Similarly, the probability F_{tm} is given by

$$F_{tm} = \left[1 - \frac{\theta}{\theta_1} \right]^n \qquad (12.6)$$

Where

n is the number of independent tests conducted.
F_{tm} is the probability that an error was missed n times.

After substituting Eqs. (12.5) and (12.6) into Eq. (12.4), we get

$$F_{ef} = \beta(1 - \beta)^n \leqslant \beta e^{-\beta n} \tag{12.7}$$

Where

$$\beta = \frac{\theta}{\theta_1}$$

The above equation can be used to calculate the approximate number of tests required for a specified value of reliability. In addition, it can be concluded from Eq. (12.7), the value of n has to be much larger than β to obtain a small value for F_{ef}.

12.2.4 Model IV

This model is concerned with calculating the program memory requirement. The following equation is used for this purpose [5]:

$$M_{re} = L_p + s_{vc} + s_{ds} \tag{12.8}$$

Where

M_{re} is the memory requirement.

L_p is the length of the program. This can be estimated with the aid of *Zipf* length and estimates of operator and operand types.

s_{vc} is the variable and constant storage length. This can be obtained by analysing input parameters and constants.

s_{ds} is the storage length of the data structure. This storage length can be obtained through the analysis of the structures and algorithms being used in the design.

12.2.5 Model V

This model can be used to calculate the cost of transferring software from one computer system to another computer system. The model was developed in 1970 [6]. The total cost of software transfer is expressed as

$$k = \Sigma M_i \frac{A\alpha_1 + B\alpha_2}{\alpha_1 \cdot \alpha_2} k_d + \Sigma k_m + k_{dt} + \Sigma k_{mat} \tag{12.9}$$

Where

$A \equiv (1 + f_{si})$
$B \equiv (1 + f_{sd} + f_{dd})$

k is the total cost of transferring software from one computer system to another.

f_{si} is the degradation factor associated with system integration.

f_{sd} is the degradation factor associated with documentation.

f_{dd} is the degradation factor associated with program instability.

α_1 is the baseline conversion rate (instructions or statements per man–day). This rate depends on the type of computer language used and on factors such as redesign, recode, and reprogram. Several values of this rate are tabulated in reference [3].

α_2 is the baseline test production rate.

M_i is the number of instructions expected to be transferred manually.

k_d is the man–day cost.

k_m is the miscellaneous cost. This includes the cost of training, keypunching, planning, etc.

k_{dt} is the cost associated with transferring data.

k_{mat} is the cost associated with machine-assisted transfer methods, for example, translation and decompilation.

12.2.6   Model VI

This mathematical model is concerned with measuring the efficiency of testing. The efficiency index is defined as follows [7]:

$$I = \frac{E_d}{E_d + E_u} \cdot 100 \tag{12.10}$$

Where

I is the efficiency measure in percentage.

E_d is the number of software errors discovered.

E_u is the number of software errors still remaining after the test.

Example 12.1

Suppose a program contains 1,200 errors and has to go through four test phases, i.e. unit test, integration, qualification, and system. For each test phase the software errors found and still remaining after the test are tabulated in Table 12.1. Calculate the value of the efficiency index for each test phase, in addition to the value of the overall index.

Table 12.1   Software Errors Found and Remaining After Each Test

Test Phase	Errors Found in the Program E_d	Errors Remaining in the Program E_u
Unit test	600	600
Integration	300	300
Qualification	150	150
System	75	75

With the aid of Eq. (12.10) and the values given in Table 12.1, for each test phase we get the following result for the efficiency index:

i. *Unit test*

$$I_u = \frac{600}{600 + 600} \cdot 100 = 50\%$$

ii. *Integration*

$$I_i = \frac{300}{300 + 300} \cdot 100 = 50\%$$

iii. *Qualification*

$$I_q = \frac{150}{150 + 150} \cdot 100 = 50\%$$

iv. *System*

$$I_s = \frac{75}{75 + 75} \cdot 100 = 50\%$$

It is to be noted that the value of the efficiency index is the same for all four test phases. From Table 12.1 the total number of errors found in the program is 1125. The total number of errors still remaining in the program is

$$E_u = 1200 - 1125 = 75$$

Thus the value of the overall efficiency index from Eq. (12.10) is given by

$$I = \frac{1125}{1125 + 75} \cdot 100$$

$$= 93.75\%$$

The overall efficiency of finding errors in the program is 93.75%. However, the value of the efficiency index was only 50% for each test phase.

12.2.7 Model VII

This model is known as McCabe's complexity model and is used to estimate the value of measure of complexity. In this model the cyclomatic number of classical graph theory is computed [8]. The program control structure is the program graph. The equation for the model is expressed as follows:

$$v(g) = b - k + 2c \qquad (12.11)$$

Where

$v(g)$ is the cyclomatic number (i.e. measure of program complexity).

c is the number of linked parts (a module in a program may be considered as a unique part).

k is the number of software processing nodes (i.e., including decision points).

b is the number of paths between the nodes.

According to McCabe [8] one should restrict modules in a program to cyclomatic complexities of 10.

12.2.8 Model VIII

This model was developed to estimate the software development time in months [1,2,3]. The duration of software development is given by

$$M = [\alpha + \beta s^{0.067}]^{-1} \qquad (12.12)$$

Where

M is the software development time (in months).

α is a constant (in this model the value of α is 99.25).

β is a constant (in this case the value of β is 0.233).

s is the estimated program size (in object code).

12.2.9 Model IX

This model is concerned with computing the performance index. In reference [9] the performance index is defined as follows:

$$I_p = \frac{f_m}{t_p} \cdot 10^6 \tag{12.13}$$

Where

I_p is the performance index.
f_m is the memory factor.
t_p is the processor time, in seconds/million operations.

Furthermore, the memory factor f_m is expressed as follows:

$$f_m = [(w - 7)\mu \cdot w_m]^\gamma / [(32{,}000)(36 - 7)]^\gamma \tag{12.14}$$

Where

γ is the weighting factor associated with exponential memory. For commercial and scientific computations, its values are 0.333 and 0.5, respectively.
μ is the number of words in memory.
w_m is the word factor associated with fixed word length and variable word length systems; its values are 1 and 2, respectively.
w is the word length (in bits).

Similarly, the processor time t_p is given by

$$t_p = T_{cpu} + T_{n0} \tag{12.15}$$

Where

T_{cpu} is the central processing unit (CPU) time given in per million operations.
T_{n0} is the non-overlapped input/output (I/O) time given in per million operations.

The central processing unit time T_{cpu} is defined by

$$T_{cpu} = f_5 \cdot t_0 + f_1 t_{fa} + f_4 t_d + f_2 t_a + f_3 t_m \tag{12.16}$$

Where

t_0 is the logic operation time given in microseconds.
f_i is the ith weighting factor representing the percentage of various operations, for $i = 1, 2, 3, 4, 5$. For scientific and commercial

computations the values of f_1, f_2, f_3, f_4, and f_5 are (0.10, 0.25), (0.1, 0.0), (0.06, 0.01), (0.02, 0.0) and (0.72, 0.74), respectively.

t_{fa} is the fixed-point addition time in microseconds.

t_d is the division time in microseconds.

t_a is the floating-point addition time in microseconds.

t_m is the multiplication time in microseconds.

The non-overlapped input/output (I/O) time T_{n0} is given by

$$T_{n0} = Q T_{pm} + (1 - Q)T_s \qquad (12.17)$$

Where

T_{pm} is the I/O system time (primary).

T_s is the I/O system time (secondary).

Q is the fraction of the I/O characters managed by the I/O system (i.e. primary).

The input/output system time (primary or secondary) can be computed from the expression given in reference [9]. The values of the commercial performance index for various IBM machines were as follows:

  i.   119 (IBM 650)
 ii.   1845 (IBM 1401)
iii.   17,469 (IBM 360/30)
 iv.   172,244 (IBM 370/135)
  v.   8353 (IBM 53/10)

12.2.10   Model X

This model demonstrates that as the manpower in a department increases to a large number, the productivity reaches a steady state value. The model will be useful to software or hardware managers in manpower planning. This model is based on the assumption that each (concerned) person in the department produces software (or hardware) reports and spends time to read software (or hardware) reports produced by others in the department [10]. The following symbols are associated with the model:

N is the average number of days to complete a software report (this time does not include the time spent reading reports produced by others, but the time spent for investigation, analysis, writing, and so on is included).

M is the total number of software reports produced annually in the department.

w is the total number of professional workers in the department.

D is the mean number of days taken to read a software report.

r is the fraction of all software reports given to a professional worker (more clearly, those reports which the professional worker is expected to read).

The following two assumptions are concerned with the model:

i.   Each professional employee reads rM number of software reports annually.

ii. A year has 240 working days.

The total time spent by a professional employee to read software reports in one year is given by

$$T_{te} = rMD \tag{12.18}$$

The total time left (in one year) for the employee to produce his or her software reports is

$$T_c = (240 - T_{te}) = (240 - rMD) \tag{12.19}$$

Dividing the right hand side of Eq. (12.19) by N yields the following number of reports to be turned out annually by the single employee:

$$R_a = \frac{(240 - rMD)}{N} \tag{12.20}$$

The total number of software reports produced annually in the department is

$$M = w \cdot \left[\frac{(240 - rMD)}{N} \right] \tag{12.21}$$

Since M appears on both sides of Eq. (12.21), by rearranging that equation explicitly in terms of M, we get

$$M = \frac{240w}{N + rDw} \tag{12.22}$$

Dividing the top and bottom of the right hand side of Eq. (12.22) with w we get

$$M = \frac{(240w)/w}{(N + rDw)/w}$$

$$= \frac{240}{(N/w) + rD} \tag{12.23}$$

When the value of w (i.e. the total number of professional workers in the department) becomes very large in Eq. (12.23), the M approaches its steady state (upper limit) value, i.e.

$$M_{ss} = \frac{240}{rD} \qquad (12.24)$$

Where

M_{ss} is the steady state value of M.

The above expression clearly demonstrates that regardless of the number of professional workers employed in the department, there is an upper limit for the productivity of software reports.

12.2.11 Model XI

This model is used to estimate the size of a new program [1,2]. The following two assumptions are associated with this model:

i.   The size of an earlier program for the same kind of application is known.
ii.   The number of major functions carried out by the analogous program (i.e. the earlier program for the same kind of application) is known.

The following equation is used to estimated the new program size (in object words):

$$W_{ns} = \left[\frac{W_{0s}}{F_0^{0.678}} \right] \cdot F_n^{0.678} \qquad (12.25)$$

Where

W_{0s} is the old program size (object words).
W_{ns} is the new program size (object words).
F_0 is the number of major functions carried out by the old program.
F_n is the number of major functions to be carried out by the new program.

12.2.12 Model XII

This model is used to estimate software marketing cost [9]. The marketing cost is composed of the following two types of major costs:

i.   Cost associated with the home office.
ii.   Cost associated with field sales.

The cost associated with field sales is expressed as

$$c_s = s_f + c \tag{12.26}$$

Where

c_s is the cost associated with field sales.
c is the commissions.
s_f is the field salaries (including overhead).

The total marketing cost per annum is given by

$$c_{tm} = c_h + s_f + c$$

$$= c_h + (s_p \cdot s_b + s_p s_a A)Z + R_c \cdot \alpha \tag{12.27}$$

Where

$Z = (1 + R_0)$
c_{tm} is the total yearly marketing cost.
C_h is the cost associated with the home office.
R_0 is the overhead rate.
s_p is the number of persons involved in sales.
A is the number of system analysts employed per salesperson.
s_a is the yearly salary of a system analyst.
α is the yearly product sales.
R_c is the commission rate.
s_b is the base yearly salary of a salesperson.

12.2.13 Model XIII

This model is concerned with estimating time taken for one processing step. More clearly, the time for processing one item of data from input to output can be obtained with the aid of this model. Thus the total time, τ, needed for a single processing step is given by [11]:

$$\tau = \sum_{i=1}^{5} \tau_i \tag{12.28}$$

Where

τ_1 is the input and output time.
τ_2 is the waiting time in the system.
τ_3 is the time associated with external operations.
τ_4 is the time associated with transmitting data in interactive operation.
τ_5 is the time associated with the central processing unit (i.e. processing time).

12.2.14 Model XIV

This model is used to estimate central processing unit time (processing time), for one processing step. This time is calculated by using the following simple equation:

$$\tau_5 = c \cdot \tau_c \tag{12.29}$$

Where

c is the number of commands needed to execute a single processing step.

τ_c is the mean time associated with executing a single command.

12.2.15 Model XV

This model is due to the effort of Maurice Halstead [12]. To predict software development course and consequences, the Halstead model provides various useful outputs [7].

According to Halstead, the program observed length and vocabulary, respectively, are given by

$$L_p = P_{0t} + P_{0d} \tag{12.30}$$

and

$$V_p = O_{pr} + O_{pd} \tag{12.31}$$

Where

L_p is the program observed length.
V_p is the program vocabulary.
P_{0i} is the number of occurrences: $i = t$ (of the operators), $i = d$ (of the operands).
O_{pr} is the total number of unique operators (e.g. keywords) contained in a program.
O_{pd} is the total number of unique operands.

The volume v of the program can be expressed as

$$v = (P_{0t} + P_{0d}) \log_2(O_{pr} + O_{pd})$$

$$= L_p \log_2 V_p \tag{12.32}$$

The number of errors, E, in a program prior to testing is given by

$$E = c \frac{V}{D_n} \tag{12.33}$$

Where

D_n is the average number of discriminations made between potential bugs in programming.

c is a constant.

12.2.16   Model XVI

This model is used to estimate memory size, s_m, in thousands of objective code words. For this purpose the following equation was developed [1,2]:

$$s_m = \alpha_1 \cdot c (F_m^{\alpha_2} \cdot s_w^{\alpha_3} / T_c^{\alpha_4})$$ (12.34)

Where

$\alpha_1 = 0.177$
$\alpha_2 = 0.337$
$\alpha_3 = 0.147$
$\alpha_4 = 0.770$

c is a constant (its values for weapon fire control, signal processing, navigation, and interfacing are 4.451, 2.573, 2.565, and 2.781, respectively).

s_w is the word size (bits).

F_m is the number of major functions required to be carried out by the software.

T_c is the processor cycle time in microseconds (associated with either retrieving or storing a word in memory of the processor).

12.3   SUMMARY

This chapter presented sixteen selective mathematical models which are concerned directly or indirectly with computer software. These models belong to various areas associated with software; such as the following:

i.   Software manpower
ii.   Software costing
iii.   Software testing
iv.   Memory size estimation
v.   Performance measurement

Models I through IV are concerned with estimating the software development cost, the software life cycle cost, the number of tests required for a defined value of reliability, and the program memory requirement, respectively.

Models V through VIII deal with estimating the cost of transferring software from one computer system to another, the efficiency of testing, the value of measure of complexity, and the software development time in months, respectively. The value of performance index, the steady state value of productivity of a department, the size of the new program, and the marketing cost can be computed with the aid of Models IX through XII, respectively.

The last group of four models can be used to estimate the time taken for processing one item of data from input to output, the central processing unit time, the number of errors in a program prior to testing, and the memory size, respectively.

12.4 EXERCISES

1. Discuss in detail the term "models for software".
2. Describe the most important components of the software life cycle cost.
3. Prove that the probability that a software error occurs in the field is given by

$$F_{ef} = \frac{m}{m_1}\left(1 - \frac{m}{m_1}\right)^n \tag{12.35}$$

Where

   m is the number of possible equally likely input values of the module causing errors.

   m_1 is the number of possible equally likely input values of the module.

   n is the number of independent tests conducted.

4. Make comparisons of models IV and XVI presented in this chapter.
5. Suppose a software program contains 800 errors and has to go through four test phases, i.e. unit test, integration, qualification, and system. For each test phase, the software errors found are still remaining after the test are tabulated in Table 12.2. Calculate the value of the efficiency index for each test phase, in addition to the value of the overall index.

Table 12.2 Software Errors Found and Remaining After Each Test

Test Phase	Errors Found in the Program E_d	Errors Remaining in the Program E_u
Unit test	400	400
Integration	200	200
Qualification	100	100
System	50	50

232   B.S. Dhillon

12.5 REFERENCES

1. J.H. Herd, J.N. Postak, and W.E. Russell, "Software Cost Estimation Study—Study Results—Reports", Prepared by Doty Associates, Inc., for United States Air Force, Report No. RADC-TR-77-220, Vol. I, Feb. 1977, Report No. ADA-042-264. Available from the National Technical Information Service (NTIS), Springfield, Virginia.

2. D.L. Doty, P.J. Nelson, and K.R. Stewart, "Software Cost Estimation Study—Guidelines for Improved Software Cost Estimating", Prepared by Doty Associates, Inc. for United States Air Force, Report No. RADC-TR-77-220, Vol. II, Feb. 1977, Report No. ADA-044-609. Available from the National Technical Information Service (NTIS), Springfield, Virginia.

3. M.E. Earles, *Factors, Formulas, and Structures for Life Cycle Costing*, Published by Eddins-Earles, Concord, Massachusetts, 1978.

4. A. Laemmel, "A Statistical Theory of Computer Program Testing", Report No. SRS 119/POLY EE 80-004, Dept. of Electrical Engineering, Polytechnic Institute of New York, 1980.

5. M.L. Shooman, *Software Engineering*, McGraw-Hill Book Company, New York, 1983.

6. W. Hahn and J. Stone, "Software Transfer Cost Estimation Technique", M70-43, MITRE Corporation, July 1970. Report No. ADA 055574. Available from the National Technical Information Service (NTIS), Springfield, Virginia.

7. R. Dunn and R. Ullman, *Quality Assurance for Computer Software*, McGraw-Hill Book Company, New York, 1982.

8. T. McCabe, "A Complexity Measure", IEEE Transactions on Software Engineering, Vol. 2, No. 4, 1976, pp. 308–320.

9. M. Phister, *Data Processing Technology and Economics*, The Santa Monica Publishing Company, Santa Monica, California, 1976.

10. F.P. Alder, "Relationships Between Organization Size and Efficiency", Management Science, Vol. 7, 1960, pp. 80–84.

11. W. End, H. Gotthardt, and R. Winkelmann, *Software Development: Manual for the Planning, Realization, and Installation of DP Systems*, John Wiley & Sons, Chichester, 1983.

12. M. Halstead, *Elements of Software Science*, Elsevier-North-Holland, Inc., New York, 1977.

APPENDIX
BIBLIOGRAPHY OF LITERATURE ON COMPUTER SYSTEM RELIABILITY

A.1 INTRODUCTION

Over the past number of years, hundreds of publications on computer system reliability have appeared [7, 113, 298]. These publications can be grouped into two major groups, i.e., computer hardware reliability and computer software reliability. Therefore this appendix presents selected references on both these areas separately. These references will provide a useful service to readers in the event they desire to probe deeper into computer system reliability. Some of the books listed in section A.2 are not entirely related to computer hardware reliability but are somewhat related to it.

A.2 COMPUTER HARDWARE RELIABILITY

Books

1. T. Anderson and B. Randell, Eds., *Computing Systems Reliability,* Cambridge University Press, Cambridge, 1979.

2. B. Beizer, *Micro-Analysis of Computer System Performance,* Van Nostrand Reinhold Co., New York, 1978.

3. B. Beizer, *The Architecture and Engineering of Digital Computer Complexes,* Plenum Press, New York, 1971.

4. K.M. Chandy and M. Reiser, Eds., *Computer Performance,* North-Holland Publishing Company, Amsterdam, 1977.

5. J.C. Cluley, *Electronic Equipment Reliability,* Macmillan Book Company, New York, 1974.

6. *Computer Systems Reliability,* Published by Infotech International Ltd., Maidenhead, England, 1974. (There is no author for this publication).

7. B.S. Dhillon and C. Singh, *Engineering Reliability: New Techniques and Applications,* John Wiley and Sons, New York, 1981.

8. M.F. Drummond, *Evaluation and Measurement Techniques for Digital Computer Systems,* Prentice-Hall, Englewood Cliffs, New Jersey, 1973.

9. D. Ferrari, *Computing System Performance Evaluation,* Prentice-Hall, Englewood Cliffs, New Jersey, 1978.

10. W. Freiberger, Ed., with the collaboration of U. Grenander, B.H. Margolin, and R.F. Tsao, *Statistical Computer Performance Evaluation*, Academic Press, New York, 1972.

11. H. Hellerman and T.F. Canroy, *Computer System Performance*, McGraw-Hill Book Co., New York, 1975.

12. G.D. Kraft and W.N. Toy, *Microprogrammed Control and Reliable Design of Small Computers*, Prentice-Hall, Inc., Englewood Cliffs, New Jersey, 1981.

13. S.A. Lebedev, Ed., *Computer Engineering*, translated from the Russian by J. Stuart, translation edited by J.P. Cleave and F.A. Sowan, Pergamon Press, New York, 1978.

14. R. Longbottom, *Computer Systems Reliability*, John Wiley & Sons, Chichester, 1980.

15. J. Martin, *Design of Realtime Computer Systems*, Prentice-Hall, Englewood Cliffs, New Jersey, 1967.

16. G.J. Myers, *Advances in Computer Architecture*, John Wiley & Sons, New York, 1982.

17. S. Osaki and T. Nishio, *Reliability Evaluation of Some Fault-Tolerant Computer Architectures*, Springer-Verlag, Berlin, 1980.

18. W.H. Pierce, *Failure-Tolerant Computer Design*, Academic Press, New York, 1965.

19. B. Randell and T. Anderson, (Eds.), *System Reliability and Structuring in Computing Systems Reliability*, Cambridge University Press, New York, 1979.

20. C.H. Saucer and K.M. Chandy, *Computer Systems Performance Modelling*, Prentice-Hall, Englewood Cliffs, New Jersey, 1981.

21. F.F. Sellers, Jr., M. Hsiao, and L.W. Bearnson, *Error Detecting Logic for Digital Computers*, McGraw-Hill Book Co., New York, 1968.

22. D.P. Siewiorek and R.S. Swarz, *The Theory and Practice of Reliable System Design*, Digital Press, New York, 1982.

23. L. Svobodova, *Computer Performance Measures and Evaluation Methods: Analysis and Applications*, American Elsevier, New York, 1976.

24. R.H. Wilcox, *Redundancy Techniques for Computing Systems*, Spartan Books, Inc., New York, 1962.

Articles

25. J.A. Abraham, "An Algorithm for the Accurate Reliability Evaluation of TMR Networks", proceedings of the International Conference on Fault-Tolerant Computing, 1973, pp. 100–105.

26. K.K. Aggarwal, Y.C. Chopra, and J.S Bajwa, "Reliability Evaluation by Network Decomposition", IEEE Transactions on Reliability, Vol. R-31, No. 4, 1982, pp. 355–358.

27. P.W. Agnew, R.E. Forbes, and C.B. Stieglitz, "An Approach to Self-Repairing Computers", Digest of the First Annual IEEE Computer Conference, 1967, pp. 198–204.

28. D.A. Anderson and G. Metze, "Design of Totally Self-Checking Circuits for *m*-out-of-*n* Codes", IEEE Transactions on Computers, Vol. C-22, 1973, pp. 263–269.

29. J.W. Anderson and J.C. Browne, "Graph Models of Computer Systems Application to Performance Evaluation of an Operating System", Proceedings of the International

Symposium on Computer Performance, Modelling, Measurement and Evaluation, Boston, Massachusetts, 1976, pp. 166–178.

30. T. Anderson, P.A. Lee, and S.K. Shrivastava, "A Model of Recoverability in Multilevel Systems", IEEE Transactions on Software Engineering, Vol. SE-4, 1978, pp. 486–494.

31. G.P. Anderson, "Operational Reliability of the Athena Computer", Proceedings of the Eighth National Symposium on Reliability and Quality Control, Washington D.C., 1962, pp. 357–366.

32. J.E. Anderson and F.J. Macri, "Multiple Redundancy Applications in a Computer", Proceedings of the Annual Symposium on Reliability, 1967, pp. 553–562.

33. J.E. Angus and L.E. James, "Combined Hardware/Software Reliability Models", Proceedings of the Annual Reliability and Maintainability Symposium, 1982, pp. 176–181.

34. W.E. Arens and D.A. Rennels, "A Fault-Tolerant Computer for Autonomous Spacecraft", Proceedings of the International Conference on Fault-Tolerant Computing, 1983, pp. 467–470.

35. J. Arlat and J.C. Laprie, "Performance-Related Dependability Evaluation of Supercomputer Systems", Microelectronics and Reliability, Vol. 24, 1984, pp. 717–742.

36. T.F. Arnold, "The Concept of Coverage and its Effect on the Reliability Model of a Repairable System", IEEE Transactions on Computers, Vol. C-22, 1973, pp. 251–254.

37. A. Avizienis, "Approaches to Computer Reliability—Then and Now", AFIPS, Proceedings of the Conference of the American Federation of Information Processing Societies, Vol. 45, 1976, pp. 401–411.

38. A. Avizienis, "Arithmetic Error Codes", Proceedings of the IEEE Symposium on Fault Tolerant Computing, 1971, pp. 118–121.

39. A. Avizienis, "Design of Fault-Tolerant Computers", Proceedings of the Conference of the American Federation of Information Processing Societies, AFIPS, Vol. 31, 1967, pp. 733–743.

40. A. Avizienis and D.A. Rennels, "Fault Tolerance Experiments with the JPL STAR Computer", Proceedings of the IEEE Computer Society International Conference, COMPCON, 1972, pp. 321–324.

41. A. Avizienis et al., "The STAR (Self-Testing and Repair) Computer", IEEE Transactions on Computers, Vol. C-20, 1971, pp. 1312–1321.

42. A. Avizienis, "Fault-Tolerant Computing: Progress, Problems, and Prospectus", Inf. Process '77, Proceedings of IFIP Congress, Toronto, August 8–12, 1977. Published by North-Holland Publishing Company (IFIP Congress Series, Vol. 7), Amsterdam and New York, 1977, pp. 405–420.

43. A. Avizienis, "Fault-Tolerant Computing: An Overview", Computer, January/February, 1971, pp. 5–8.

44. A. Avizienis, "Fault-Tolerant Systems", IEEE Transactions on Computers, Vol. C-25, 1976, pp. 1304–1312.

45. A. Avizienis, F.P. Mathur, D.A. Rennels, J.A. Rohr, and D.K. Rubin, "The STAR (Self-Testing and Repair) Computer: An Investigation of the Theory and Practice of Fault-Tolerant Computer Design", IEEE Transactions on Computers, Vol. C-20, 1971, pp. 1312–1321.

46. A. Avizienis and B. Parhami, "A Fault-Tolerant Parallel Computer System for Signal Processing", Proceedings of the International Symposium on Fault-Tolerant Computing, 1974, pp. 2–8 to 2–13.

47. D.O. Baechler, "Aerospace Computer Characteristics and Design Trends", Computer, January/February, 1971, pp. 46–56.

48. M. Ball and F. Hardie, "Majority Voter Considerations for a TMR Computer", Computer Design, April 1969, pp. 100–104.

49. M. Ball and F. Hardie, "IBM Proposes Triple Redundant Aerospace Computer", Computer Design, Vol. 6, November 1967, p. 34.

50. M.D. Beaudry, "A Statistical Analysis of Failures in the Slack Computer Center", Proceedings of the IEEE Computer Society International Conference, 1979, pp. 49–52.

51. M.D. Beaudry, "Performance Considerations for Reliability Analysis: A Statistical Case Study", Proceedings of the International Symposium on Fault-Tolerant Computing, 1978, p. 198.

52. M.D. Beaudry, "Performance-Related Reliability Measures for Computing Systems", IEEE Transactions on Computers, Vol. C-27, 1978, pp. 540–547.

53. D.J. Bendz, R.W. Gedney, and J. Rasile, "Cost/Performance Single-Chip Module", IBM Journal of Research and Development, Vol. 26, 1982, pp. 278–285.

54. R. Bernhard, "The 'No-Downtime' Computer", IEEE Spectrum, 1980, pp. 33–37.

55. D. Bernhardt and E. Schmitter, "The Fault-Tolerant System BFS—An Application of Reliability in a Multimicrocomputer System", in Reliability in Electrical and Electronic Components and Systems, Edited by E. Lauger and J. Moltoft, North-Holland Publishing Co., Amsterdam, 1982, pp. 621–624.

56. B. Benaert, G. Florin, P. Lonc and S. Natkin, "Evaluation of Computer Systems Dependability Using Stochastic Petri Nets", Proceedings of the International Symposium on Fault-Tolerant Computing, 1981, pp. 79–81.

57. H. Birecki, S. Naberhuis, and T. Anthony, "Reliability and Performance of Magnetic Recording Media", Proceedings of the IEEE Computer Society International Conference, 1985, pp. 83–85.

58. L. Boi and P. Michel, "Design and Principles of a Fault-Tolerant System", Proceedings of the International Conference on Software Engineering, 1978, pp. 207–214.

59. L. Boi and P. Michel, "An Approach to a Fault-Tolerant System Architecture", Proceedings of Fifth Annual Symposium on Computer Architecture, 1978, pp. 123–130.

60. L.A. Boone, H.L. Liebergot, and R.M. Sedmak, "Availability, Reliability, and Maintainability Aspects of the Sperry UNIVAC 1100/60", Proceedings of the Tenth International Symposium on Fault-Tolerant Computing, 1980, pp. 3–9.

61. B. Borgerson, "A Fail-Soften System for Time Sharing Use", Proceedings of the IEEE Symposium on Fault Tolerant Computing, 1972, pp. 197–200.

62. B.R. Borgerson and R.F. Freitas, "A Reliability Model for Gracefully Degrading and Standby-Sparing Systems", IEEE Transactions on Computers, Vol. C-24, 1975, pp. 517–525.

63. B. Borgerson, "Dynamic Configuration of System Integrity", Proceedings of the Conference of the American Federation of Information Processing Societies, Vol. 41, 1972, pp. 89–96.

64. B.R. Borgerson and R.F. Freitas, "A Reliability Modelling Technique for Self-Repairing Computer Systems", IEEE Transactions on Computers, Vol. C-24, 1975, pp. 569–625.

65. D.C. Bossen and M.Y. Hsiao, "A System Solution to the Memory Soft Error Problem", IBM Journal of Research and Development, Vol. 24, 1980, pp. 390–397.

66. D.C. Bossen and M.Y. Hsiao, "ED/FI: A Technique for Improving Computer System RAS", Proceedings of the International Symposium on Fault-Tolerant Computing, 1981, pp. 2–7.

67. W.G. Bouricius, W.C. Carter and P.R. Schneider, "Reliability Modelling Techniques for Self-Repair Computer Systems", Proceedings of the Twelfth ACM (Association of Computing Machinery) National Conference, 1969, pp. 295–309.

68. W.G. Bouricius, W.C. Carter and D.C. Jessep, "Reliability Modeling for Fault-Tolerant Computers", IEEE Transactions on Computers, Vol. C-20, 1971, pp. 1306–1311.

69. T.A. Bratz, "Application of Computers at Bart", Proceedings of IEEE Computer Society International Conference, 1971, pp. 39–40.

70. J.L. Bricker, "A Unified Method for Analysing Mission Reliability for Fault-Tolerant Computers", IEEE Transactions on Reliability, Vol. R-22, 1973, pp. 72–77.

71. J.L. Bricker and W.L. Martin, "Reliability of Modular Computer Systems with Varying Configuration and Load Requirements", Proceedings of IEEE Computer Society International Conference, 1972, pp. 333–335.

72. D.B. Brosius and J. Jurison, "Design of a Voter Comparator Switch for Redundant Computer Modules", Proceedings of IEEE Symposium on Fault-Tolerant Computing, 1973, pp. 113–118.

73. W.G. Brown, J. Tierney, and R. Wasserman, "Improvement of Electronic-Computer Reliability Through the Use of Redundancy", IRE Transactions on Electronic Computers, Vol. EC-10, 1961, pp. 407–416.

74. J.C. Browne, "A Critical Overview of Computer Performance Evaluation", Proceedings of the International Conference on Software Engineering, 1976, pp. 138–145.

75. M. Budwen, H. Hecht, G.G. Lonardo, R. Schmiesing, and J.J. Stiffler, "Recovery Strategies for the Fault-Tolerant Spaceborne Computer", Proceedings of the IEEE Computer Society International Conference, 1979, pp. 54–58.

76. W.L. Bunce, "Hardware and Software: An Analytical Approach", Proceedings of the Annual Reliability and Maintainability Symposium, 1980, pp. 209–213.

77. D.D. Burchby, L.W. Keren, and W.A. Sturm, "Specification of the Fault-Tolerant Spaceborne Computer (FTSC)", Proceedings of the IEEE Symposium on Fault-Tolerant Computing, 1976, pp. 129–133.

78. R.G. Cantarella, "The Reliability of Periodically Repaired $n-1/n$ Parallel Redundant System", IEEE Transactions on Computers, Vol. C-32, 1983, pp. 597–598.

79. W.C. Carter and P.R. Schneider, "Design of Dynamically Checked Computers", Proceedings of the Congress of the International Federation of Information Processing Societies, Edinburgh, Scotland, August 1968, pp. 878–883.

80. W.C. Carter, H.C. Montgomery, R.J. Preiss, and H.J. Reinheimer, "Design of Serviceability Features for the IBM System/360", IBM Journal of Research and Development, Vol. 8, 1963, pp. 115–126.

81. W.C. Carter and W.G. Bouricius, "A Survey of Fault Tolerant Computer Architecture and its Evaluation", Computer, Vol. 4, No. 1, 1971, pp. 9–16.

82. X. Castillo, S.R. McConnel, and D.P. Siewiorek, "Derivation and Calibration of a Transient Error Reliability Model", IEEE Transactions on Computers, Vol. C-31, 1982, pp. 658–671.

83. X. Castillo and D.P. Siewiorek, "A Performance-Reliability Model for Computing Systems", Proceedings of the Tenth International Symposium on Fault-Tolerant Computing, 1980, pp. 187–192.

84. X. Castillo and D.P. Siewiorek, "Workload, Performance and Reliability of Digital Computing Systems", Proceedings of the International Symposium on Fault-Tolerant Computing, 1981, pp. 84–89.

85. T.J. Cerniglia, "Ferrite Core Reliability by 'Hands-off' Quality Control", Quality Progress, February 1971, pp. 14–17.

86. R. Chattergy and U.W. Pooch, "Analysis of the Availability of Computer Systems Using Computer-Aided Algebra", Proceedings of the Conference of the Association for Computing Machinery (ACM), 1978, pp. 586–591.

87. J. Chavade and Y. Crouzet, "The P.A.D.: A Self-Checking LSI Circuit for Fault-Detection in Microcomputers", Proceedings of the IEEE Symposium on Fault-Tolerant Computing, 1982, pp. 55–62.

88. R.C. Cheek, "Fail-Safe Power and Environmental Facilities for a Large Computer Installation", Proceedings of the Conference of the American Federation of Information Processing Societies, Vol. 33, 1968, pp. 51–56.

89. V. Cherkassky, E. Opper, and M. Malek, "Reliability and Fault Diagnosis Analysis of Fault-Tolerant Multistage Interconnection Network", Proceedings of the IEEE Symposium on Fault-Tolerant Computing, 1984, pp. 246–251.

90. T.C.K. Chou and J.A. Abraham, "Performance/Availability Model of Shared Resource Multiprocessors", IEEE Transactions on Reliability, Vol. R-29, 1980, pp. 70–74.

91. T.C.K. Chou and J.A. Abraham, "Load Redistribution Under Failure in Distributed Systems", IEEE Transactions on Computers, Vol. C-32, 1983, pp. 799–808.

92. D.K. Chow, "Availability of Some Repairable Computer System", IEEE Transactions on Reliability, Vol. R-24, 1975, pp. 64–66.

93. M.L. Ciaceli, "Fault Handling on the IBM 4341 Processor", Proceedings of the IEEE Symposium on Fault-Tolerant Computing, 1981, pp. 9–12.

94. M.D. Cin, "Availability Analysis of a Fault-Tolerant Computer System", IEEE Transactions on Reliability, Vol. R-29, 1980, pp. 265–268.

95. P. Ciompi and L. Simoncini, "The Boundary Graphs: An Approach to the Diagnosability with Repair of Digital Systems", Proceedings of Texas Conference on Computing Systems", University of Texas, November 7–8, 1974, pp. 9-3-1–9-3-9.

96. D.S. Cleverly, "Product Quality Level Monitoring and Control for Logic Chips and Modules", IBM Journal of Research and Development, Vol. 27, No. 1, 1983, pp. 4–10.

97. W.T. Comfort, "A Fault-Tolerant System Architecture for Navy Applications", IBM Journal of Research and Development, Vol. 27, 1983, pp. 219–236.

98. P. Cooke, "The Design of Microcomputer Systems", Microelectronics and Reliability, Vol. 18, 1978, pp. 127–131.

99. R.W. Cook, W.H. Sisson, T.F. Storey, and W.N. Toy, "Maintenance Design of a Central Processor for Electronic Switching Systems", Proceedings of Texas Conference on Computing Systems, University of Texas, November 7–8, 1974, pp. 9-1-1–9-3-9.

100. A.E. Cooper and W.T. Chow, "Development of On-Board Space Computer Systems", IBM Journal of Research and Development, Vol. 26, No. 1, January 1976, pp. 5–19.

101. R.B. Conn, N.A. Alexandridis, and A. Avizienis, "Design of a Fault-Tolerant Modular Computer with Dynamic Redundancy", Proceedings of the Conference of the American Federation of Information Processing Societies (AFIPS), Vol. 41, 1972, pp. 1057–1067.

102. M.L. Cortes and R.K. Iyer, "Device Failures and System Activity: A Thermal Effects Model", Proceedings of the IEEE Symposium on Fault-Tolerant Computing, 1984, pp. 71–76.

103. A. Costes, C. Landrault, and J.C. Laprie, "An Approach Towards a Unified Design Methodology for Gracefully-Degradable Periodically-Maintained Computers", Proceedings of the IEEE Symposium on Fault Tolerant Computing, 1978, pp. 200.

104. A. Costes, J.E. Doncet, C. Landrault, and J.C. Laprie, "SURF—A Program for Dependability Evaluation of Complex Fault-Tolerant Computing Systems", Proceedings of the IEEE Symposium on Fault-Tolerant Computing, 1981, pp. 72–78.

105. A. Costes, C. Landrault, and J.C. Laprie, "Reliability and Availability Models for Maintained Systems Featuring Hardware Failures and Design Faults", IEEE Transactions on Computers, Vol. C-27, No. 6, 1978.

106. B. Courtois, "Some Results About the Efficiency of Simple Mechanisms for the Detection of Microcomputer Malfunctions", Proceedings of the IEEE Symposium on Fault Tolerant Computing, 1979, pp. 71–74.

107. G.W. Cox and B.D. Carroll, "A Memory System Reliability Model", Proceedings of the IEEE Symposium on Fault Tolerant Computing, 1977, pp. 203.

108. C. Curry and T. Amendt, "The Computer in the Street", Microelectronics and Reliability, Vol. 18, 1978, pp. 9–13.

109. D.N. Cutler, R.H. Eckhouse, Jr., and M.R. Pellegrini, "The Nucleus of a Real-Time Operating System (A Tutorial on the Internals of RSX-11M)", Proceedings of the Association for Computing Machinery (ACM), 1976, pp. 241–246.

110. H.H. Damon, "Controlling the Quality Computer Systems", Quality Progress, February 1970, pp. 35–36.

111. D. Damskez, "Totally Distributed, Redundantly Structured Hardware and Software Local Computer Control Network", IEEE Transactions on Power Apparatus and Systems, Vol. PAS-102, 1983, pp. 127–133.

112. N.D. Deans and D.P. Mann, "Development of a New Hardware Reliability Simulator", Reliability Engineering, Vol. 5, 1983, pp. 181–195.

113. B.S. Dhillon and K.I. Ugwu, Bibliography of Literature on Computer Hardware Reliability, Microelectronics and Reliability, Vol. 26, 1986, pp. 131–154.

114. D.C. Dorrough, "A Methodical Approach to Analyzing and Synthesizing a Self-Repairing Computer", IEEE Transactions on Computers, Vol. C-18, 1969, pp. 22–42.

115. H. Dussault and H. Hecht, "Reliability of Current Fault Tolerant Systems", Proceedings of IEEE Computer Society International Computer Software and Application Conference (COMPSAC), 1984, pp. 432–438.

116. W. Dzida, S. Herda, and W.D. Itzfeldt, "User-Perceived Quality of Interactive Systems", Proceedings of the International Conference on Software Engineering, 1978, pp. 188–197.

117. M. Eden, "A Note on Error Detection in Noisy Logical Computers", Information and Control, Vol. 2, 1959, pp. 310-313.

118. F.D. Erwin and E. Bersoff, "Modular Computer Architecture Strategy for Long Term Missions", American Federation of Information Processing Societies (AFIPS), Conference Proceedings, Vol. 35, 1969, pp. 337-345.

119. P.P. Fasang and S.F. Daniels, "Microbit I—A Microcomputer with Built-In Diagnostics", in Reliability in Electrical and Electronic Components and Systems, Edited by E. Lauger and J. Moltoft, North-Holland Publishing Co., Amsterdam, 1982, pp. 625-629.

120. E.A. Feustelt, "Tagged Architectures and Protection: Message Systems", Proceedings of Texas Conference on Computing Systems, University of Texas, Austin, November 17-18, 1975, pp. 2A-3.1-2A-3.3.

121. R.J. Filene and W.M. Daly, "The Reliability Impact of Mission Abort Strategies on Redundant Flight Computer Systems", IEEE Transactions on Computers, July 1974, pp. 739-743.

122. R.J. Filene and A.I. Green, "A Simple Executive for a Fault-Tolerant, Real-Time Microprocessor", Proceedings of IEEE Computer Society International Conference (COMPCON), 1971, pp. 35-36.

123. E. Fiorentino and E.C. Soistman, "Combined Hardware/Software Reliability Predictions", Proceedings of the Annual Reliability and Maintainability Symposium, 1985, pp. 169-176.

124. B.J. Flehinger, "Reliability Improvements Through Redundancy at Various System Levels", IBM Journal of Research and Development, Vol. 2, 1958, pp. 148-158.

125. R.E. Forbes, D.H. Rutherford, and C.B. Stieglitz, "A Self Diagnosable Computer", American Federation of Information Processing Societies (AFIPS), Conference Proceedings, 1965, pp. 1073-1100.

126. H.A. Freeman and G. Metze, "Fault-Tolerant Computers Using Dotted Logical Redundancy Techniques", IEEE Transactions on Computers, Vol. C-21, 1972, pp. 867-871.

127. D.G. Furchtgott and J.F. Meyer, "A Performability Solution Method for Degradable Nonrepairable Systems", IEEE Transactions on Computers, Vol. C-33, 1984, pp. 550-554.

128. K. Gallyas and J. Endrenyi, "Computing Methods and Devices for the Reliability Evaluation of Large Power System", IEEE Transactions on Power Apparatus and Systems, Vol. Pas-100, 1981, pp. 1250-1258.

129. H. Garcia-Molina, "Reliability Issues for Completely Replicated Distributed Databases", Proceedings of the IEEE Computer Society International Conference (COMPCON), 1980, pp. 442-449.

130. H. Garcia-Molina and J. Kent, "Evaluating Response Time in a Faulty Distributed Computing System", IEEE Transactions on Computers, Vol. C-34, 1985, pp. 101-109.

131. H. Garcia-Molina, "Elections in a Distributed Computing System", IEEE Transactions on Computers, Vol. C-31, 1982, pp. 48-59.

132. F.A. Gay and M.L. Ketelsen, "Performance Evaluation for Gracefully Degrading Systems", Proceedings of the IEEE Symposium on Fault Tolerant Computing, 1979, pp. 51-57.

133. R.M. Geist, K.S. Trivedi, J.B. Dugan, and M.K. Smotherman, "Modeling Imperfect Coverage in Fault-Tolerant Computer Systems", Proceedings of the 14th Fault-Tolerant Computing Symposium, June 1984, pp. 85–91.

134. T. Giamo, "Validation of a Computer Performance Model of the Exponential Queueing Network Family", Proceedings of International Symposium on Computer Performance and Modelling, Measurement and Evaluation, Cambridge, Massachusetts, March, 1976, pp. 44–57.

135. D.C. Gilley, "A Fault Tolerant Spacecraft", Proceedings of the IEEE Symposium on Fault Tolerant Computing, 1972, pp. 105–109.

136. A.L. Goel and I. Soenjoto, "Models for Hardware/Software System Operational Performance Evaluation", IEEE Transactions on Reliability, Vol. R-30, 1981, pp. 232–239.

137. N.S. Goel and G. Karpovsky, "Functional Testing of Computer Hardware and Data-Transmission Channels Based on Minimizing the Magnitude of Undetected Errors", IEE Proceedings of Computers and Digital Techniques (UK), Vol. 129, NO. 5, September 1982, pp. 169–181.

138. A.L. Goel and J.B. Soenjoto, "Hardware-Software Availability: A Cost Based Trade Off Study", Proceedings of the Annual Reliability and Maintainability Symposium, 1983, pp. 303–309.

139. J. Goldberg, "A Survey of the Design and Analysis of Fault-Tolerant Computers", in Reliability and Fault Tree Analysis, Edited by R.E. Barlow, J.B. Fussell, N.D. Singpurwalla, Society of Industrial and Applied Mathematics (SIAM), Philadelphia, 1975, pp. 687–731.

140. J. Goldberg, "New Problems in Fault-Tolerant Computing", Proceedings of the IEEE Symposium on Fault Tolerant Computing, June 1975, pp. 29–34.

141. W. Gorke, "Reliability Definitions for Complex Software and Hardware Systems", in Reliability in Electrical and Electronic Components and Systems, Edited by E. Lauger and J. Moltoft, North-Holland Publishing Co., Amsterdam, 1982, pp. 630–633.

142. A. Goyal, G.J. Lipovski, and M. Malek, "Reliability in Ring Networks", Proceedings of the IEEE Computer Society International Conference (COMPCON), 1982, pp. 417–453.

143. R.A. Grueninger, "An Approach to Field Repair of Avionics Computers", Proceedings of the Annual Symposium on Reliability, 1970, pp. 292–299.

144. R.H. Gumpertz, "Combining Tags with Error Codes", Proceedings of Tenth Annual International Symposium on Computer Architecture, Stockholm, Sweden, 1983, pp. 160–165.

145. D.E. Haberman, "Fail-Safe Synchronization of Redundant Microprocessor Control Systems", Proceedings of the IEEE Vehicular Technology Conference, 1982, pp. 427–431.

146. W.B. Hall, "Some Aspects of Quality Control in Computer Tube Applications", Proceedings of the First National Symposium on Quality Control and Reliability in Electronics, New York, November 12–13, 1954, pp. 19–21.

147. F.M. Hall, R.A. Paul, and W.E. Snow, "Hardware/Software FMECA", Proceedings of the Annual Reliability and Maintainability Symposium, 1983, pp. 320–327.

148. M. Hamer, "Reliability Modelling Considerations for a Real-Time Control System", Proceedings of the IEEE Symposium on Fault Tolerant Computing, 1974, pp. 2-2-2-7.

149. M. Hamilton and S. Zeldin, "Reliability in Terms of Predictability", Proceedings of the
      IEEE Computer Society International Computer Software and Application Conference
      (COMPSAC), 1978, pp. 657–662.

150. D.R. Haring, "A Technique for Improving the Reliability of Certain Classes of Threshold
      Elements", IEEE Transactions on Computers, October 1968, pp. 997–998.

151. R.P. Hassett and E.H. Miller, "Multi-Threading Design of a Reliable Aerospace Com-
      puter", IEEE Transactions on Aerospace and Electronic Systems, Vol. 2, 1966, pp.
      147–158.

152. R.D. Haynes and W.E. Thompson, "Hardware and Software Reliability and Confidence
      Limits to Computer-Controlled Systems", Microelectronics and Reliability, Vol. 20,
      1980, pp. 109–122.

153. H. Hecht and J.J. Stiffler, "Redundancy Allocations in the Fault-Tolerant Spaceborne
      Computer", Proceedings of the IEEE Symposium on Fault Tolerant Computing, 1978,
      p. 197.

154. H. Hecht, "Economics of Reliability for Spacecraft Computers", Proceedings of the Relia-
      bility and Maintainability Symposium, 1972, pp. 554–564.

155. H. Hecht, "Figure of Merit for Fault-Tolerant Space Computers", IEEE Transactions on
      Computers, Vol. C-22, 1973, pp. 246–251.

156. H. Hecht, "Can Software Benefit from Hardware Experience?", Proceedings of the Annual
      Reliability and Maintainability Symposium, 1975, pp. 480–484.

157. S.G. Hibben, "Soviet Computer Reliability", Datamation, August 1967, pp. 22–25.

158. R.O. Hippert, L.R. Palounek, J. Provetero, and R.O. Skatrud, "Reliability, Availability,
      and Serviceability Design Considerations for the Super-Market and Retail Store Sys-
      tems", IBM Systems Journal, 1975, pp. 81–95.

159. A.L. Hopkins, "A Prognosis of Fault Tolerant Digital Control Systems", Proceedings of
      the IEEE Computer Society International Conference, 1972, 329–332.

160. S.H. Hosseini, J.G. Kuhl, and S.M. Reddy, "A Diagnosis Algorithm for Distributed Com-
      puting System with Dynamic Failure and Repair", IEEE Transactions on Computers,
      Vol. 33, 1984, pp. 223–233.

161. R.T. Howard, "Optimization of Indium-Lead Alloys for Controlled Collapse Chip Connec-
      tion Application", IBM Journal of Research and Development, Vol. 26, 1982, pp.
      372–378.

162. M.Y. Hsiao, W.C. Carter, J.W. Thomas, and W.R. Stringfellow, "Reliability, Availability,
      and Serviceability of IBM Computer Systems: A Quarter Century of Progress", IBM
      Journal of Research and Development, Vol. 25, 1981, pp. 453–465.

163. S.C. Hu, "A Probabilistic Approach of Designing More Reliable Logic Gates with Asym-
      metric Input Faults", IEEE Transactions on Computers, October 1975, pp. 1012–1014.

164. E.W. Husband and S.A. Szygenda, "Synthesis and Analysis of a Cost Effective, Ultrareli-
      able, High Speed Semiconductor Memory System", IEEE Transactions on Reliability,
      Vol. R-25, 1976, pp. 217–223.

165. K. Hwang and T. Chang, "Combinatorial Reliability Analysis of Multi-Processor Comput-
      ers", IEEE Transactions on Reliability, Vol. R-31, 1982, pp. 469–473.

166. R.D. Hynes and W.E. Thompson, "Hardware and Software Reliability Confidence Limits
      for Computer Controlled Systems", Microelectronics and Reliability, Vol. 20, 1980,
      pp. 109–122.

167. A.D. Ingle and D.P. Siewiorek, "Reliability Models for Multiprocessor Systems with and without Periodic Maintenance", Proceedings of the IEEE Symposium on Fault Tolerant Computing, 1977, pp. 3–9.

168. A.D. Ingle and D.P. Siewiorek, "Reliability of Microprocessor Structures", Proceedings of the IEEE Computer Society International Conference (COMPCON), 1976, pp. 24–29.

169. A.D. Ingle and D.P. Siewiorek, "A Reliability Model for Various Switch Designs in Hybrid Redundancy", IEEE Transactions on Computers, Vol. C-25, 1976, pp. 115–133.

170. R.K. Iyer, "Reliability Evaluation of Fault-Tolerant Systems—Effect of Variability in Failure Rates", IEEE Transactions on Computers, Vol. C-33, 1984, pp. 197–200.

171. R.K. Iyer, S.E. Butner, and E.J. McCluskey, "A Statistical Failure/Load Relationship: Results of a Multicomputer Study", IEEE Transactions on Computers, Vol. C-31, 1982, pp. 697–706.

172. L.A. Jack, L.L. Kinney, and R.O. Memory, "Comparison of Alternative Self Check Techniques in Semiconductor Memories", Proceedings of the IEEE Computer Society International Conference (COMPCON), 1977, pp. 170–174.

173. S.E. James, "Evolution of Real-Time Computer Systems for Manned Space Flight", IBM Journal of Research and Development, Vol. 25, 1981, pp. 417–428.

174. E. Johnson, "Redundancy for On-Line Computer Control Systems", Reliability Engineering, Vol. 4, 1983, pp. 105–125.

175. C. Kaiser, J. Langet, and J.F. Poitvin, "Design of a Continuously Available Distributed Real-Time System", Proceedings of the IEEE Symposium on Fault Tolerant Computing, 1978, pp. 195–196.

176. M. Kameyama and T. Higudin, "Design of Dependent-Failure-Tolerant Microcomputer System Using Triple-Modular Redundancy", IEEE Transactions on Computers, Vol. C-29, 1980, pp. 202–205.

177. T. Kanai, "An Improvement of Reliability of Memory System with Skewing Reconfiguration", IEEE Transactions on Computers, Vol. C-30, 1981, pp. 811–812.

178. S. Kaneda and E. Fujiwara, "Single Byte Error Correcting—Double Byte Error Detecting Codes for Memory Systems", IEEE Transactions on Computers, Vol. C-31, 1982, pp. 596–602.

179. J.F. Keeley, "System/370—Reliability from a System Viewpoint", Proceedings of the IEEE Computer Society International Conference (COMPCON), 1971, pp. 33–34.

180. G. Kasouf and D.A. McGoye, "R/M Design for Long Term Dormant Storage", Proceedings of the Annual Reliability and Maintainability Symposium, 1984, pp. 168–176.

181. M.G. Keinzle and K.C. Sevcik, "A Systematic Approach to the Performance Modeling of Computer Systems", Proceedings of the Fourth International Symposium on Modeling and Performance Evaluation of Computer Systems, Vienna, February 1979.

182. W. Kell and J. Staller, "A Computer Designer Looks at Maintainability Aspects of Micro-Molecular Designs", Proceedings of the Aerospace Reliability and Maintainability Conference, Washington D.C., May 6–8, 1963, pp. 526–529.

183. V. Kini and D.P. Siewiorek, "Automatic Generation of Symbolic Reliability Functions for Processor-Memory-Switch Structures", IEEE Transactions on Computers, Vol. C-31, 1982, pp. 752–771.

184. H. Kinzinger, K. Kuspert, K. Meyer-Wegener, and P. Peinl, "Integrated Environment for Performance Measurement and Evaluation in a DB/DC System", Computer Performance, Vol. 5, 1984, pp. 207–221.

185. T.F. Klaschka, "A Method for Redundancy Scheme Performance Assessment", Proceedings of the IEEE Symposium on Fault Tolerant Computing, 1971, pp. 69–73.

186. M.B. Kline, "Software and Hardware R & M: What are the Differences?", Proceedings of the Annual Reliability and Maintainability Symposium, 1980, pp. 179–185.

187. A.J. Knight, "Meeting Performance and Reliability Targets", Computer Performance, Vol. 2, 1981, pp. 30–37.

188. L.J. Koczela, "A Three-Failure-Tolerant Computer System", IEEE Transactions on Computers, November 1971, pp. 1389–1393.

189. R. Konakovsky, "Safety Evaluation of Computer Hardware and Software", Proceedings of the IEEE Computer Society Software and Application Conference (COMPSAC), 1978, pp. 559–564.

190. R.L. Koppel and I.R. Maltz, "Cost, Performance, and Reliability Tradeoffs in Semiconductor Memory Systems", Proceedings of the IEEE Computer Society International Conference (COMPCON), 1976, pp. 218–222.

191. I. Koren and M. Berg, "A Module Replacement Policy for Dynamic Redundancy Fault Tolerant Computing Systems", Proceedings of the IEEE Symposium on Fault Tolerant Computing, 1981, pp. 90–95.

192. D.O. Koval and H.F. Ewasechko, "Digital Computer Systems Reliability", Proceedings of the Annual Reliability and Maintainability Symposium, 1985, pp. 69–76.

193. D.O. Koval, "Microprocessor Outage Frequency and Duration Monitor", Proceedings of the IEEE International Electrical and Electronic Conference and Exposition, Toronto, 1981, pp. 24–25.

194. D.O. Koval, H.F. Ewasechko, and G.W. Yip, "Reliability Performance and Modeling of a Large Digital Computer System", 4th International Conference on Reliability and Maintainability, France, 1984, Vol. 1, Part 1, pp. 221–227.

195. D.O. Koval, H.F. Ewasechko, and G.W. Yip, "Impact of Power System Disturbances on Computer Systems", 15th Annual Pittsburg Conference on Modeling and Simulation Proceedings, Published by the Instrument Society of America, 1984, pp. 1–5.

196. L. Kristiansen, "Swedish Hardware/Software Reliability", Proceedings of the Annual Reliability and Maintainability Symposium, 1983, pp. 297–302.

197. R.E. Kuehn, "Computer Redundancy: Design, Performance and Future", IEEE Transactions on Reliability, Vol. R-18, 1969, pp. 3–11.

198. J.G. Kuhl and S.M. Reddy, "Distributed Fault-Tolerant for Large Multiprocessor Systems", Proceedings of the Seventh Annual Symposium on Computer Architecture, France, May 6–8, 1980, pp. 23–30.

199. D.J. Kunshier, "Fail-Soft Design in a Multiprocessor Computer System", in Reliability in Electrical and Electronic Components and Systems, Edited by E. Lauger and J. Moltoft, North-Holland Publishing Co., Amsterdam, 1982, pp. 641–644.

200. C. Landrault and J.C. Laprie, "Reliability and Availability Modeling of Systems Featuring Hardware and Software Faults", Proceedings of the Seventh Annual International Conference on Fault-Tolerant Computing, Los Angeles, June 28–30, 1977, pp. 10–15.

201. A. Langsford, "Reliable Inter-Process Communication", Proceedings of the First European Seminar on Real Time Systems, 1972, pp. 123–126.

202. J.C. Laprie, "Dependability Modeling of Computing Systems", International Federation on Information Processing Societies (IFIP), Working Conference: Reliable Computing and Fault-Tolerance in the 80's, London, September 26–29, 1979, pp. 110–114.

203. J.C. Laprie and A. Costes, "Dependability: A Unifying Concept for Reliability Computing", Proceedings of the IEEE Symposium on Fault Tolerant Computing, 1982, pp. 18–21.

204. J.C. Laprie, A. Costes, and C. Landrault, "Parametric Analysis of 2-Unit Redundant Computer Systems with Corrective and Preventive Maintenance", IEEE Transactions on Reliability, Vol. R-30, June 1981, pp. 139–144.

205. J.C. Laprie, "On Computer System Dependability: Faults, Errors and Failures", Proceedings of the IEEE Computer Society International Conference (COMPCON), 1985, pp. 256–259.

206. J.C.B. Leite, and P.G. Depledge, "Availability Modelling of Multi-Processors", IEE Proceedings of Computer and Digital Techniques (UK), Vol. 130, 1983, pp. 165–168.

207. C. Leung and J. Dennis, "Design of a Fault Tolerant Packet Communication Computer Architecture", Proceedings of the IEEE Symposium on Fault Tolerant Computing, October 1980, pp. 328–335.

208. H.O. Levyt and R.B. Conn, "A Simulation Program for Reliability Prediction of Fault Tolerant Systems", Proceedings of the IEEE Symposium on Fault Tolerant Computing, 1975, pp. 104–109.

209. H. Leibergot, "Fault Absorption by Hardware and Software", Proceedings of the IEEE Symposium on Fault Tolerant Computing, 1975, p. 231.

210. C.S. Lin, "A Structured Functional Testing Approach", Proceedings of the IEEE Computer Society International Conference (COMPCON), 1981, pp. 198–202.

211. T.S. Liu, "The Role of a Maintenance Processor for a General-Purpose Computer System", IEEE Transactions on Computers, Vol. C-33, June 1984, pp. 507–517.

212. F. Lombardi, "Availability Modelling of Ring Microcomputer Systems", Microelectronics and Reliability, Vol. 22, 1982, pp. 295–308.

213. F. Lombardi and O.J. Davies, "Availability Analysis of Fault Tolerant Microcomputer Systems with Periodic Preventive Replacement", Proceedings of the Eighth EUROMICRO Symposium on Microprocessing and Microprogramming, Antwerp, December 9–10, 1982, pp. 185–191.

214. L. Longbottom, "Analysis of Computer Systems Reliability and Maintainability", The Radio and Electronic Engineer, Vol. 42, December 1972, pp. 110–114.

215. J. Losq, "A Highly Efficient Redundancy Scheme: Self-Purging Redundancy", IEEE Transactions on Computers, Vol. C-25, 1976, pp. 569–578.

216. J. Losq, "Effects of Failures on Gracefully Degradable System", Proceedings of the IEEE Symposium on Fault Tolerant Computing, 1977, pp. 29–34.

217. J. Losq, "Enumeration of the Critical Fault Patterns in Fault-Tolerant Computing Systems", Proceedings of the IEEE Symposium on Fault-Tolerant Computing, 1978, pp. 31–36.

218. D.W. Lowry, "Maintainability Demonstration Test Performed on a Computer System", Proceedings of the Annual Symposium on Reliability, 1970, pp. 308–318.

219. R.E. Lyons and W. Vanderkulk, "The Use of Triple Modular Redundancy to Improve Computer Reliability", IBM Journal of Research and Development, Vol. 6, 1962, pp. 200–209.

220. F.P. Maison, "The MECRA: A Self-Repairable Computer for Highly Reliable Process", IEEE Transactions on Computers, Vol. C-20, 1971, pp. 1382–1393.

221. Y.K. Malaiya and S.Y.H. Su, "Reliability Measure of Hardware Redundancy Fault Tolerant Digital Systems with Intermittent Faults", IEEE Transactions on Computers, Vol. 30, 1981, pp. 600–604.

222. E. Manning, "On Computer Self-Diagnosis: Part I and II", IEEE Transactions on Electronic Computers, Vol. 15, 1966, pp. 873–890.

223. L.R. Marino, "The Effect of Asynchronous Inputs on Sequential Network Reliability", IEEE Transactions on Computers, Vol. C-26, 1977, pp. 1082–1090.

224. E.C. Martinez, "Storage Reliability with Periodic Test", Proceedings of the Annual Reliability and Maintainability Symposium, 1984, pp. 181–185.

225. C.J. Masreliez, "Reliability Enhancement Through Monitored Redundancy", Proceedings of the IEEE Symposium on Fault Tolerant Computing, 1975, p. 227.

226. F.P. Mathur, "On Reliability Modeling and Analysis of Ultra-Reliability Fault-Tolerant Digital Systems", IEEE Transactions on Computers, November 1971, pp. 1376–1382.

227. F.P. Mathur and A. Avizienis, "Reliability Analysis and Architecture of a Hybrid Redundant Digital System", American Federal of Information Processing Societies (AFIPS), Conference Proceedings, Vol. 36, 1970, pp. 375–384.

228. F.P. Mathur, "Reliability Modeling and Analysis of a Dynamic TMR System Utilizing Standby Spares", Proceedings of the Seventh Annual Allerton Conference on Circuits and Systems, October 20–22, 1969, pp. 115–120.

229. F.P. Mathur and P.T. de Sousa, "Reliability Modelling and Analysis of General Modular Redundant Systems", IEEE Transactions on Reliability, Vol. R-24, 1975, pp. 296–299.

230. F.P. Mathur and A. Avizienis, "Reliability Analysis and Architecture of a Hybrid-Redundant Digital System: Generalized Triple Modular Redundancy with Self-Repair", American Federation of Information Processing Societies (AFIPS), Conference Proceedings, Vol. 36, Spring 1970, pp. 375–383.

231. R.E. Matick, "Comparison of Memory Chip Organizations vs. Reliability in Virtual Memories", IEEE Transactions on Reliability, Vol. R-32, 1983, pp. 48–58.

232. R.A. Maxion and D.E. Morgan, "The Application of Artificial Intelligence Techniques to Reliable and Fault-Tolerant Computing", Proceedings of the IEEE Symposium on Fault Tolerant Computing, 1984, pp. 285–290.

233. G.B. McCarter and J. Gold, "Large Digital Computer Dependability Measurement", Proceedings of the Fourth National Symposium on Reliability and Quality Control in Electronics, Washington D.C., January 6–8, 1958, pp. 95–112.

234. E.J. McCluskey, "Hardware Fault-Tolerant", Proceedings of the IEEE Computer Society International Conference (COMPCON), 1985, pp. 260–263.

235. E.J. McCluskey and R.C. Ogus, "Comparative Architecture of High-Availability Computer Systems", Proceedings of the IEEE Computer Society International Conference (COMPCON), 1977, pp. 288–293.

236. G.A. McLintock, "Bubble Memory Increases Data Storage Reliability", Engineering Digest, April 1985, pp. 20–28.

237. S.R. McConnel, D.P. Siewiorek, and M.M. Tsao, "The Measurement and Analysis of Transient Errors in Digital Computer Systems", Proceedings of the Ninth International Symposium on Fault-Tolerant Computing, 1979, pp. 67–70.

238. C.V. McNeil and G.C. Randa, "Self-Correcting Memory—the Basis of a Reliable Computer", Electronic Design, Vol. 13, 1965, pp. 28–31.

239. E.H. Melan, R.T. Curtis, J.K. Ho, J.G. Koens, and G.A. Snyder, "Quality and Reliability Assurance Systems in IBM Semiconductor Manufacturing", IBM Journal of Research and Development, Vol. 26, 1982, pp. 613–624.

240. P.M. Melliar-Smith and R.L. Schwartz, "Formal Specification and Mechanical Verification of SIFT: A Fault-Tolerant Flight Control System", IEEE Transactions on Computers, Vol. C-31, 1982, pp. 616–630.

241. C. Merand, F. Browaeys, J.P. Queille, and G. Garmain, "Hardware and Software Design of Fault-Tolerant Computer Copra", Proceedings of the Ninth Annual International Symposium on Fault-Tolerant Computing, Madison, Wisconsin, June 20–22, 1979, p. 167.

242. P.M. Merryman and A.A. Avizienis, "Modeling Transient Faults in TMR Computer System", Proceedings of the Annual Reliability and Maintainability Symposium, 1975, pp. 333–339.

243. J.F. Meyer, "Closed-Form Solutions of Performability", IEEE Transactions on Computers, Vol. C-31, 1982, pp. 648–657.

244. J.F. Meyer, "Computation-Based Reliability Analysis", IEEE Transactions on Computers, Vol. C-25, 1976, pp. 578–584.

245. J.F. Meyer and L.T. Wu, "Evaluation of Computing Systems Using Functionals of a Markov Process", Proceedings of the Fourth Annual Conference on Systems Science, Honolulu, Hawaii, January 1981, pp. 74–83.

246. J.F. Meyer, D.G. Furchtgott, and L.T. Wu, "Performability Evaluation of the SIFT Computer", IEEE Transactions on Computers, Vol. C-29, June 1980, pp. 501–509.

247. J.F. Meyer, "On Evaluating the Performability of Degradable Computing Systems", IEEE Transactions on Computers, Vol. C-29, August 1980, pp. 720–731.

248. E.H. Miller, "Reliability Aspects of the RCS/USAF Variable Instruction Computer", Proceedings of the Aerospace Computer Symposium, Santa Monica, 1966, pp. 12–19.

249. D.R. Miller, "Reliability Calculation Using Randomization for Markovian Fault-Tolerant Computing Systems", Proceedings of the IEEE Symposium on Fault Tolerant Computing, 1983, pp. 284–289.

250. H. Mine and K. Hatayama, "Performance Evaluation of a Fault-Tolerant Computing System", Proceedings of the IEEE Symposium on Fault-Tolerant Computing, 1979, pp. 59–62.

251. H. Mine and K. Hatayama, "Performance Related Reliability Measures for Computing Systems", Proceedings of the International Symposium on Fault-Tolerant Computing, 1979, pp. 59–62.

252. I. Mitrani and P.J.B. King, "Multiserver Systems Subject to Breakdowns: An Empirical Study", IEEE Transactions on Computers, Vol. C-32, 1983, pp. 96–98.

253. C. Moore, W. Leahy, C.L. Longenecker, W.P. Hamilton, J.P. Whooley, R.B. Squires, D.R. Swann, H. Mehta, T.C. Lee, J.O. Crowne, and A.B. Long, "Power Plant Computer Reliability Survey", IEEE Transactions on Power Plant Apparatus and Systems, Vol. PAS-97, 1978, pp. 1115–1123.

254. M. Morgan, "The Management of Hardware Redundancies in Coptex", Proceedings of the Third International Conference on Software Engineering for Telecommunication Switching Systems, Finland, June 27–29, 1978, pp. 70–74.

255. D.E. Muller, "Evaluation of Logical and Organizational Methods for Improving the Reliability and Availability of a Computer", Proceedings of the First IEEE Computer Conference, 1967, pp. 103–107.

256. J.A. Munarin, "Dynamic Workload Model for Performance/Reliability Analysis of Gracefully Degrading Systems", Proceedings of the IEEE Symposium on Fault-Tolerant Computing, 1983, pp. 290–295.

257. T. Nakagawa, K. Yasui, and S. Osaki, "Optimum Maintenance Policies for a Computer System with Restart", Proceedings of the IEEE Symposium on Fault-Tolerant Computing, 1981, pp. 148–150.

258. H. Nakazawa, "A Decomposition Method for Computing System Reliability by Boolean Expression", IEEE Transactions on Reliability, Vol. R-26, 1977, pp. 250–252.

259. H. Nakazawa, "A Decomposition Method for Computing System Reliability by a Matrix Expression", IEEE Transactions on Reliability, Vol. R-27, 1978, pp. 342–344.

260. Y.W. Ng and A. Avizienis, "A Unifying Reliability Model for Closed Fault-Tolerant Systems", Proceedings of the IEEE Symposium on Fault Tolerant Computing, 1975, p. 224.

261. Y.W. Ng and A. Avizienis, "A Unified Reliability Model for Fault-Tolerant Computers", IEEE Transactions on Computers, Vol. C-29, 1980, pp. 1002–1011.

262. A.A. Nilsson, Comment on "The Reliability of Periodically Repaired $n-1/n$ Parallel Redundant Systems", IEEE Transactions on Computers, Vol. C-33, 1984, p. 681.

263. K.C. Norris and A.H. Landzberg, "Reliability of Controlled Collapse Interconnections", IBM Journal of Research and Development, May 1969, pp. 266–271.

264. F.J. O'Brien, "Rollback Point Insertion Strategies", Proceedings of the IEEE Symposium on Fault-Tolerant Computing,, 1976, pp. 136–142.

265. R.C. Ogus, "Fault-Tolerant of the Iterative Cell Array Switch for Hybrid Redundancy", IEEE Transactions on Computers, Vol. C-23, 1974, pp. 667–681.

266. H. Ohlet, W. Binroth, and Roger Haboush, "Statistical Model for a Failure Mode and Effects Analysis and its Application to Computer Fault-Tracing", IEEE Transactions on Reliability, Vol. R-27, 1978, pp. 16–22.

267. P.J.P. O'Reilly and J.L. Hammod, "An Efficient Algorithm for Generating the Busy/Idle Periods of a Channel Using CSMA and Loaded by an Arbitrary Number of Stations", Proceedings of the IEEE Computer Society International Conference (COMPCON), Washington, D.C., September 20–23, 1982, pp. 427–436.

268. T.I. Oren, "Model Reliability in Interactive Modelling", Proceedings of the World Conference on Systems Simulation, 1982, pp. 201–203.

269. S. Osaki, "Performance/Reliability Measures for Fault-Tolerant Computing Systems", IEEE Transactions on Reliability, Vol. R-33, 1984, pp. 268–271.

270. Y.G. Park and J.W. Cho, "Fault Diagnosis of Bit-Slice Processor", Proceedings of the Tenth International Symposium on Computer Architecture, Stockholm, Sweden, 1983, pp. 166–172.

271. N.G. Parke and P.C. Barr, "The SERF Fault Tolerant Computer: Implementation and Reliability Analysis", Proceedings of the IEEE Symposium on Fault-Tolerant Computing, 1973, pp. 27–32.

272. J.H. Parsons and J.H. Rubel, "A Case History Developing an Airborne Digital Computer", Proceedings of the Second National Symposium on Quality Control and Reliability in Electronics, Washington, D.C., January 9–10, 1956, pp. 84–98.

273. V.B. Patki and B.N. Chatterji, "Reliability Modelling of Computer Systems", Journal of Electronics Engineering (India), Vol. XXIV, 1983, pp. 683–694.

274. V.B. Patki, A.B. Patki, and B.N. Chatterji, "Reliability and Maintainability Considerations in Computer Performance Evaluation", IEEE Transactions on Reliability, Vol. R-32, 1983, pp. 433–436.

275. A. Pedar and V.V.S. Sarma, "Computer-Based Reliability Analysis in Real Time Applications, IEEE Transactions on Reliability, Vol. R-27, 1978, pp. 345–346.

276. F.J. Perpiglia, T.W. Schaible, and M.E. Ryan, "Burroughs B7700 Systems Architecture and Reliability", Proceedings of the Texas Conference on Computing Systems, University of Texas, Austin, November 7–8, 1974, pp. 9-2-1–9-2-10.

277. J. Peterson and W. Bulgren, "Studies in Markov Models of Computer Systems", Annual Proceedings of the Association for Computing Machinery (ACM), 1975, pp. 102–107.

278. R. Piskar, "Hardware/Software Availability for a Phone System", Proceedings of the Annual Reliability and Maintainability Symposium, 1983, pp. 310–315.

279. E.F. Platz, "Solid Logic Technology Computer Circuits—Billion Hours Reliability Data", Microelectronics and Reliability, Vol. 8, 1969, pp. 55–59.

280. J.H. Powell, "Hardware/Software Reliability Considerations in the Design of Microprocessor Controlled Industrial Safety Systems", Proceedings of the Third International Conference on Reliability and Maintainability, Toulouse, France, October 18–21, 1982, pp. 143–149.

281. D. Powell, "RHEA: A System for Reliability and Survivable Interconnection of Real-Time Processing Elements", Proceedings of the IEEE Symposium on Fault-Tolerant Computing, June 1978, pp. 117–122.

282. W.E. Quillin, "Reliability of Multi-Processor Systems", Proceedings of the First European Seminar on Real Time Systems, 1972, pp. 114–118.

283. C.V. Ramamoorthy, "Fault-Tolerant Computing: An Introduction and an Overview", IEEE Transactions on Computers, Vol. C-20, 1971, pp. 1241–1244.

284. C.V. Ramamoorthy and G.S. Ho, "Fault Tree Analysis of Computer Systems", Proceedings of the National Computer Conference, 1977, pp. 13–17.

285. B. Randell, P.A. Lee, and P.C. Treleaven, "Reliability Issues in Computing System Design", Computing Surveys, Vol. 10, 1978, pp. 123–165.

286. A.V. Reddi, "Shared-Memory Performance of Multiple Computer Terminals in Parallel Distributed Information-Processing Systems", Computer Performance, Vol. 5, 1984, pp. 55–63.

287. D.A. Rennels and A. Avizienis, "RMS: A Reliability Modeling System for Self-Repairing Computers", Proceedings of the Third International Symposium on Fault-Tolerant Computing, Palo Alto, California, June 1973, pp. 131–135.

288. D. Rennels, "Architecture for Fault-Tolerant Spacecraft Computers", Proceedings of IEEE, Vol. 66, 1978, pp. 1255–1268.

289. H.C. Rickers and P.F. Manno, "Microprocessor and LSI Microcircuit Reliability-Prediction Model", IEEE Transactions on Reliability, Vol. R-29, 1980, pp. 196–202.

290. J.G. Robinson, "The Pluribus Fault-Tolderant Multiprocessor", Proceedings of the IEEE Computer Society International Conference (COMPCON), 1979, pp. 45–48.

291. J.C. Rogers, "System Availability—An Operating System Viewpoint", Proceedings of the IEEE Computer Society International Conference, 1971, pp. 31–32.

292. M. Ruschitzka, "Performance Evaluation of Computer Systems and Networks", Proceedings of the Tenth IMACS World Congress on System Simulation and Scientific Computation, 1982, pp. 231–232.

293. P. Russel, "High Availability in Industrial Control", Systems International (GB), October 1982, Vol. 10, pp. 56–58.

294. T.F. Schwab and S.S. Yau, "An Algebraic Model of Fault-Masking Logic Circuits", IEEE Transactions on Computers, Vol. C-32, 1983, pp. 809–825.

295. R.L. Schwartz and P.M. Melliar-Smith, "Specifying and Verifying Ultra Reliability and Fault-Tolerant Properties", Proceedings of the IEEE Computer Society International Conference, 1983, pp. 71–76.

296. R.M. Sedmak and H.L. Liebergot, "Fault-Tolerance of a General Purpose Computer Implemented by Very Large Scale Integration", IEEE Transactions on Computers, Vol. C-29, 1980, pp. 492–500.

297. Y.S. Sherif and N.A. Kheir, "Reliability and Failure Analysis of Computer Systems", Computers and Electrical Engineering, Vol. 11, 1984, pp. 151–157.

298. R.A. Short, "The Attainment of Reliable Digital Systems Through the Use of Redundancy: A Survey", IEEE Computer Group News, Vol. 2, March 1968, pp. 2–11.

299. R.A. Short and J. Golberge, "Soviet Progress in the Design of Fault Tolerant Digital Machines", IEEE Transactions on Computers, Vol. C-20, 1971, pp. 1337–1352.

300. R.E. Shostak, M.W. Green, K.N. Levitt, and J.H. Wensley, "Proving the Reliability of a Fault-Tolerant Computer Design", Proceedings of the IEEE Computer Society International Conference, 1977, pp. 283–287.

301. S.K. Shrivastava and F. Panzieri, "The Design of a Reliable Remote Procedure Call Mechanism", IEEE Transactions on Computers, Vol. C-31, 1982, pp. 692–697.

302. D.P. Siewiorek and R.S. Swarz, "Reliability and Maintainability Features in the VAX-11/750", Proceedings of the IEEE Symposium on Fault Tolerant Computing, 1981, p. 8.

303. D.P. Siewiorek, V. Kini, R. Joobbani, and H. Bellis, "A Case Study of Cmmp, Cm, and C.Vmp: Part II—Predicting and Calibrating Reliability of Multiprocessor Systems", Proceedings of the IEEE, Vol. 66, 1978, pp. 1200–1220.

304. D.J. Simkins and J.V. Bukowski, "Bayesian Reliability Evaluation of Computer Systems", Computers and Electrical Engineering, Vol. 11, 1984, pp. 79–86.

305. C. Singh, "Reliability Modeling of TMR Computer Systems with Repair and Common Mode Failures", Microelectronics and Reliability, Vol. 21, No. 2, 1981, pp. 259–262.

306. J.R. Sklaroff, "Redundancy Management Technique for Space Shuttle Computers", IBM Journal of Research and Development, Jan. 1976, pp. 20–28.

307. I.M. Soi and K.K. Aggarwal, "Maintenance of Reliable Real Time Systems: Hardware Versus Software Tradeoffs", Microelectronics and Reliability, Vol. 22, 1982, pp. 357–361.

308. I.M. Soi and K. Gopal, "Hardware Vs. Software Reliability—A Comparative Study", Microelectronics and Reliability, Vol. 20, 1980, pp. 881–885.

309. A.K. Sood, S. Akhtar, and M. Alam, "Markov Models for Performance Evaluation of Multiple Bus Local Area Computer Network", Proceedings of IEEE International Symposium on Circuits and Systems, 1985, pp. 715–718.

310. R.J. Spillman, "A Fail-Safe Redundant Architecture for Fault-Tolerant Computing", Proceedings of the Annual Conference of the Association for Computing Machinery, 1977, pp. 372–376.

311. S. Srivastava and I.M. Soi, "Hardware Vs. Software Maintainability: A Comparative Study", Microelectronics and Reliability, Vol. 22, 1982, pp. 1077–1079.

312. J. Staudhammer, C.A. Combs, and G. Wilkinson, "Analysis of Computer Peripheral Interference", Proceedings of the Annual Conference of the Association for Computing Machinery, 1967, pp. 97–101.

313. J.J. Stiffler, "Architectural Design for Near-100% Faul Coverage", Proceedings of the IEEE Symposium on Fault-Tolerant Computing, 1976, pp. 134–137.

314. J.J. Stiffler and A.H. VanDoren, "FTSC—Fault Tolerant Spaceborne Computer", Proceedings of the IEEE Symposium on Fault-Tolerant Computing, 1979, p. 143.

315. J.J. Stiffler, "How Computers Fail", IEEE Spectrum, October 1981, pp. 44–46.

316. J.J. Stiffler, "The Reliability of a Fault-Tolerant Configuration Having Variable Coverage", IEEE Transactions on Computers, Vol. C-27, 1978, pp. 1195–1197.

317. E.M. Stiles, "Meeting Computer/QC Challenges of the '705'", Quality Progress, January 1972, pp. 7–9.

318. A.C. Stover, "Quality Problems with Automatic Test Equipment", American Society for Quality Control Quality Congress Transactions, Detroit, 1982, pp. 771–776.

319. S.Y.H. Su and E. DuCasse, "Hardware Redundancy Reconfiguration Scheme for Tolerating Multiple Module Failures", IEEE Transactions on Computers, Vol. 29, 1980, pp. 254–258.

320. N. Sullivan, "Tymnet-Maintenance Considerations in a Very Large Network", Proceedings of the Fifth Data Communications Symposium, Snowbird, Utah, September 27–29, 1977, pp. 3/1–3.

321. R.S. Swarz, "Reliability and Maintainability Enhancements for the VAX-11/780", Proceedings of the IEEE Symposium on Fault-Tolerant Computing, 1978, pp. 24–28.

322. T. Takaoka and H. Mine, "N-Fail-Safe Logical Systems", IEEE Transactions on Computers, Vol. C-20, 1971, pp. 536–542.

323. O. Tasar and V. Tasar, "A Study of Intermittent Faults in Digital Computers", Proceedings of the American Federation of Information Processing Societies Conference, Dallas, Texas, Vol. 46, 1977, pp. 807–811.

324. M.N. Tendolkar and R.L. Swann, "Automated Diagnostic Methodology for the IBM 3081 Processor Complex", IBM Journal of Research and Development, Vol. 26, 1982, pp. 78–88.

325. S.M. Thatte and J.A. Abraham, "Test Generation for Microprocessors", IEEE Transactions on Computers, Vol. C-29, 1980, pp. 429–441.

326. E.L. Thomas, "Application of Unified Data Base Technology", Proceedings of the Annual Reliability and Maintainability Symposium, 1984, pp. 192–196.

327. W.E. Thompson, "System Hardware and Software Reliability Analysis", Proceedings of the Annual Reliability and Maintainability Symposium, 1983, pp. 316–319.

328. N. Tokura, T. Kasami, and A. Hashimoto, "Failsafe Logic Nets", IEEE Transactions on Computers, March 1971, pp. 323–330.

329. O. Tosun, "Dynamic Decision Elements for 3-Unit Systems", IEEE Transactions on Reliability, Vol. R-26, 1977, pp. 335–338.

330. W.N. Toy, "Error Switch of Duplicated Processing in the No 2 ESS", Proceedings of the IEEE Symposium on Fault-Tolerant Computing, 1971, pp. 108–109.

331. D.C. Trindade and L.D. Haugh, "Estimation of the Reliability of Computer Components From Field Renewal Data", Microelectronics and Reliability, Vol. 20, 1980, pp. 205–218.

332. K. Trivedi, J.B. Dugan, R. Geist, and M. Smotherman, "Hybrid Reliability Modelling of Fault-Tolerant Computers Systems", Computer and Electrical Engineering, Vol. 11, 1984, pp. 87–108.

333. M.A. Tyler, "Hard Facts on Hardware Reliability", Datamation, Vol. 30, 1984, pp. 82–96.

334. J.B.J. Van Baal, "Hardware/Software FMEA Applied to Airplane Safety", Proceedings of the Annual Reliability and Maintainability Symposium, 1985, pp. 250–255.

335. D.R. Vinograd, "What's A System to Do?—Assuring System Data Integrity", Proceedings of the IEEE Computer Society International Conference, 1971, pp. 31–37.

336. J.F. Wakerly, "Transient Failures in Triple Modular Redundancy Systems with Sequential Modules", IEEE Transactions on Computers, Vol. C-24, May 1975, pp. 570–573.

337. W.K.S. Walker, C.W. Sundberge, and C.J. Black, "A Reliable Spaceborne Memory with a Single Error and Erasure Correction Scheme", IEEE Transactions on Computers, Vol. C-28, July 1979, pp. 493–500.

338. J.F. Wakerly, "Microcomputer Reliability Improvement Using Triple-Modular Redundancy", Proceedings of the IEEE, Vol. 64, 1976, pp. 889–895.

339. J.F. Wakerly, "Reliability of Microcomputer Systems Using Triple Modular Redundancy", Proceedings of the IEEE Computer Society International Conference, 1976, pp. 23–26.

340. J.J. Wallace and W.W. Barnes, "Designing for Ultrahigh Availability: The Unix RTR Operating System", Computer, August 1984, pp. 31–39.

341. S.Q. Wang and K. Lovelace, "Improvement of Memory Reliability By Single Bit-Error Correction", Proceedings of the IEEE Computer Society International Conference, 1977, pp. 175–178.

342. Y.W. Yak, T.S. Dillon, K.E. Forward, "The Effect of Imperfect Periodic Maintenance on Fault-Tolerant Computer Systems", Proceedings of the IEEE Symposium on Fault-Tolerant Computing, 1984, pp. 66–70.

343. C.B. Weinstock and M.W. Green, "Reconfiguration Strategies for the SIFT Fault-Tolerant Computer", Proceedings of the IEEE Computer Society International Computer Software and Application Conference, 1978, pp. 645–650.

344. A.Y. Wei, K. Hiraishi, R. Cheng, and R.H. Campbell, "Application of the Fault-Tolerant Deadline Mechanism to a Satellite On-Board Computer System", Proceedings of the IEEE Symposium on Fault-Tolerant Computing, 1980, pp. 107–109.

345. J.H. Wensley, "Validation of the Fault-Tolerance in the August Systems Computer", Proceedings of the IEEE Computer Society International Computer Conference, 1983, pp. 293–301.

346. J.H. Wensley, M.W. Green, K.N. Levitt, and R.E. Shostak, "The Design, Analysis, and Verification of the SIFT Fault-Tolerance System", Proceedings of the International Conference on Software Engineering, 1976, pp. 458–469.

347. J.H. Wensley, et al., "SIFT: Design and Analysis of a Fault-Tolerant Computer for Aircraft Control", Proceedings of IEEE, Vol. 66, Oct. 1978, pp. 1240–1255.

348. M.V. Wilkes, "Self-Repairing Computers", IRE Transactions on Electronic Computers", Vol. EC-10, 1961, pp. 93–94.

349. S.E. Woodard and G. Metze, "Self-Checking Alternating Logic: Sequential Circuit Design", Conference Proceedings of the Fifth Annual Symposium on Computer Architecture, April 3-5, 1978, pp. 114–122.

350. W.A. Wulf, "Reliable Hardware/Software Architecture", IEEE Transactions on Software Engineering, Vol. SE-1, 1975, pp. 233–240.

351. H. Wyle, and G.J. Burnett, "Some Relationships Between Failure Detection Probability and Computer System Reliability", Proceedings of the American Federation of Information Processing Societies (AFIPS) Conference, Vol. 31, 1967, pp. 745–756.

352. M. Yaacob, M.G. Hartley, and P.G. Depledge, "Operational Fault-Tolerant Microcomputer for Very High Reliability", IEE Proceedings—Computer and Digital Techniques (UK), Vol. 130, 1983, pp. 90–94.

353. K. Yasui, T. Nakagawa, and Y. Sawa, "Reliability Analysis of Computer System with Retry", Transactions Institute of Electrical and Communication Engineering (Japan), 1981, Vol. 64, p. 569.

354. M.A. Young, "Predelivery Steps Towards Reliable Computers", Proceedings of the Fourth Annals of Reliability and Maintainability Conference, Los Angeles, July 28-30, 1965, pp. 229–239.

355. E. Yourdon, "Reliability of Real-Time Systems—Part 1—Different Concepts of Reliability", Modern Data, January 1972, pp. 36–42.

356. E. Yourdon, "Reliability of Real-Time Systems—Part 2—The Causes of System Failures", Modern Data, February 1972, pp. 50–56.

357. E. Yourdon, "Reliability of Real-Time Systems—Part 3—The Causes of System Failures Continued", Modern Data, March 1972, pp. 36–40.

358. E. Yourdon, "Reliability of Real-Time Systems—Part 4—Examples of Real-Time System Failures", Modern Data, April 1972, pp. 52–57.

359. E. Yourdon, "Reliability of Real-Time Systems—Part 5—Approaches to Error Recovery", Modern Data, May 1972, pp. 38–52.

360. E. Yourdon, "Reliability of Real-Time Systems—Part 6—Approaches to Error Recovery Continued", Modern Data, June 1972, pp. 38–36.

361. J. Zika "Availability of Data Communications Network and Network Based Computer Systems", Computer Performance, Vol. 4, 1983, pp. 134–140.

362. K. Zukauskas and J. Karosas, "The Theoretical Analysis of Redundant Systems" Proceedings of the IEEE Symposium on Fault-Tolerant Computing, 1973, pp. 125–130.

363. R. Zussman, "Forecasting Computer System Reliability with a Hand-Held Programmable Calculator", Computer Design, Vol. 18, 1979, pp. 141–149.

A.3 COMPUTER SOFTWARE RELIABILITY

Books and Conference Proceedings

1. B. Boehm, et al., *Characteristics of Software Quality,* North-Holland Publishing Company, New York, 1978.

2. *Computing Surveys: Special Issues on Software Reliability* I. Software Validation, Computing Surveys, Vol. 8, No. 3, September 1976. II. Fault-Tolerant Software, Computing Surveys, Vol. 8, No. 4, December 1976.

3. J.D. Cooper, M.J. Fischer, Eds., *Software Quality Management,* Petrocelli Books, New York, 1979.

4. R. Dunn and R. Ullman, *Quality Assurance for Computer Software,* McGraw-Hill Book Company, New York, 1982.

5. B.S. Dhillon and C. Singh, *Engineering Reliability: New Techniques and Applications,* John Wiley & Sons, New York, 1981.

6. R.L. Glass, *Software Reliability Guidebook,* Prentice-Hall, Englewood Cliffs, New Jersey, 1979.

7. H. Kopetz, *Software Reliability,* The McMillan Press Limited, London, 1979.

8. D.K. Lloyd and M. Lipow, *Reliability: Management, Methods and Mathematics,* Prentice-Hall Inc., Englewood Cliffs, New Jersey, 1979.

9. J. Martin and C. McClure, *Software Maintenance,* Prentice-Hall Inc., Englewood Cliffs, New Jersey, 1983.

10. G.J. Meyers, *Software Reliability: Principles and Practice,* John Wiley & Sons, New York, 1976.

11. G.J. Meyers, *Reliability Software Through Composite Design,* Petrocelli/Charter, New York, 1975.

12. M.L. Shooman, *Software Engineering,* McGraw-Hill Book Company, New York, 1983.

13. *Software Reliability,* Vols. I & II, Edited by R.L.D. Rees, Infotech State of the Art Report, Published by Infotech International Limited, Maidenhead, England, 1977.

14. T.A. Thayer, M. Lipow, and E.C. Nelson, *Software Reliability: A Study of Large Project Reality,* TRW Series of Software Technology, Vol. 2, North-Holland Publishing Company, Amsterdam, 1978.

15. M.G. Walker, *Managing Software Reliability: The Paradigmatic Approach,* North-Holland Publishing Company, New York, 1981.

Articles

16. F. Akiyama, "An Example of Software System Debugging", Proceedings of the International Federation of Information Processing Societies (IFIP) Congress, Vol. 1, Amsterdam, August 1971, North-Holland, pp. 353–359.

17. S.J. Amster and M. Shooman, "Software Reliability: An Overview", in Reliability and Fault-Tree Analysis, Edited by Barlow, Fussell, and Singpurwalla, Society for Industrial and Applied Mathematics, Philadelphia, 1975, pp. 655–685.

18. P.G. Anderson, "Redundancy Techniques for Software Quality", Proceedings of the Annual Reliability and Maintainability Symposium, 1978, pp. 86–93.

19. T. Anderson, "Software Fault-Tolerance: A System Supporting Fault-Tolerant Software", in Software Reliability, Infotech State of the Art Report, Vol. 2, Infotech International Limited, Maidenhead, England, 1977, pp. 1–14.

20. T. Anderson and R. Kerr, "Recovery Blocks in Action: A System Supporting High Reliability", Proceedings of the International Conference on Software Engineering, 1976, pp. 447–457.

21. J.E. Angus, R.E. Schafer, and A. Sukert, "Software Reliability Model Validation", Proceedings of the Annual Reliability and Maintainability Symposium, 1980, pp. 191–199.

22. J.E. Angus and L.E. James, "Combined Hardware/Software Reliability Models", Proceedings of the Annual Reliability and Maintainability Symposium, 1982, pp. 176–181.

23. W. Ansaldi, I. Ruello, and F. Tosielli, "Fault Tolerant Software Techniques for High Reliable Computer Systems", in Mini and Microcomputers and their Applications (M. Mastronardi, ed.), A Publication of the International Society for Mini and Microcomputers (ISMM), Basi, Italy, June 5–8, 1984, pp. 19–20.

24. A. Avizienis, "Computer System Reliability: An Overview", In Computer Systems Reliability, Infotech State of the Art Report, Infotech International Limited, Maidenhead, England, 1974.

25. A. Avizienis, "Fault-Tolerance and Fault-Intolerance: Complimentary Approachs to Reliable Computing", Proceedings of the International Conference on Reliable Software, IEEE, 1975, pp. 458–464.

26. R.G. Babb and L.L. Tripp, "An Engineering Framework for Software Standards", Proceedings of the Annual Reliability and Maintainability Symposium, 1980, pp. 214–219.

27. R.E. Barone and D.R. Harkness, "Innovations in Software Quality Management", American Society for Quality Control, ASQC, Technical Conference Transactions, 1972, pp. 152–156.

28. F.B. Bastani and C.V. Ramamoorthy, "A Methodology for Assessing the Correctness of Control Programs", Computer and Electrical Engineering, Vol. 11, 1984, pp. 115–144.

29. F.B. Bastani, "On the Uncertainty in the Correctness of Computer Programs", Proceedings of the IEEE Computer Software and Application Conference (COMPSAC), 1982, pp. 109–118.

30. V.W. Bateman, "Software Quality—Key to Productivity", American Society for Quality Control (ASQC) Quality Conference Transactions, 1982, pp. 767–770.

31. R.G. Bennets, "A Comment on Reliability Evaluation of Software", 1973 NATO Generic Conference, NATO Advanced Study Institute on Generic Techniques of System Reliability Assessment, North-Holland Book Company, New York, 1974.

32. R.W. Berger, "Microcomputers and Software Quality Control", American Society for Quality Control (ASQC) Technical Conference Transactions, 1978, pp. 328–332.

33. E.R. Berlekamp, "Algebraic Codes for Improving the Reliability of Tape Storage", American Federation of Information Processing Society Conference Proceedings, Vol. 44, 1975, pp. 497–499.

34. W.R. Bezanson, "Reliable Software Through Requirement Definition Using Data Abstractions", Microelectronics and Reliability, Vol. 17, 1976, pp. 85–92.

35. B. Bhargava, "Software Reliability in Real-Time Systems", American Federation of Information Processing Societies (AFIPS) Conference, Vol. 50, 1981, pp. 297–309.

36. B.S. Bloom, M.J. McPheters, S.H. Tsiang, "Software Quality Control", Proceedings of the IEEE Symposium on Computer Software Reliability, 1973, pp. 50–55.

37. B.W. Boehm, "Software and Its Impact: A Quantitative Assessment", Datamation Magazine, May 1973, pp. 48–59.

38. B.W. Boehm, R.K. McClean, and D.B. Urfsiq, "Some Experience with Automated Aids to the Design of Large-Scale Reliability Software", Proceedings of the International Conference on Reliable Software, IEEE, 1975, pp. 105–113.

39. B.W. Boehm, J.R. Brown, and M. Lipow, "Quantitative Evaluation of Software Quality", Proceedings of the Second International Conference on Software Engineering, October 1976, pp. 592–605.

40. B.W. Boehm, J.R. Brown, H. Kaspar, M. Lipow, G.J. McLeoad, and M.J. Merrit, "Characteristics of Software Quality", TRW Software Series Report TRW-SS-73-09, December 1973, Redondo Beach, California.

41. T.L. Booth and C.A. Wiecek, "Performance Abstract Data Types as a Tool in Software Performance Analysis and Design", IEEE Transactions on Software Engineering, Vol. SE-6, 1980, pp. 138–151.

42. P.I.P. Boulton and M.A.R. Kittler, "Estimating Program Reliability", The Computer Journal, Vol. 22, 1979, pp. 328–331.

43. J.B. Bowen, "Are Current Approaches Sufficient for Measuring Software Quality", Software Engineering Notes, Vol. 3, 1978, pp. 148–155.

44. W.D. Brooks and P.W. Weiler, "Software Reliability Analysis", IBM Technical Report FSD-77-0009, International Business Machines Corporation, Federal Systems Division, Gaithersberg, Maryland, 1977.

45. J.R. Brown and M. Lipow, "Testing for Software Reliability", Proceedings of the International Conference on Reliable Software, IEEE, 1975, pp. 518–527.

46. J.R. Brown and H.N. Buchanan, "The Quantitative Measurement of Software Safety and Reliability", TRW Report SDP-1776-2H, 1973, Redondo Beach, California.

47. J.R. Brown, "A Case for Software Test Tools", Proceedings of the TRW Symposium on Reliability, Cost-Effective, Secure Software, TRW Software Series SS-74-14, March 1974, Redondo Beach, California.

48. J.V. Bukowski and J.H. Goodman, "A Software Design Assistance Tool", Proceedings of the Annual Reliability and Maintainability Symposium, 1985, pp. 265–269.

49. W.L. Bunce, "Hardware and Software: An Analytical Approach", Proceedings of the Annual Reliability and Maintainability Symposium, 1980, pp. 209–213.

50. M. Calderbank, "The Use of a Front End Computer to Increase the Availability of a Central Computer Facility", Software Systems Engineering, Published by Online Conferences Limited, Uxbridge, England, 1976, pp. 227–234.

51. L.C. Carpenter and L.L. Tripp, "Software Design Validation Tool", Proceedings of the International Conference on Reliable Software, IEEE, 1975, pp. 395–400.

52. C.L. Carpenter, Jr. and G.E. Musine, "Measuring Software Product Quality", Quality Progress, May 1984, pp. 14–20.

53. P.A. Caspi and E.F. Kouka, "Stopping Rules for a Debugging Process Based on Different Software Reliability Models", Proceedings of the IEEE Symposium on Fault-Tolerant Computing, 1984, pp. 114–119.

54. P.V. Catiglione and W.W. Thompson, "Implementation and Measurable Output of Software Quality Assurance", Proceedings of the Annual Reliability and Maintainability Symposium, 1983, pp. 107–112.

55. J.P. Cavano, "Software Reliability Measurement: Prediction, Estimation, and Assessment", The Journal of System and Software, Vol. 4, 1984, pp. 269–275.

56. J.P. Cavano and J.A. McCall, "A Framework for the Measurement of Software Quality", Software Engineering Notes, Vol. 3, 1978, pp. 133–139.

57. W.C. Cave and A.B. Salisbury, "Controlling the Software Life Cycle—The Project Management Task", IEEE Transactions on Software Engineering, Vol. SE-4, 1978, pp. 326–334.

58. K.M. Chandy, J.C. Brown, C.W. Dissly, and W.R. Uhsiq, "Analytical Models for Rollback and Recovery Strategies in Data Base Systems", IEEE Transactions on Software Engineering, Vol. SE-1, 1975, pp. 100–110.

59. H.Y. Chang, "Hardware Maintainability and Software Reliability of Electronic Switching Systems", in Computer Systems Reliability, Infotech International Ltd., Maidenhead, England, C.J. Bunyan, Ed., 1974.

60. L. Chen and A. Avizienis, "N-Version Programming: A Fault-Tolerance Approach to Reliability of Software Operation", Eighth International Conference on Fault-Tolerant Computing, Toulouse, France, June 1978, pp. 195–200.

61. H.B. Chenoweth, "Modified Musa Theoretic Software Reliability", Proceedings of the Annual Reliability and Maintainability Symposium, 1981, pp. 353–356.

62. R.C. Cheung, "A User-Oriented Software Reliability Model", IEEE Transactions on Software Engineering, Vol. SE-6, 1980, pp. 118–125.

63. T.S. Chow, "Advances in Software Quality Assurance", Proceedings of the IEEE Computer Software and Application Conference (COMPSAC), 1982, p. 351.

64. J.R. Connet, E.J. Pasternak, and B.D. Wagner, "Software Defenses in Real-Time Systems", Proceedings of the Second IEEE Symposium on Fault-Tolerant Computing, June 1972, pp. 94–99.

65. J.D. Cooper, "MIL-STD-1679 (NAVY)", Proceedings of the Annual Reliability and Maintainability Symposium, 1979, pp. 352–355.

66. J.D.S. Continho, "Software Reliability Growth" Proceedings of the IEEE Symposium on Computer Software Reliability, 1973, pp. 58–64.

67. J.D.S. Continho, "Special Army Requirements for Tactical Data Systems", Proceedings of the Annual Reliability and Maintainability Symposium, 1976, pp. 440–445.

68. P.R. Cox, "Elements of a Software Quality Control Program", Proceedings of the Association of Computing Machinery (ACM) National Conference, 1982, pp. 2–4.

69. G.R. Craig, W.L. Hetrick, M. Lipow, and T.A. Thayer, "Software Reliability Study", TRW Systems Group, Interim Technical Report, RADC-TR-74-250, October 1974, Redondo Beach, California.

70. L.H. Crow and N.D. Singpurwalla, "An Empirically Developed Fourier Series Model for Describing Software Failures", IEEE Transactions on Reliability, Vol. R-33, 1984, pp. 176–183.

71. L.M. Culpepper, "A System for Reliability Engineering Software", IEEE Transactions of Software Engineering, Vol. SE-1, 1975, pp. 174–178.

72. C.J. Dale and L.N. Harris, "Approaches to Software Reliability Prediction", Proceedings of the Annual Reliability and Maintainability Symposium, 1982, pp. 167–175.

73. B.K. Daniels, "Software Reliability", Reliability Engineering, Vol. 4, 1983, pp. 199–234.

74. D. DeAngelis and J.A. Lauro, "Software Recovery in the Fault-Tolerant Spaceborne Computer", Proceedings of the IEEE Symposium on Fault-Tolerant Computing, 1976, pp. 143–147.

75. R. DeMillo, R. Lipton, and F. Sayward, "Program Mutation as a Tool for Managing Large Scale Software Development", American Society for Quality Control Technical Conference Transactions, 1978, pp. 341–346.

76. R.A. DeMillo, "Mutation Analysis as a Tool for Software Quality Assurance", Proceedings of the IEEE Computer Software and Application Conference (COMPSAC), 1980, pp. 390–393.

77. P.J. Denning, "Fault-Tolerant Operating Systems", Computing Surveys, Vol. 8, 1976, pp. 359–389.

78. J.C. Dickson, J.L. Hesse, and A.C. Kientz, "Quantitative Analysis of Software Reliability", Proceedings of the Annual Reliability and Maintainability Symposium, 1972, pp. 148–157.

79. J. Donahoo and D. Swearingen, "Software Maintenance Technology", Proceedings of the IEEE Computer Software and Application Conference (COMPSAC), 1980, pp. 394–400.

80. R.H. Dunn, "Software Quality Assessment", Proceedings of the IEEE Computer Software and Application Conference, 1984, pp. 516–517.

81. R.H. Dunn and R.S. Ullman, "Modularity is not a Matter of Size", Proceedings of the Annual Reliability and Maintainability Symposium, 1979, pp. 342–345.

82. L. Duvall, Jon Martens, D. Swearingen, and J. Donahoo, "Data Needs for Software Reliability Modelling", Proceedings of the Annual Reliability and Maintainability Symposium, 1980, pp. 200–207.

83. W.R. Elmendorf, "Fault-Tolerant Programming", Proceedings of the International Symposium on Fault-Tolerant Computing, 1972, pp. 79–83.

84. B. Elspas, K.N. Lewitt, and R.J. Waldinger, "An Assessment of Techniques for Proving Program Correctness", Computing Surveys, Vol. 4, 1972, pp. 99–147.

85. B. Elspas, M.W. Green, and K.N. Lewitt, "Software Reliability", Computer, Vol. 4, 1971, pp. 21–27.

86. A. Endres, "An Analysis of Errors and Their Causes in System Programs", IEEE Transactions on Software Engineering, Vol. 1, 1975, pp. 140–149.

87. J.G. Estep, "A Software Reliability and Availability Model", Proceedings of the IEEE Symposium on Computer Software Reliability, 1973, p. 101.

88. A.R. Ets, and W.E. Thompson, "Combined Hardware and Software Reliability Specification and Test", Proceedings of the 5th International Conference on Software Engineering, San Diego, March 1981, pp. 85–90.

89. M.E. Fagan, "Design and Code Inspection to Reduce Errors in Program Developments", IBM Systems Journal, 1976, pp. 202–203.

90. A.R. Ferrer and E.B. Fowlkes, "Relating Computer Program Maintainability to Software Measures", American Federation of Information Processing Societies (AFIPS), Conference Proceedings, 1979, pp. 1003–1012.

91. E. Fiorentino and E.C. Soistman, "Combined Hardware/Software Reliability Predictions", Proceedings of the Annual Reliability and Maintainability Symposium, 1985, pp. 169–176.

92. K.F. Fischer, "A Program for Software Quality Assurance", American Society for Quality Control (ASQC) Technical Conference Transactions, 1978, pp. 333–340.

93. K.F. Fischer and M.G. Walker, "Improved Software Reliability Through Requirements Verification", IEEE Transactions on Reliability, Vol. R-28, 1979, pp. 233–240.

94. K.F. Fischer, "A Methodology for Developing Quality Software", American Society for Quality Control Technical Conference Transactions, 1979, pp. 364–371.

95. M.J. Fisher, "Software QA Standards—The Coming Revolution", The Journal of Systems and Software, Vol. 2, 1981, pp. 357–362.

96. R.J. Flynn, "Design of Computer Software", Proceedings of the Annual Reliability and Maintainability Symposium, 1975, pp. 476–479.

97. E. Forman and N.D. Singpurwalla, "Optimal Time Intervals for Testing Hypotheses on Computer Software Errors", IEEE Transactions on Reliability, Vol. R-28, 1979, pp. 250–253.

98. E.H. Forman, "Statistical Models and Methods for Measuring Software Reliability", D.Sc. Dissertation, School of Engineering and Applied Science, The George Washington University, Washington, D.C., 1974.

99. L.D. Fosdick and L.J. Osterwell, "Data Flow Analysis in Software Reliability", Computing Surveys, Vol. 8, 1976, pp. 306–330.

100. R.A. Foster, "Software Quality Assurance is a Profitable Investment", American Society for Quality Control (ASQC) Technical Conference Transactions, 1976, pp. 370–374.

101. J.R. Fragola and J.F. Spahn, "Software Error Effect Analysis: A Quantitative Design Tool", Proceedings of the IEEE Symposium on Computer Software Reliability, 1973, pp. 90–93.

102. R. Foulkes and M.P. Mills, "Software Configuration Management and Its Contribution to Reliability Program Management", IEEE Transactions on Reliability, Vol. R-32, 1983, pp. 289–292.

103. L.A. Fry, "Joint Logistics Commanders (JLC) Software Workshop", Proceedings of the Annual Reliability and Maintainability Symposium, 1981, pp. 223–224.

104. M.S. Fujii, "A Comparison of Software Assurance Methods", Proceedings of the Software Quality and Assurance Workshop, San Diego, November 1978, Sponsored by National Association for Computing Machinery, pp. 27–32.

105. J.E. Gaffney, Jr., "Metrics in Software Quality Assurance", Proceedings of the Association of Computing Machinery (ACM) National Conference, 1981, pp. 126–130.

106. J.E. Gaffney, Jr. and M.G. Spiegel, "An Overview of the 1981 ACM Sigmetrics Workshop/Symposium on Measurement and Evaluation of Software Quality", Proceedings of the Association of Computing Machinery (ACM) National Conference, 1981, pp. 131–135.

107. T.F. Gannon and S.D. Shapiro, "An Optimal Approach to Fault Tolerant Software Systems Design", IEEE Transactions on Software Engineering, Vol. SE-4, 1978, pp. 390–409.

108. J.D. Gannon and J.J. Horning, "The Impact of Language Design of Reliable Software", Proceedings of the International Conference on Reliable Software, IEEE, 1975, pp. 10–22.

109. S.L. Gerhart, "A Unified View of Current Program Testing and Proving-Theory and Practice", Software Reliability, in Infotech State of the Art Report, Infotech International Limited, Maidenhead, England, 1977, pp. 71–100.

110. S.L. Gerhart and L. Yelowitz, "Observations of Fallibility in Applications of Modern Programming Methodologies", IEEE Transactions on Software Engineering, Vol. 2, 1976, pp. 195–207.

111. T. Gilb, "Software Metrics Technology: Some Unconventional Approaches to Reliable Software", Software Reliability, in Infotech State of the Art Report, Infotech International Limited, Maidenhead, England, 1977, pp. 101–115.

112. T. Gilb, "Distinct Software: A Redundancy Technology for Reliable Software", Software Reliability in Infotech State of the Art Report, Infotech International Limited, Maidenhead, England, 1977, pp. 117–133.

113. E. Girard and J.C. Rault, "A Programming Technique for Software Reliability", Proceedings of the IEEE Symposium on Computer Software Reliability, New York, May 1973, p. 44.

114. S.A. Gloss-Soler, "Assuming Software Quality: The Need for Standards Development and Application", Proceedings of the IEEE Computer Software and Application Conference, 1984, p. 342.

115. A.L. Goel and K. Okumoto, "Time-Dependent Error-Detection Rate Model for Software Reliability and Other Performance Measures", IEEE Transactions on Reliability, Vol. R-28, No. 3, August 1979, pp. 206–211.

116. A.L. Goel and J.B. Soenjoto, "Hardware–Software Availability: A Cost Based Trade-Off Study", Proceedings of the Annual Reliability and Maintainability Symposium, 1983, pp. 303–309.

117. D.I. Good, R.L. London, and W.W. Bledsoe, "An Interactive Program Verification System", IEEE Transactions on Software Engineering, Vol. SE-1, 1975, pp. 59–67.

118. W. Gorke, "Reliability Definitions for Complex Software and Hardware Systems", In Reliability in Electrical and Electronic Components and Systems, North-Holland Publishing Company, 1982, pp. 630–633.

119. K.K. Govil, "Incorporation of Executive Time Concept in Several Software Reliability Models", Reliability Engineering, Vol. 7, 1984, pp. 235–249.

120. J.J. Greene, C.P. Hollocker, M.A. Jones, and T.C. Pingel, "Developing a Software Quality Assurance Program Based on the IEEE Standard 730-1981", Proceedings of the IEEE Computer Software and Application Conference, 1982, pp. 257–262.

121. S.J. Greenspan and C.L. McGowan, "Structuring Software Development for Reliability", Microelectronics and Reliability, Vol. 17, 1978, pp. 75–84.

122. A.C. Grinath and P.H. Vess, "Making SQA Work: The Development of a Software Quality System", Quality Progress, July 1983, pp. 18–23.

123. M. Gubitz and K.O. Ott, "Quantifying Software Reliability by a Probabilistic Model", Reliability Engineering, Vol. 5, 1983, pp. 157–171.

124. "Guidelines for Software Quality Assurance", Group Report SDP-3055, TRW Systems, Redondo Beach, California, September 1974.

125. F.M. Hall, R.A. Paul, and W.E. Snow, "Hardware/Software FMECA", Proceedings of the Annual Reliability and Maintainability Symposium, 1983, pp. 320–327.

126. F. Hall, "Computer Program Stress Testing", Proceedings of the Annual Reliability and Maintainability Symposium, 1985, pp. 256–261.

127. G. Hallendal, A. Hedin, and A. Ostrand, "Estimating Software Failure Rates When the Failure Rate is Very Small", in Software Systems Engineering, pp. 295–307, Published by Online Conferences Limited, Uxbridge, England, 1976.

128. P.A. Hamilton and J.D. Musa, "Measuring Reliability of Computer Centre Software", Proceedings of the Third International Conference on Software Engineering, 1978, pp. 29–38.

129. S.L. Hantler and J.C. King, "An Introduction to Proving the Correctness of Programs", Computing Surveys, Vol. 8, 1976, pp. 331–353.

130. W.P. Harris, "Quality and Aerospace Software", Proceedings of the Annual Conference of the American Society for Quality Control, 1970, p. 43.

131. R. Hartwick and R. Rubey, "Quantitative Measurement of Program Quality", Proceedings of the 23rd Association of Computing Machinery National Conference, 1968, pp. 671–677.

132. R.D. Haynes and W.E. Thompson, "Combined Hardware and Software Availability", Proceedings of the Annual Reliability and Maintainability Symposium, 1981, pp. 365–370.

133. R.D. Haynes and W.E. Thompson, "Hardware and Software Reliability and Confidence Limits for Computer-Controlled Systems", Microelectronics and Reliability, Vol. 20, 1980, pp. 109–122.

134. H. Hecht, "Mini-Tutorial on Software Reliability", Proceedings of the IEEE Computer Software and Application Conference, 1980, pp. 383–385.

135. H. Hecht, "Fault-Tolerant Software", IEEE Transactions on Reliability, Vol. R-28, 1979, pp. 227–232.

136. H. Hecht, "Current Issues in Fault-Tolerant Software", Proceedings of the IEEE Computer Software and Application Conference, 1980, pp. 603–607.

137. H. Hecht, "Can Software Benefit from Hardware Experience?", Proceedings of the Annual Reliability and Maintainability Symposium, 1975, pp. 480–484.

138. H. Hecht, "Allocation of Resources for Software Reliability", Proceedings of the IEEE Computer Society International Conference, 1981, pp. 74–82.

139. H. Hecht, "Fault-Tolerant Software for Real-Time Applications", Computer Surveys, Vol. 8, December 1976, pp. 391–407.

140. H. Hecht, "Fault-Tolerant Software", IEEE Transactions on Reliability, Vol. R-28, 1979, pp. 227–232.

141. J. Hesse, A. Kientz, J. Dickson, and M. Shooman, "Quantitative Analysis of Software Reliability", Proceedings of the Annual Reliability Symposium, IEEE, New York, January 1972, pp. 100–106.

142. J. Hentinck and D. Smith, "Software Reliability Report", Plant Records Center, System Sciences Company, Los Angeles, Report PRC R-1470, September 1972.

143. J. Hirvensalo and R. Sepponen, "Quality Control and Verification of Software", in Reliability in Electrical and Electronic Components and Systems, North-Holland Publishing Company, 1982, pp. 634–637.

144. J.J. Horning, H.C. Laner, P.M. Melliar-Smith, and B. Randell, "A Program Structure for Error Detection and Recovery", Lecture Notes on Computer Science, Vol. 16, Springer-Verlag, New York, pp. 171–187.

145. W.E. Howden, "Empirical Studies of Software Validation", Microelectronics and Reliability, Vol. 19, 1979, pp. 39–47.

146. J.M. Howell, "A Software Evaluation: Results and Recommendations", Proceedings of the Annual Reliability and Maintainability Symposium, 1983, pp. 113–117.

147. P.P. Howley, Jr., "Software Quality Assurance for Reliable Software", Proceedings of the Annual Reliability and Maintainability Symposium, 1968, pp. 73–78.

148. P. Hsia, "Software Reliability—Theory and Practice", Computer and Electrical Engineering, Vol. 11, 1984, pp. 145–149.

149. K. Ishikawa, "Interactive Software for Graphical QC Analysis", American Society for Quality Control Annual Conference Transactions, 1984, pp. 208–213.

150. Z. Jelinski and R. Moranda, "Software Reliability Research", in Statistical Computer Performance Evaluation, edited by W. Frieberger, Academic Press, New York, 1972, pp. 465–484.

151. H. Jensen and K. Vairavan, "A Comparative Study of Software Metrics for Real Time Software", Proceedings of the IEEE Computer Software and Application Conference, 1982, pp. 96–99.

152. J.P. Johnson, "Software Reliability Measurement Study", GIDEP Report No. 195.45.00.00-BA-01. Available from GIDEP Operations Centre, Corona, California, 1975.

153. T.C. Jones, "Measuring Program Quality and Productivity", IBM Systems Journal, Vol. 17, No. 1, 1978, pp. 75–81.

154. R.D. Joshi, "Software Development for Reliable Software Systems", The Journal of Systems and Software, Vol. 3, 1983, pp. 107–121.

155. F. Kamigo, "Software Quality Control—A Project Management View", Proceedings of the IEEE Computer Society International Conference, 1981, p. 318.

156. K. Kant, "Error Recovery in Concurrent Processes", Proceedings of the IEEE Computer Software and Application Conference, 1980, pp. 608–614.

157. S. Katz and Z. Manna, "Towards Automatic Debugging of Programs", International Conference on Reliable Software, IEEE, 1975, pp. 143–155.

158. R.H. Keegan and R.C. Howard, "Approximation Method for Estimating Meaningful Parameters for a Software-Controlled Electro-Mechanical System", Proceedings of the Annual Reliability and Maintainability Symposium, 1976, pp. 434–439.

159. P.A. Keiller, B. Littlewood, D.R. Miller, and A. Sofer, "Comparison of Software Reliability Predictions", Proceedings of the 13th International Fault Tolerant Computing Symposium, Milan, June 1983, pp. 128–134.

160. K.H. Kim, "An Implementation of a Programmer-Transparent Scheme for Coordinating Concurrent Processes in Recovery", Proceedings of the IEEE Computer Software and Application Conference, 1980, pp. 615–621.

161. K.H. Kim and C.V. Ramamoorthy, "Structure of an Efficient Duplex Memory for Processing Fault-Tolerant Programs", Proceedings of the 5th Annual Conference on Computer Architecture, April 1978, pp. 131–138.

162. K.H. Kim and C.V. Ramamoorthy, "Fault-Tolerant Parallel Programming and its Supporting System Architecture", American Federation of Information Processing Society Conference Proceedings, Vol. 45, 1976, pp. 413–423.

163. J. King, "A New Approach to Program Testing", International Conference on Reliable Software, IEEE, 1975, pp. 50–56.

164. J.C. King, "Proving Programs to be Correct", Proceedings of the International Symposium on Fault-Tolerant Computing, IEEE, 1971, pp. 130–133.

165. M.B. Kline, "Software and Hardware R & M: What are the Differences?", Proceedings of the Annual Reliability and Maintainability Symposium, 1980, pp. 179–185.

166. R.K. Klobert, "Quest for Reliable Software", Proceedings of the Summer Computer Simulation Conference, July 1977, pp. 700–704.

167. K.S. Koch and P. Kubat, "Quick and Simple Procedures to Assess Software Reliability and Facilitate Project Management", The Journal of Systems and Software, Vol. 2, 1981, pp. 271–276.

168. G. Koch and P.J.C. Spreij, "Software Reliability as an Application of Martingale's Flitering Theory", IEEE Transactions on Reliability, Vol. R-32, 1983, pp. 342–345.

169. T.E. Konchan, "Software Reliability and the Musa Model", American Society for Quality Control Annual Conference Transactions, 1983, pp. 101–107.

170. W. Kremer, "Birth–Death and Bug Counting", IEEE Transactions on Reliability, Vol. R-32, 1983, pp. 37–47.

171. L. Kristiansen, "Swedish Hardware/Software Reliability", Proceedings of the Annual Reliability and Maintainability Symposium, 1983, pp. 297–302.

172. R. Kubat and H.S. Koch, "Pragmatic Testing Protocols to Measure Software Reliability", IEEE Transactions on Reliability, Vol. R-32, 1983, pp. 338–341.

173. P. Kubat and H.S. Koch, "Managing Test-Procedures to Achieve Reliable Software", IEEE Transactions on Reliability, Vol. R-32, 1983, pp. 299–303.

174. N.G. Leveson and P.R. Harvey, "Software Fault Tree Analysis", The Journal of Systems and Software, Vol. 3, 1983, pp. 173–181.

175. N.G. Leveson and P.R. Harvey, "Analysing Software Safety", IEEE Transactions on Software Engineering, Vol. SE-9, 1983, pp. 569–579.

176. N.G. Leveson and J.L. Stolzy, "Safety Analysis of ADA Programs Using Fault-Trees", IEEE Transactions on Reliability, Vol. R-32, 1983, pp. 479–484.

177. N.G. Leveson, "Software Safety from a Software Viewpoint", Proceedings of the 5th International System Safety Conference, 1981, Vol. 2, pp. 111-E-1–111-E-19.

178. M. Lipow and T.A. Thayer, "Prediction of Software Failures", Proceedings of the Annual Reliability and Maintainability Symposium, 1977, pp. 489–494.

179. M. Lipow, "Quantitative Demonstration and Cost Considerations of Software Fault Removal Methodology", Quality and Reliability Engineering International, Vol. 1, 1985, pp. 27–35.

180. M. Lipow, "Prediction of Software Failures", The Journal of System and Software, Vol. 1, 1979, pp. 71–75.

181. M. Lipow, "A New Approach to Software Reliability", Proceedings of the Annual Reliability and Maintainability Symposium, 1985, pp. 262–264.

182. B.H. Liskov, "A Design Methodology for Reliable Software Systems", Proceedings of the American Federation of Information Processing Societies Conference, Vol. 41, 1972, pp. 191–199.

183. C.R. Litecky and G.B. Davis, "A Study of Errors, Error-Proneness, and Error-Diagnosis in COBOL", Proceedings of the Association of Computing Machinery National Conference, Vol. 19, 1976, pp. 33–37.

184. B. Littlewood and P.A. Keiller, "Adaptive Software Reliability Modelling", Proceedings of the IEEE Symposium on Fault-Tolerant Computing, 1984, pp. 108–113.

185. B. Littlewood, "What Makes a Reliable Program—Few Bugs, or a Small Failure Rate?", American Federation of Information Processing Societies Conference Proceedings, 1980, pp. 707–720.

186. B. Littlewood, "The Littlewood-Verrall Model for Software Reliability Compared with Some Rivals", The Journal of Systems and Software, Vol. 1, No. 3, 1980, pp. 251–258.

187. B. Littlewood, "Software Reliability Model for Modular Program Structure", IEEE Transactions on Reliability, Vol. R-28, 1979, pp. 241–246.

188. B. Littlewood, "A Critique for the Jelinski-Moranda Model for Software Reliability", Proceedings of the Annual Reliability and Maintainability Symposium, 1981, pp. 357–364.

189. B. Littlewood and J.L. Verrall, "A Bayesian Reliability Growth Model for Computer Software", Proceedings of the IEEE Symposium on Computer Software Reliability, 1973, pp. 70–77.

190. B. Littlewood, "How to Measure Software Reliability and How Not To", IEEE Transactions on Reliability, Vol. R-25, 1979, pp. 103–110.

191. B. Littlewood, "A Bayesian Differential Debugging Model for Software Reliability", Proceedings of the Workshop on Quantitative Software Models, IEEE, Kiamesha, New York, October 1979, pp. 170–181.

192. B. Littlewood, "A Reliability Model for Markov Structural Software", Proceedings of the International Conference on Reliable Software, IEEE, 1975, pp. 204–207.

193. B. Littlewood, "A Semi-Markov Model for Software Reliability with Failure Costs", Proceedings of the Symposium on Software Engineering, New York, April 1976, pp. 281–300.

194. B. Littlewood, "Theories on Software Reliability: How Good are They, and How Can They be Improved?", IEEE Transactions on Software Engineering, Vol. SE-6, 1980, pp. 489–500.

195. R.L. London, "Bibliography on Proving The Correctness of Computer Programs", in Machine Intelligence, Edinburgh University Press, Edinburgh, 1970, pp. 569–580.

196. R.L. London, "Proving Programs Correct: Some Techniques and Examples", BIT, Vol. 10, 1979, pp. 168–185.

197. R.L. London, "A View of Program Verification", Proceedings of the International Conference on Reliable Software, IEEE, 1975, pp. 534–545.

198. R.L. London, "Software Reliability Through Proving Programs Correct", Proceedings of the International Symposium on Fault-Tolerant Computing, March 1971, pp. 125–129.

199. W.H. MacWilliams, "Reliability of Large Real Time Control Software Systems", Proceedings of the IEEE Symposium on Computer Software Reliability, 1973, pp. 1–6.

200. Z.J. Manna, "The Correctness of Programs", Journal of Computer and System Sciences, Vol. 3, 1969, pp. 119–127.

201. D. Marca, "Software Manufacturing and Large Software Maintenance", Proceedings of the IEEE Computer Society International Conference, 1984, pp. 312–315.

202. R.J. Martin, "The Need for Management of Software Maintenance", Proceedings of the IEEE Computer Software and Application Conference, 1983, pp. 83–84.

203. V.D. Matney, "Software Quality Assurance of Electronics Development Programs", American Society for Quality Control Technical Conference Transactions, 1975, pp. 56–59.

204. J.A. McCall and M.A. Herndon, "Quality Assessment: A Missing Element in Software Maintenance", Proceedings of the IEEE Computer Software Application Conference, 1983, pp. 87–88.

205. J.C. McCall, "An Introduction to Software Quality Metrics", Chapter 8 in Software Quality Management, Cooper and Fischer Eds., Petrocelli Books, New York, 1979.

206. J.A. McCall and P.K. Richards, F. Walters, "Factors in Software Quality: Concept and Definitions of Software Quality", RADC-TR-77-369, Rome Air Development Centre, New York, 3 Vols., November 1977.

207. J. McKissick, Jr. and R.A. Price, "The Software Development Notebook—A Proven Technique", Proceedings of the Annual Reliability and Maintainability Symposium, 1979, pp. 346–351.

208. K.S. Mendis, "A Software Quality Assurance Program for the 80's", American Society for Quality Control Technical Conference Transactions, 1980, pp. 379–388.

209. K.S. Mendis, "Software Quality Assurance Staffing Problems", American Society for Quality Control, Congress Transactions, 1983, pp. 108–112.

210. K.S. Mendis, "Quantifying Software Quality", Quality Progress, May 1982, pp. 18–22.

211. M.J. Merritt et al., "Characteristics of Software Quality", Report 25201-6001-RU-00, TRW Systems, Redondo Beach, California, December 1973.

212. E.F. Miller, Jr., "Position Statement–Software Quality Assurance (SQA) Tools", Proceedings of the IEEE Computer Software and Application Conference, 1982, pp. 352.

213. J.S. Miller and W.H. Vandever, Jr., "On Software Quality", Proceedings of the IEEE Symposium on Fault-Tolerant Computing, 1972, pp. 84–88.

214. E. Miller, "Special Mini-Tutorial on Software Quality Assurance", Proceedings of the IEEE Computer Software and Application Conference, 1980, pp. 381–382.

215. E.F. Miller, Jr., "Program Testing Tools and Their Uses", in Software Reliability, Infotech State of the Art Report, Infotech International Limited, Maidenhead, England, 1977, pp. 183–216.

216. E.F. Miller, Jr., "Testing for Software Reliability", in Software Reliability, Infotech State of the Art Report, Infotech International Limited, Maidenhead, England, 1977, pp. 217–241.

217. H.D. Mills, "On the Development of Large Reliability Programs", Proceedings of the IEEE Symposium on Computer Software Reliability, 1973, pp. 155–159.

218. H.D. Mills, "How to Write Correct Programs and Know It", Proceedings of the International Conference on Reliable Software, IEEE, 1975, pp. 363–370.

219. R.T. Mittermeir, "Optimal Test-Effort for Software Systems", in Reliability in Electrical

and Electronic Components and Systems, North-Holland Publishing Company, 1982, pp. 650–654.

220. I. Miyamoto, "Toward an Effective Software Reliability Evaluation", Proceedings of the International Conference on Software Engineering, 1979, pp. 46–55.

221. I. Miyamoto, "Software Reliability in On Line Real Time Environment", Proceedings of the International Conference on Reliable Software, IEEE, 1975, pp. 194–203.

222. Y. Mizuno, "Panel Session: Software Product Quality", Proceedings of the IEEE Computer Society International Conference, Fall 1981, pp. 316.

223. Y. Mizuno, "Bugs to Improve Software Quality", Proceedings of the IEEE Computer Society International Conference, Fall 1981, p. 319.

224. R. Moawad and R. Troy, "Assessment of Software Reliability Models", Proceedings of the IEEE Computer Software and Application Conference, 1982, pp. 110–115.

225. R. Moawad, "Comparison of Concurrent Software Reliability Models", Proceedings of the International Conference on Software Engineering, 1984, pp. 222–229.

226. S.N. Mohanity, "Models and Measurements for Quality Assessment of Software", Computing Surveys, Vol. 11, No. 3, 1979, pp. 251–275.

227. P.B. Moranda, "A Comparison of Software Error-Rate Models", Proceedings of the Texas Conference on Computing Systems, IEEE, 1975, pp. 2A-6.1–2A-6.9.

228. P.B. Moranda, "Event-Altered Rate Models for General Reliability Analysis", IEEE Transactions on Reliability, Vol. R-28, 1979, pp. 376–381.

229. P.B. Moranda and Z. Jelinski, "Software Reliability Predictions", Proceedings of the 6th Triennial World Congress, Published by the International Federation of Automatic Control, August 1975, pp. 60–67.

230. P.B. Moranda, "Prediction of Software Reliability During Debugging", Annual Reliability and Maintainability Symposium Proceedings, 1975, pp. 327–332.

231. R. Motley, "SQA Perspective on Quality Measurement and Evaluation Throughout the Software Life Cycle", Proceedings of the IEEE Computer Software and Application Conference, 1982, pp. 354–355.

232. R.B. Mulock, "Program Correctness, Software Reliability, Today's Capabilities", Proceedings of the International Symposium on Fault-Tolerant Computing, March 1971, pp. 137–139.

233. R.B. Mulock, "Software Reliability Engineering", Proceedings of the Annual Reliability and Maintainability Symposium, 1972, pp. 586–593.

234. R.B. Mulock, "Software Reliability", Annual Symposium on Reliability and Maintainability Proceedings, 1969, p. 495.

235. J.D. Musa, "The Measurement and Management of Software Reliability", Proceedings of the IEEE, Vol. 68, 1980, pp. 1131–1143.

236. J.D. Musa, "Software Reliability Measurement: The State of the Art", in Reliability in Electrical and Electronic Components and Systems, North-Holland Publishing Company, 1982, pp. 655–662.

237. J.D. Musa and K. Okumoto, "A Logarithmic Poisson Execution Time Model for Software Reliability Measurement", Proceedings of the International Conference on Software Engineering, 1984, pp. 230–238.

238. J.D. Musa, "Software Reliability Measurement", The Journal of Systems and Software, Vol. 1, 1980, pp. 223-241.

239. J.D. Musa, "Software Reliability Measures Applied to Systems Engineering", Conference Proceedings of the American Federation of Information Processing Societies, 1979, pp. 941-946.

240. J.D. Musa, "A Theory of Software Reliability and Its Application", IEEE Transactions on Software Engineering, Vol. SE-1, 1975, pp. 312-327.

241. J.D. Musa, "Validation of Execution Time Theory on Software Reliability", IEEE Transactions on Reliability, Vol. R-28, 1979, pp. 181-191.

242. G.J. Myers, "Storage Concept in a Software-Reliability-Directed Computer Architecture", Conference Proceedings of the 5th Annual Symposium on Computer Architecture, April 3-5, 1978, pp. 107-113.

243. P. Naur, "Software Reliability", in Software Reliability, Infotech State of the Art Report, Infotech International Limited, Maidenhead, England, 1977, pp. 243-251.

244. E.C. Nelson, "A Statistical Basis for Software Reliability Assessment", TRW Software Series Report TRW-SS-73-03, Redondo Beach, California, March 1973.

245. E.C. Nelson, "Estimating Software Reliability from Test Data", Microelectronics and Reliability, Vol. 17, 1978, pp. 67-74.

246. J.L. Ogdin, "Designing Reliable Software", Datamation, Vol. 18, 1972, pp. 71-78.

247. M. Ohba, S. Yamada, K. Takeda, and S. Osaki, "S-Shaped Software Reliability Growth Curve: How Good is it?", Proceedings of the IEEE Computer Software and Application Conference, 1982, pp. 38-44.

248. K. Okumoto and A.L. Goel, "Optimum Release Time for Software Systems Based on Reliability and Cost Criteria", The Journal of Systems and Software, Vol. 1, 1980, pp. 315-318.

249. D.L. Parnas, "The Influence of Software Structure on Reliability", International Conference on Reliable Software, IEEE, 1975, pp. 353-362.

250. D.L. Parnas and H. Wurges, "Response to Undesired Events in Software Systems", Proceedings of the International Conference on Software Engineering, 1976, pp. 437-446.

251. D.E. Peercy, "A Software Maintainability Evaluation Methodology", IEEE Transactions on Software Engineering, Vol. SE-7, 1981, pp. 343-351.

252. R.A. Pikul and R.T. Wojcik, "Software Effectiveness: A Reliability Growth Approach", Proceedings of the Symposium on Computer Software Engineering, IEEE, April 1976, pp. 531-546.

253. R. Piskar, "Hardware/Software Availability for a Phone System", Proceedings of the Annual Reliability and Maintainability Symposium, 1983, pp. 310-315.

254. R.M. Poston, "Software Quality Assurance Implementation", Proceedings of the IEEE Computer Software and Application Conference, 1982, pp. 356-357.

255. "Power Plant Computer Reliability Survey", IEEE Transactions on Power Apparatus and Systems, Vol. PAS-97, 1978, pp. 1115-1123.

256. R.R. Prudhomme, "New Software Methodologies and Quality Software", American Society for Quality Control Technical Conference Transactions, 1979, pp. 357-63.

257. R.R. Prudhomme, "Software Verification and Validation and SQA", American Society for Quality Control Technical Conference Transactions, 1980, pp. 397–404.

258. C.V. Ramamoorthy, Y.R. Mok, F.B. Bastani, and G. Chin, "Application of a Methodology for the Development and Validation of Reliable Process Control Software", Proceedings of the IEEE Computer Software and Application Conference, 1980, pp. 622–633.

259. C.V. Ramamoorthy, R.E. Meeker, and J. Turner, "Design and Construction of An Automated Software Evaluation System", Proceedings of the IEEE International Symposium on Computer Software Reliability, 1973, pp. 28–37.

260. C.V. Ramamoorthy, R.C. Cheung, and K.H. Kim, "Reliability and Integrity of Large Computer Programs", in Computer Systems Reliability, Infotech International Ltd., 1974, pp. 617–710.

261. C.V. Ramamoorthy and S.F. Ho, "Testing Large Software with Automated Software Evaluation Systems", IEEE Transactions on Software Engineering, Vol. SE-1, No. 1, 1975, pp. 46–58.

262. B. Randell, "System Structure for Software Fault-Tolerance", IEEE Transactions on Software Engineering, Vol. SE-1, 1975, pp. 220–232.

263. J.R. Rao, "A Definition of Software Reliability Dependent on Program Behavior", Proceedings of the Texas Conference on Computing Systems, 1975, pp. 2A-5.1–2A-5.4.

264. J.C. Rault, "An Approach Towards Reliable Software", Proceedings of the International Conference on Software Engineering, 1979, pp. 220–230.

265. J.C. Rault, "Extension of Hardware Fault Detection Models to the Verification of Software", in Program Test Methods, Ed. W.C. Hetzel, Prentice-Hall, Englewood Cliffs, N.J., 1973, pp. 255–262.

266. D.J. Reifer, "Automated Aides for Reliable Software", Proceedings of the International Conference on Reliable Software, IEEE, 1975, pp. 131–142.

267. D.J. Reifer, "A New Assurance Technology for Computer Software", Proceedings of the Annual Reliability and Maintainability Symposium, 1976, pp. 446–451.

268. D.J. Reifer, "Software Failure Modes and Effects Analysis", IEEE Transactions on Reliability, Vol. R-28, 1979, pp. 247–249.

269. H. Remus and S. Zilles, "Prediction and Management of Program Quality", Proceedings of the 4th International Conference on Software Engineering, September 1979, pp. 341–350.

270. T.J. Roberts, "Maintaining Quality After the Software is Released", American Society for Quality Control Conference Transactions, 1977, pp. 157–166.

271. L. Robinson, "On Obtaining Reliable Software for a Secure Operating Systems", Proceedings of the International Conference on Reliable Software", IEEE, 1975, pp. 267–284.

272. H. Roggenbauer, "Software Reliability for Computerized Control and Safety Systems in Nuclear Power Plants", Atomic Energy Review, Vol. 15, 1977, pp. 793–800.

273. J.A. Ronaback, "Software Reliability—How it Affects System Reliability", Microelectronics and Reliability, Vol. 14, 1975, pp. 121–140.

274. D.J. Rossetti and R.K. Iyer, "Software Related Failures on the IBM 3081: A Relationship with System Utilization", Proceedings of the IEEE Computer Software and Application Conference, 1982, pp. 45–54.

275. R.J. Rubey, "Planning for Software Reliability", Proceedings of the Annual Reliability and Maintainability Symposium, 1977, pp. 495–499.

276. R.J. Rubey, "Quantitative Aspects of Software Validation", Proceedings of the International Conference on Reliable Software, IEEE, 1975, pp. 246–251.

277. G. Rzevski, "Identification of Factors Which Cause Software Failure", Proceedings of the Annual Reliability and Maintainability Symposium, 1982, pp. 157–161.

278. J.L. Saurter, "Reliability in Computer Programs", Mechanical Engineering, Vol. 91, February 1969, pp. 24–27.

279. R.E. Schafer, et al., "Validation of Software Reliability Models", Rome Air Development Centre, Report No. RADC-TR-79-147, Griffiss AFB, New York, June 1979.

280. G.J. Schick and R.W. Wolverton, "Achieving Reliability in Large-Scale Software Systems", Proceedings of the Annual Reliability and Maintainability Symposium, 1974, pp. 302–319.

281. G.J. Schick and R.W. Wolverton, "An Analysis of Competing Software Reliability Models", IEEE Transactions on Software Engineering, Vol. SE-4, 1978, pp. 104–120.

282. G.J. Schick and C. Lin, "Use of a Subjective Prior Distribution for the Reliability of Computer Software", The Journal of Systems and Software, Vol. 1, 1980, pp. 259–266.

283. B. Schneiderman, "Human Factors Experiments for Developing Quality Software", in Software Reliability, Infotech State of the Art Report, Infotech International Ltd., Maidenhead, England, 1977, pp. 261–276.

284. N.F. Schneidewind, "Application of Program Graphs and Complexity Analysis to Software Development Testing", IEEE Transactions on Reliability, Vol. R-28, 1979, pp. 192–198.

285. N.F. Schneidewind, "The Application of Hardware Reliability Principles to Computer Software", in Software Quality Management, Cooper and Fishcher, Eds., Petrocelli Books, New York, 1979, Chapter II.

286. N.F. Schneidewind, "An Approach to Software Reliability Prediction and Quality Control", American Federation of Information Processing Societies Conference Proceedings, Vol. 41, 1972, pp. 837–847.

287. N.F. Schneidewind, "Analysis of Error Processes in Computer Software", Proceedings of the International Conference on Reliable Software, IEEE, 1975, pp. 337–346.

288. R.K. Scott, J.W. Gault, D.F. McAllister, and J. Wings, "Experimental Validation of Six Fault-Tolerant Software Reliability Models", Proceedings of the IEEE Symposium on Fault-Tolerant Computing, 1984, pp. 102–107.

289. J.G. Shantikumar, "A Binomial Model for Software Performance Prediction", Proceedings of the 18th Allerton Conference on Communication, Control and Computing, October 8–10, 1980, pp. 524–533.

290. J.G. Shantikumar, "A State- and Time-Dependent Error Occurrence-Rate Software Reliability Model with Imperfect Debugging", American Federation of Information Processing Societies Conference Proceedings (AFIPS), Vol. 50, 1981, pp. 311–315.

291. W.K. Sharpley, Jr., "Software Maintenance Planning for Embedded Computer Systems", Proceedings of the IEEE Computer Software and Application Conference, 1977, pp. 520–526.

292. M.L. Shooman, "Models, Data and Analysis—A Summary of MR1 Symposium", Proceedings of the IEEE Computer Society International Conference, 1976, pp. 334–336.

293. M.L. Shooman and A.K. Trivedi, "A Many-State Markov Model for Computer Software Performance Parameters", IEEE Transactions on Reliability, Vol. R-25, 1976, pp. 66–68.

294. M.L. Shooman, "Software Reliability: A Historical Perspective", IEEE Transactions on Reliability, Vol. R-33, 1984, pp. 48–55.

295. M.L. Shooman and G. Richeson, "Reliability of Shuttle Mission Control Center Software", Proceedings of the Annual Reliability and Maintainability Symposium, 1983, pp. 125–135.

296. M.L. Shooman, "Structural Models for Software Reliability Prediction", Proceedings of the 2nd International Conference on Software Engineering, 1976, pp. 268–275.

297. M.L. Shooman, "Software Reliability: Measurement and Models", Proceedings of the Annual Reliability and Maintainability Symposium, 1975, pp. 485–491.

298. M.L. Shooman and M.I. Bolsky, "Types, Distribution, and Test Correction Times for Programming Errors", Proceedings of the International Conference on Reliable Software, IEEE, 1975, pp. 347–362.

299. M.L. Shooman, "Operational Testing and Software Reliability During Program Development", Proceedings of the IEEE Symposium on Computer Software Reliability, 1973, pp. 51–57.

300. M.L. Shooman, "Probablistic Models for Software Reliability Prediction", in Statistical Computer Performance Evaluation, W. Freiberger, Eds., Academic Press, New York, 1972, pp. 485–502.

301. M.L. Shooman and S. Natarajan, "Effect of Manpower Development and Error Generation on Software Reliability", Proceedings of the Symposium on Computer Software Engineering, New York, Vol. XXIV, April 20–22, 1976, pp. 155–170.

302. S.K. Shrivasta and J. Banatre, "Reliable Resource Allocation Between Unreliable Processes", IEEE Transactions on Software Engineering, Vol. SE-4, 1978, pp. 230–241.

303. D.J. Simkins, "Systems Software Reliability Model", Proceedings of the Annual Reliability and Maintainability Symposium, 1982, pp. 162–165.

304. D.J. Simkins, "Software Performance Modeling and Management", IEEE Transactions on Reliability, Vol. R-32, 1983, pp. 293–298.

305. C.E. Skrukrud, "A Systems Approach to Software Quality Control", American Society for Quality Control Conference Transactions, 1979, pp. 348–356.

306. H.M. Sneed and A. Merey, "Automated Software Quality Assurance", Proceedings of the IEEE Computer Software and Application Conference, 1982, pp. 239–247.

307. I.M. Soi and K.K. Aggarwal, "Maintenance of Reliable Real Time Systems: Hardware Versus Software Tradeoffs", Microelectronics and Reliability, Vol. 22, 1982, pp. 357–361.

308. I.M. Soi and K. Gopal, "Detection and Diagnosis of Software Malfunctions", Microelectronics and Reliability, Vol. 18, 1978, pp. 353–356.

309. I.M. Soi and K. Gopal, "Some Aspects of Reliable Software Packages", Microelectronics and Reliability, Vol. 19, 1979, pp. 379–386.

310. I.M. Soi and K. Gopal, "Hardware vs. Software Reliability—A Comparative Study", Microelectronics and Reliability, Vol. 20, pp. 881–885.

311. L.J. Stucki and G.L. Foshee, "New Assertion Concepts for Self-Metric Software Validation", Proceedings of the International Conference on Reliable Software, IEEE, 1975, pp. 59–71.

312. N. Sugiura and M. Yamamoto, "On the Software Reliability", Microelectronics and Reliability, Vol. 13, 1973, pp. 529–533.

313. A.N. Sukert, "A Four-Project Empirical Study of Software Error Prediction Models", Proceedings of the IEEE Computer Software and Application Conference, 1978, pp. 577–582.

314. A.N. Sukert and A.L. Goel, "A Guidebook for Software Reliability Assessment", Proceedings of the Annual Reliability and Maintainability Symposium, 1980, pp. 186–190.

315. A.N. Sukert, "Empirical Validation of Three Software Error Prediction Models", IEEE Transactions on Reliability, Vol. R-28, 1978, pp. 199–205.

316. A.N. Sukert, "All Multi-Project Comparison of Software Reliability Models", Proceedings of the American Institute of Aeronautics and Astronautics Conference (Computers in Aerospace), 1977, pp. 413–421.

317. A.N. Sukert, "An Investigation of Software Reliability Models", Proceedings of the Annual Reliability and Maintainability Symposium, 1977, pp. 478–484.

318. S.G. Szabo, "A Scheme for Producing Reliable Software", Proceedings of the International Symposium on Fault-Tolerant Computing, 1975, pp. 151–155.

319. E.F. Thomas, "Pitfalls of Software Quality Assurance Management", Proceedings of the Annual Reliability and Maintainability Symposium, 1983, pp. 101–106.

320. W.E. Thompson, "System Hardware and Software Reliability Analysis", Proceedings of the Annual Reliability and Maintainability Symposium, 1983, pp. 316–319.

321. W.E. Thompson and P.O. Chelson, "Software Reliability Testing for Embedded Computer Systems", IEEE Transactions on Reliability, Vol. R-28, 1979, pp. 201–202.

322. G.D. Tice, Jr., "Management Policy and Practice for Quality Software", American Society for Quality Control Conference Transactions, 1983, pp. 369–372.

323. G.D. Tice, Jr., "Gaining Acceptance for Software", Quality Progress, April 1981, pp. 24–26.

324. S.J. Trivedi, "Tutorial: Software Quality, Key to Reliable Software", American Society for Quality Control Conference Transactions, 1982, pp. 884–885.

325. A.K. Trivedi and M.L. Shooman, "A Many-State Markov Model for the Estimation and Prediction of Computer Software Performance Parameters", Proceedings of the International Conference on Reliable Software, IEEE, 1975, pp. 208–220.

326. R. Troy and R. Moawad, "Assessment of Software Reliability Models", Proceedings of the IEEE Computer Software and Application Conference, 1982, pp. 28–37.

327. R. Ullman and R. Dunn, "A Software QC Tutorial", American Society for Quality Control Conference Transactions, 1979, pp. 780–781.

328. J.B.I. VanBaal, "Hardware/Software FMEA Applied to Airplane Safety", Proceedings of the Annual Reliability and Maintainability Symposium, 1985, pp. 250–255.

329. P. Velardi and R.K. Iyer, "A Study of Software Failures and Recovery in the MVS Operating System", IEEE Transactions on Computers, Vol. C-33, 1984, pp. 564–568.

330. V. Vemuri and J.V. Cornacchio, "Figures of Merit for Software Quality", Proceedings of the IEEE Computer Software and Application Conference, 1980, pp. 744–750.

331. C.F. Vera, "A Problem with Computerized Systems", Proceedings of the Annual Reliability and Maintainability Symposium, 1985, pp. 150–152.

332. F.W. VonHenke and D.C. Luckam, "A Methodology for Verifying Programs", Proceedings of the International Conference on Reliable Software, IEEE, 1975, pp. 156–164.

333. J.K. Wall and P.A. Ferguson, "Program Software Reliability Prediction", Proceedings of the Annual Reliability and Maintainability Symposium, 1977, pp. 485–489.

334. M.G. Walter, "A Theory of Software Reliability", Datamation, September 1978, pp. 211–214.

335. G.F. Walters and J.A. McCall, "The Development of Metrics for Software R & M", Proceedings of the Annual Reliability and Maintainability Symposium, 1988, pp. 79–85.

336. G.F. Walters and J.A. McCall, "Software Quality Metrics for Life-Cycle Cost-Reduction", IEEE Transactions on Reliability, Vol. R-28, 1979, pp. 212–220.

337. R.S. Wang, "Program With Measurable Structure", American Society for Quality Control Conference Transactions, 1980, pp. 389–396.

338. B. Wegbreit, "Some Remarks on Software Correctness and Program Verification", in Software Reliability, Infotech State of the Art Report, Infotech International Ltd., Maidenhead, England, 1977, pp. 397–401.

339. L. Weissman, "An Interface System for Improving Reliability of Software Systems", Proceedings of the IEEE International Symposium on Computer Software Reliability, 1973, pp. 136–140.

340. B.B. White, "Program Standards Help Software Maintainability", Proceedings of the Annual Reliability and Maintainability Symposium,, 1978, pp. 94–98.

341. M.H. Whitworth and P.A. Szulewski, "The Measurement of Control and Data Flow Complexity in Software Designs", Proceedings of the IEEE Computer Software and Application Conference, 1980, pp. 735–743.

342. H.E. Williams, "Software Systems Reliability: A Raytheon Project History", RADC-TR-77-188, Technical Report, Rome Air Development Centre, Air Force Systems Command, Griffiss Air Force Base, New York, June 1977.

343. R.D. Williams, "Managing the Development of Reliable Software", Proceedings of the International Conference on Reliable Software, IEEE, 1975, pp. 3–8.

344. O.L. Williamson, G.G. Dorris, A.J. Rybert, and W.E. Straight, "A Software Reliability Program", Proceedings of the Annual Reliability Symposium, 1970, pp. 420–428.

345. M. Writh, "An Assessment of the Programming Language Pascal", IEEE Transactions on Software Engineering, Vol. SE-1, 1975, pp. 192–198.

346. R.W. Wolverton and G.J. Schick, "Assessment of Software Reliability", TRW Software Series, Report TRW-SS-73-04, September 1972, Redondo Beach, California.

347. R.W. Wolverton, "Software Reliability Modelling, Prediction and Measurement Methodology", TRW Systems Group Report 6600.7-99/74, Redondo Beach, California, July 1974.

348. D.E. Wright and B.D. Carroll, "An Automated Data Collection System for the Study of Software Reliability", Proceedings of the IEEE Computer Software and Application Conference, 1978, pp. 571–576.

349. W.A. Wulf, "Reliable Hardware/Software Architecture", IEEE Transactions on Software Engineering, Vol. SE-1, 1975, pp. 233–240.

350. S. Yamada, M. Ohba, and S. Osaki, "S-Shaped Reliability Growth Modelling for Software Error Detection", IEEE Transactions on Reliability, Vol. R-32, 1983, pp. 475–478.

351. S. Yamada, M. Ohba, and S. Osaki, "S-Shaped Software Reliability Growth Models and Their Applications", IEEE Transactions on Reliability, Vol. R-33, 1984, pp. 289–292.

352. S.S. Yan, J.S. Collofello, "Some Stability Measures for Software Maintenance", IEEE Transactions on Software Engineering, Vol. SE-6, 1980, pp. 545–552.

353. S.S. Yan and J.S. Collofello, "Design Stability Measures for Software Maintenance", Proceedings of the IEEE Computer Software and Application Conference, 1982, pp. 100–108.

354. B.H. Yin and J.W. Winchester, "The Establishment and Use of measures to Evaluate the Quality of Software Designs", Proceedings of the Software Quality and Assurance Workshop, Association of Computing Machinery, November 1978, pp. 45–52.

AUTHOR INDEX

SUBJECT INDEX

classification, 201
geometric, 212
history, 199
Jelinski-Moranda, 202
Musa, 209
Schick, Wolverton, 207
Shooman, 204
Weibull, 211
Software reliability model classifications, 201
Bayesian, 201
calendar time, 201
execution, 201
input space, 201
semi-Markov, 201
Software testing, 181, 189, 191
big bang, 191–192
bottom-up, 191–192
definition, 3
integration, 191–192
modified sandwich, 191, 193
modified top-down, 191, 193
module, 191–192
performance, 191
regression, 191, 193
sandwich, 191–192
top-down, 191–192
Software test tools, 193
code auditor, 194
output comparators, 194
Software quality assurance
benefits, 177
engineers, 174
functions, 168

manager, 173
organization, 173
records, 170
standards, 176
Space computer, 160
Spacecraft, 160–161
Statistical quality control, 30
System availability, 88, 101
System reliability, 88
Structured flow charts, 186

T
Telephone exchanges, 129
Terminals, 74
Terminal control unit, 124
Timing analyzer, 183
Top-down programming, 183, 187–188
Trace program, 183
Transient fault, 87
Transistors, 1
Transition probability, 94
Triple Modular Redundant System, 62, 67

V
Variance, definition, 12
of parallel system, 39
of series system, 38
of standby system, 46

W
Warnier-Orr diagram, 186
Weibull distribution, 14